Christian Beginnings

GEZA VERMES

Christian Beginnings

From Nazareth to Nicaea

Yale

UNIVERSITY

PRESS

New Haven and London

3-21-14
LN
$30.00

First published in the United States in 2013 by Yale University Press.
First published in the United Kingdom in 2012 by Penguin Books Ltd.

Yale University Press books may be purchased in quantity for educational, business, or promotional use. For information, please e-mail
sales.press@yale.edu (U.S. office) or sales@yaleup.co.uk (U.K. office).

Printed in the United States of America.

Library of Congress Control Number: 2012946575
ISBN 978-0-300-19160-8 (cloth: alk. paper)

A catalogue record for this book is available from the British Library.

This paper meets the requirements of ANSI/NISO Z39.48-1992 (Per-
manence of Paper).

10 9 8 7 6 5 4 3 2

Contents

For Margaret and Ian with love

List of Abbreviations

Acts	Acts of the Apostles
Am.	Amos
Ant.	Flavius Josephus, *Jewish Antiquities*
ap	Apocryphon
Apol.	Justin, *Apology*
b	Babylonian Talmud
Barn.	Barnabas
Ber.	Berakhot (Benedictions)
CD	Cairo Damascus Document
Chron.	Chronicles
Clem.	Clement
Col.	Colossians
Cor.	Corinthians
D	Damascus Document from Qumran
Deut.	Deuteronomy
Did.	Didache (The Teaching of the Twelve Apostles)
Ecclus	Ecclesiasticus (Wisdom of Jesus ben Sira)
EH	Eusebius, *Ecclesiastical History*
En.	Enoch
Eph.	Ephesians
Esdr.	Esdras
Exod.	Exodus
Gen.	Genesis
Gal.	Galatians
H	Hodayot (Thanksgiving hymns)
Hab.	Habakkuk
Heb.	Hebrews
Hos.	Hosea

Isa.	Isaiah
Jas.	James
Jer.	Jeremiah
Jn	John
Jub.	Jubilees
Ket.	Ketubot (Marriage deeds)
LAB	Pseudo-Philo, *Liber Antiquitatum Biblicarum*
Lev.	Leviticus
Lk.	Luke
m	Mishnah
Mac.	Maccabees
Mal.	Malachi
Meil.	Meilah (Sacrilege)
Mic.	Micah
Mk	Mark
Mt.	Matthew
Ned.	Nedarim (Vows)
Num.	Numbers
p	Pesher (Commentary)
P.	Papyrus
Pes.	Pesahim (Passover)
Pet.	Peter
Phil.	Philippians
Praep. Ev.	Eusebius, *Praeparatio Evangelica*
Ps	Psalms
Q	Qumran Cave
Rev.	Revelation
Rom.	Romans
S	Serekh (Rule)
Sam.	Samuel
Shab.	Shabbat (Sabbath)
Strom.	*Stromateis* (Miscellanies)
t	Tosefta
Taan.	Taanit (Fasting)
Test.	Testament
Thess	Thessalonians
Thom.	Thomas
Tim.	Timothy

War	Flavius Josephus, *Jewish War*
Wisd.	Wisdom
y	Jerusalem Talmud
Zech.	Zechariah
4Q200	Hebrew Tobit
4Q242	Prayer of Nabonidus
4Q372	Narrative composition
4Q502	Marriage ritual
4Q510–11	Songs of the Sage

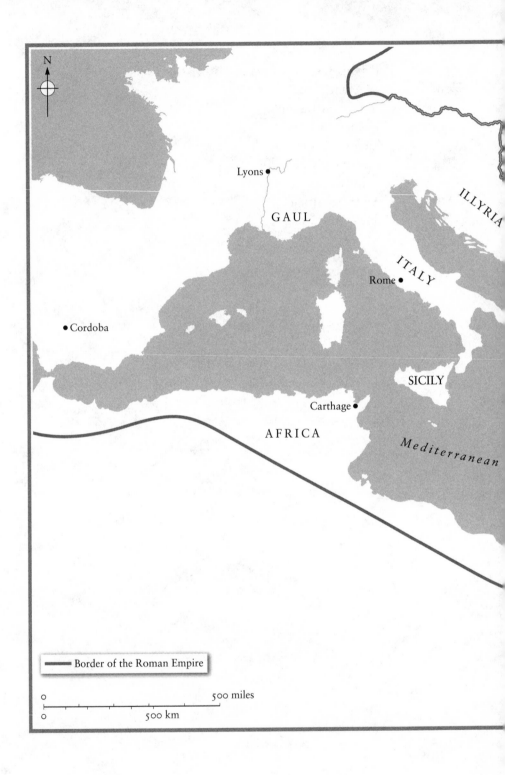

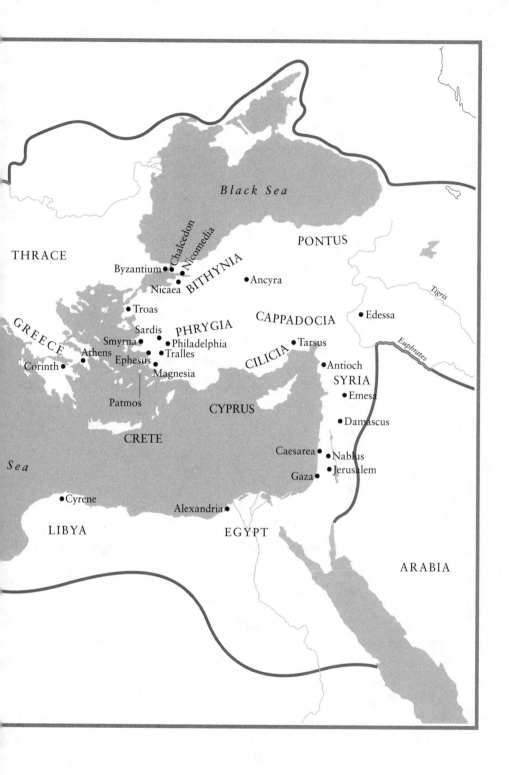

THRACE

Black Sea

PONTUS

Chalcedon
Nicomedia
Byzantium
Nicaea
BITHYNIA

Ancyra

Troas

CAPPADOCIA

Edessa

Tigris

GREECE

Sardis
PHRYGIA
Smyrna
Philadelphia
Athens
Tralles
Ephesus
Magnesia

Tarsus

CILICIA

Antioch

SYRIA

Euphrates

Corinth

Patmos

CYPRUS

Emesa

Damascus

CRETE

Caesarea
Nablus
Gaza
Jerusalem

Sea

Cyrene

Alexandria

LIBYA

EGYPT

ARABIA

Introduction

More than forty years have passed since my initial venture into the 'Jesus' field that culminated with *Jesus the Jew* in 1973. After the publication of twelve further books on the topic, it occurred to me in 2008 to round off the series with a very different book: an attempt to sketch the historical continuity between Jesus portrayed in his Galilean charismatic setting and the first ecumenical council held at Nicaea in AD 325, which solemnly proclaimed his divinity as a dogma of Christianity.

In this attempt at tracing the evolutionary curve, particular emphasis will be laid on the impact of charismatic Judaism on Jesus and on budding Palestinian Christianity. Equally important to note is the influence of Hellenistic thought and mysticism on the early church, which within decades from the crucifixion became very largely Greek in speech and thought. The trend started with Paul and the Fourth Gospel and was responsible from the second century onwards for the impact of Platonic philosophy on the formulation of Christian theological ideas. The final crucial thrust stemmed from the pressure exerted by the emperor Constantine on the bishops of the Nicene Council, compelling them to bear in mind the reverberations of their ongoing religious disputes on the civic peace of the Roman state.

To grasp the full picture, let us first glance at Judaism. As a religion, it essentially applied to persons born into the Jewish nation. In his turn, Jesus himself also exclusively addressed the Jews and ordered his envoys to turn only to 'the lost sheep of Israel'. However, Judaism also accepted Gentile proselytes who were willing to profess the uniqueness of God and embrace all the religious obligations of the Mosaic Law. Ritual initiation was achieved through proselyte baptism, conferred on both male and female candidates, and through the circumcision of all the male aspirants. It goes without saying that a certain amount of missionary activity was pursued among Gentiles in various periods of Jewish history including the age of Jesus, but how widely it was practised in those days and how deeply the eschatological idea of Israel being the light of the nations penetrated Jewish consciousness continue to be the subject of scholarly debate (see M. Goodman, *Mission and Conversion*, 1994). Admission of Gentiles into the early Judaeo-Christian community is originally presumed to have followed conversion to Judaism. The first members of the Jesus movement could hardly have imagined a non-Jew becoming their companion. However, less than twenty years after the crucifixion, the church authorities, urged by Paul, relented and abolished the condition of prior acceptance of the Mosaic Law, including circumcision for converts. They only obliged Gentile candidates for church membership to abide by a few basic rules similar to the Noachic laws which prohibited idol worship, the consumption of blood and certain sexual acts abhorrent to Jews.

Beneath the essentially Law-based Judaism there existed also a current of less formal religion. It was linked to and fed by the prophets, the influential mouthpieces of God, and was sustained down to the age of the rabbis by charismatic holy men. This religion demanded a devout attitude towards the Deity whose protection was solicited against illness, premature death, injustice and war as well as for the poor, the widow and the fatherless. Divine goodwill was also sought for a long and happy life and the well-being of the family, and occasionally in the late biblical period, for the privilege of escaping the underworld in some mysterious way and joining God beyond the grave in some form of afterlife.

In the early stages of biblical history Judaism represented not so much monotheism, the claim that there is only one God, but monolatry, which means that, practically ignoring the pantheon of the other peoples, the Jews revered only their own God. The Bible contains no rational argument against polytheism; the primitive assertion that the foreign deities are idols made by men out of wood, stone or precious metals hardly rates as an intellectual proof of the non-existence of other divine beings (although it continued to be repeated by both Jews and Christians for centuries). In practice, Jews had to resist the social and political attraction of the religions of their neighbouring peoples (Canaanites, Philistines), and even more so those of their Egyptian, Assyrian, Babylonian, Persian, Greek and Roman overlords. The worship of foreign gods was seen not so much as an erroneous act as the breach of a mystical monogamous matrimony between the heavenly King and his bride, the chosen people of Israel. It was only under the influence of the prophets of the exilic and post-exilic period in the sixth century BC that proper monotheism, the idea of a single God responsible for the creation of the world and mankind, entered Jewish consciousness, together with the conviction that only this God would ultimately be duly recognized by the whole human race. Monotheism remained the battle cry of the Jews whereas Christians were subjected to criticism by both Jews and pagans for falsely claiming to be monotheists.

Regarding the nature of the Jewish religion, one point is definitely beyond dispute: intellectual religious speculation as such played no part in Hebrew or Aramaic Jewish literature written in the Second Temple period after the Babylonian exile, or in the later centuries of Mishnah, Midrash and Talmud. The works of Philo and Josephus' *Against Apion* form the main exceptions in this field in antiquity. They were, however, composed in Greek either for Gentile readers or for Jews imbued with Hellenism. Jews produced no theological treatises in a Semitic language before the tenth century AD with the one possible exception of the first century BC 'Instruction on the two Spirits' incorporated into the Cave 1 manuscript of the Qumran Community Rule, in which the divine purpose of creation and the destiny of mankind are summarily expounded.

Judaism was primarily a religion of deeds. Apart from subscribing to a single doctrinal proposition concerning the oneness of God, it essentially amounted to a way of life. In the Temple or the synagogue, at home or in the workplace, religion was enacted through obedience to rules believed to have been laid down by the Deity. These rules, above all the Law of Moses, were handed down and interpreted by the caste of the Levitical priests, who were considered the divinely appointed guardians of justice and piety. Their monopoly remained uncontested until the second century BC when lay intellectuals, the Pharisees, whose authority stemmed from their learning, began to challenge them. The leadership of the Pharisees was to be taken over by their heirs, the rabbis, after the destruction of the Temple.

The religion of Jesus was essentially an appeal for eschatological action but subsequent Christianity, though it also insisted on deeds and for a time remained eschatological, was turned by Paul and John into a religion of believing. Notwithstanding its Jewish roots, it developed into a fundamentally distinct movement, which had already become creed-based with Ignatius of Antioch from the start of the second century AD, and took a philosophical turn with Justin in the mid-second century. The features dominating Christianity were belief concerning the nature of the Deity, the definition of Jesus Christ's person and of his work of salvation, and the redemptive function of the one true church. On authentic faith depended whether someone was within the church or outside it. Personal conduct in the religious domain came second to belief. Repentance, though early Christian rigorists allowed it only once after baptism, healed sin, and through penance every wrong could be put right as long as faith persisted.

Compared to Judaism, Christianity's cosmopolitan character constituted the second essential difference. Within decades after the crucifixion, the church turned away from the Jewish Temple and soon after AD 70 Christian supersessionism began, founded on the view that the destruction of Jerusalem and its sanctuary proved the rejection of Judaism by God and its replacement by a new people of God. Also by the end of the first century, increasing Jewish unresponsiveness to the preaching of the apostles and missionaries brought about an ever-increasing Hellenistic-Gentile takeover of the Jesus movement. They were preoccupied with the role of Christ in the salvation of mankind, his superterrestrial pre-existence entailing divine generation prior to time and his instrumentality in the creation of the cosmos before history began. The way of thinking of the Church Fathers was very different from that of Jesus. The principal task the prophet from Nazareth set in front of his Galilean followers was the pursuit of the Kingdom of God in the immediacy of the here and now. By the early fourth century the practical, charismatic Judaism preached by Jesus was transformed into an intellectual religion defined and regulated by dogma.

This book is meant to guide readers along the evolutionary path from the Jesus of history towards the Christ deified at the Council of Nicaea.

G. V.

Oxford, July 2011

I

Charismatic Judaism from
Moses to Jesus

The idea of charisma, envisaged in general terms, was first put on the map by the renowned German sociologist Max Weber (1864–1920):

> The charismatic hero does not deduce his authority from codes and statutes, as is the case with the jurisdiction of office; nor does he deduce his authority from traditional customs or feudal vows of faith, as is the case with patrimonial power. The charismatic leader gains and maintains authority solely by proving his strength in life. If he wants to be a prophet, he must perform miracles; if he wants to be a war lord, he must perform heroic deeds. (H. H. Gerth (ed.), *From Max Weber: Essays in Sociology*, 1979, pp. 248–9)

The phrase 'charismatic Judaism' was introduced into the biblical scholars' terminology in 1973 in my *Jesus the Jew*. As some readers may find the phrase baffling, I will start this book with a survey of the phenomenon in the scriptural narrative from the early stages of Israelite history to the first century AD, in other words, from Moses to Jesus.

The ordinary, formal, non-charismatic Jewish religion of the Old Testament age was centred on Temple and Torah, that is, the Law of Moses. The Bible reports that after the exodus from Egypt, the Israelites first worshipped in a mobile tent-sanctuary in the wilderness of Sinai, and after the settlement in Canaan they did so in numerous temples in various Palestinian locations; finally, following the closure of the provincial cult places, they worshipped in a single sanctuary in the capital, Jerusalem.

The Torah, on the other hand, represented a continuously evolving obligatory religious teaching relating to the Jewish way of life. Both the conduct of worship and the instruction and enforcement of the law were in the hands of a hereditary priesthood – first of the whole tribe of Levi and then, from the late seventh century BC onwards when only Jerusalem functioned, of the privileged priestly family of Aaron. From the mid-second century BC onwards, the lay Pharisees began to compete with the priests as interpreters of the Law, including the rules relating to Temple ceremonies.

A little earlier rivalry broke out within the ranks of the priesthood too. After the murder of the high priest Onias III in 171 BC, his son, Onias IV, turned his back on Jerusalem and set up a competing sanctuary at Leontopolis in the delta of the Nile in Egypt. Indeed, his descendants continued to officiate there until their schismatic centre of worship had to share the fate of Jerusalem, being destroyed by the Romans in AD 73/74. When the family of the Maccabees had taken over the pontificate in Jerusalem in 152 BC, their opponents, the Qumran Essenes, abandoned the national sanctuary and substituted for it a spiritual Temple within their community in which prayer and holy life replaced offerings and sacrifices, although they hoped to take charge of the national cult in the capital again at the end of time. Despite these internal upheavals, Jerusalem remained the focal point of cultic activity, especially during the three annual pilgrim festivals for most Palestinian Jews as well as for the pious visitors from the Diaspora. Temple worship came to an end in AD 70 with the destruction of Jerusalem at the end of the great uprising of the Jews against Rome. From then on the synagogues, already religious centres outside Jerusalem in the Holy Land and beyond its borders, became the only focal points of Jewish cultic activity.

Yet ever since the early centuries, beside the organized type of priestly religion there existed another variety. It claimed to be based on direct contact with the divine. On the highest level, this stream was represented by revelation-based prophetic Judaism. It was the religion of Moses at the burning bush and on the summit of Mount Sinai, and inherited by the Old Testament prophets, prominent figures who remonstrated with the rulers of Israel and sought to inspire the people. Their words have survived in the Bible.

On a less exalted level, there was also throughout the ages a popular religion, cut off from the public centres and priestly officialdom but equally marked by charismatic manifestations of ecstasy and wonder. As it was not part of mainstream religiosity and was often in conflict with kings and temple personnel, it was only sporadically recorded. It persisted nevertheless until the age of Jesus and beyond, indeed down to modern times both among Jews in the phenomenon of the Hasidic *Wunderrebbe* and among Pentecostal Christians of diverse denomination. Without this kind of charismatic Judaism the typical features of the religion of Jesus and early Christianity cannot be truly grasped.

THE BIBLICAL PERIOD

Charisma, or the display of divinely granted power, is attested in the Bible from Mosaic times to the epoch of the New Testament, but its most emphatic biblical pageant occurred roughly between 1000 and 800 BC. The trend was connected with three early prophetic figures – Samuel, Elijah and Elisha – who were also known as 'men of God'. To comprehend the kernel of charismatic Judaism, the concepts of 'prophet' and 'man of God' need therefore to be scrutinized.

To begin with prophecy, according to the English dictionary definition a prophet is a teacher who foretells the future, and 'to prophesy' is a transitive verb that implies the conveyance of a divine message. The Hebrew root *nun-bet-aleph* ('to prophesy') transmits a notion very different from the corresponding terms in Greek, Latin or modern languages. It does not refer to the announcement of a heavenly plan or instruction but instead, using the reflexive form of the verb, it describes the prophesying state. In fact, such an individual was seen as experiencing prophetic frenzy or ecstasy, caused by the divine spirit responsible for the prophet's strange behaviour. The nearest modern equivalent is the demeanour of Muslim mystics known as Sufis or whirling dervishes, who in the course of an ecstatic dance cut and wound themselves, or (in a less extreme form) the trance of exalted worshippers in Pentecostal churches.

The state of 'prophecy' first appears in a toned-down form in the first five books of the Bible, the Pentateuch. Moses, a visionary endowed with miraculous power, was its representative par excellence. Before transmitting the divine Law to the Jews he was under the spell of the spirit of God.

Never since has arisen in Israel a prophet like Moses, whom the Lord knew face to face. He was unequalled for all the signs and wonders that the Lord sent him to perform in the land of Egypt, against Pharaoh and all his servants and his entire land, and for all the mighty deeds and all the terrifying displays of power that Moses performed in the sight of Israel. (Deut. 34:10–12)

The spirit that inspired Moses was transferred also on to the seventy elders of his council. On that particular occasion they all behaved as prophets (Num. 11:24–5). Moreover, two of them, Eldad and Medad, did not so to speak sober up, and spirit-possessed they carried on prophesying (Num. 11:26–9).

However, the main evidence relating to charismatic prophecy is contained in later stories. For example, the Books of Samuel and Kings regularly refer to the ecstatic bands of the 'sons of prophets' linked to the local Jewish sanctuaries. Saul, the future first king of Israel, was seen in their company in the proximity of the shrine of Gibeah. They produced rapturous music, and their ecstasy was contagious. So Samuel announced to Saul: 'The spirit of the Lord will possess you, and you will be in a prophetic frenzy along with them and be turned into a different person' (1 Sam. 10:6, 10).

Pagan cultic prophets served also in the high places of worship of the Canaanite deity, Baal. In the ninth century BC the prophet Elijah single-handedly confronted and eliminated 450 of Baal's prophets on Mount Carmel. Whether the Jewish 'sons of prophets' wounded themselves with swords and lances as the Canaanites did (1 Kings 18:28) is not explicitly stated. Yet even three hundred years later, the Jewish prophet Zechariah asserted that wounds on a man's body revealed his prophetic status (Zech. 13:6).

The popular religion in the period of Samuel, Saul and David was filled with spirits and ghosts. In a telling anecdote Saul, facing the threat of the powerful army of the Philistines, first sought to discover through legitimate means God's plan for the outcome of the impending battle. When the Israelite prophets and dream interpreters turned out to be useless, in his despair the king turned to forbidden intermediaries (1 Sam. 28:3–20). But finding wizards proved difficult, as Saul had wiped them out earlier in his reign, in obedience to the Torah that outlawed sorcery (Lev. 20:27). Nevertheless, his men managed to ferret out the only female medium still hiding in the country, the notorious witch of Endor. She was ordered to summon up the spirit of the recently deceased Samuel from the underworld to find out from him the fate in store for the king and his host. Samuel announced imminent and total disaster: 'The Lord will give Israel along with you into the hands of the Philistines; and tomorrow you and your sons shall be with me; the Lord will also give the army of Israel into the hands of the Philistines' (1 Sam. 28:19).

In addition to the practitioners of the occult and to the ecstatic 'sons of prophets', we also find outstanding personalities designated as 'men of God'. Their activity has been described in a magisterial essay by J. B. Segal ('Popular Religion in Ancient Israel', 1976). Such persons were seen as possessing specific God-given qualities, enabling them to proclaim and demonstrate before kings and princes the authority of their divine patron, to take care and solve the problems of common people, and, above all, to heal the sick. Their peculiar power was directly attributed to the active presence of God's spirit in them. The folkloristic context in which they appear constitutes the natural setting of charismatic Judaism.

As mentioned earlier, Samuel, Elijah and Elisha are the chief representatives of this class, but they also bear the title of 'seer' or prophet. Samuel told Saul, whom he was soon to anoint as ruler of his people, not only how to find his father's stray donkeys, but also what to do with Israel's enemies (1 Sam. 9:1–21). The 'men of God' were not meek and mild: Samuel himself massacred the Amalekite enemies of the Jews, and Elijah did the same to the prophets of Baal after miraculously defeating them in a contest that proved the superiority of his God (1 Kings 18). He is also reported to have brought down lightning on soldiers dispatched to arrest him (2 Kings 1:9–12). The story recalls the two impulsive apostles of Jesus who wanted to punish with fire from heaven the unwelcoming Samaritans (Lk. 9:54). A shocking episode relates to Elisha who cursed and killed a group of impertinent children (2 Kings 2:23–4) as the young Jesus did to a playmate, according to the apocryphal Gospel of Thomas (Greek text B), for having hit him with a stone. Usually, however, the charismatic power of the ancient men of God served generous and loving purposes. They are typified by Elijah and his successor, Elisha, the heir of a 'double share of his spirit' (2 Kings 2:9).

Unsophisticated in appearance and wearing, like his future reincarnation, John the Baptist in the Gospels, a furry cloak and a leather loincloth (2 Kings 1:8; see Mt. 3:4) Elijah like Moses (see Exod. 33) was granted a vision of God on Mount Horeb, which the prophet reached after travelling forty days without food or drink (1 Kings 19:8). His mystical experience is presented even more dramatically than that of the Lawgiver. Instead of hiding in a cleft of the rock like Moses when the Lord went past him (Exod. 33:21–3), Elijah was allowed to experience directly the divine encounter, which started with a fright and ended gently in a communion of silence. It was in a quiet whisper that God chose to reveal himself to Elijah, thus insinuating the inward depth and beauty and the mystical quality of the charismatic religion.

> Now there was a great wind, so strong that it was splitting mountains and breaking rocks in pieces before the Lord, but the Lord was not in the wind; and after the wind an earthquake, but the Lord was not in the earthquake; and after the earthquake a fire, but the Lord was not in the fire; and after the fire a still small voice. (1 Kings 19:11–12)

Both Elijah and Elisha were celebrated wonder-workers. Elijah is depicted as randomly appearing and disappearing (1 Kings 18:12) until at the end he suddenly vanished, taken to heaven by a whirlwind and a chariot and horses of fire (2 Kings 2: 11). His cloak, inherited by Elisha, was seen as a miracle-working instrument (2 Kings 2:7–8, 13–14). Elijah, having been fed by ravens while hiding in a wadi (1 Kings 17:2–6), miraculously multiplied flour and oil for the Sidonian widow, whose charity provided him with bed and board during the great famine (1 Kings 17). Also adopting a peculiar yoga-type praying position, he produced rain that restored life in the country after a long drought (1 Kings 18:41–5).

Both Elijah and Elisha were worshipped as healers. Elijah revived the son of the widow who sheltered him. Like Abraham before the destruction of Sodom and Gomorrah (Gen. 18:22–33), Elijah reproached God for his unfair treatment of the widow, and resuscitated the boy by transmitting to him his own life force:

> He took him from her bosom, carried him up into the upper chamber . . . and laid him on his own bed. He cried out to the Lord, 'O Lord my God, have you brought calamity even upon the widow with whom I am staying, by killing her son?' Then he stretched himself upon the

child three times, and cried out to the Lord, 'O Lord my God, let this child's life come into him again.' The Lord listened to the voice of Elijah; the life of the child came into him again, and he revived. Elijah took the child ... and gave him to his mother; then Elijah said, 'See, your son is alive.' (1 Kings 17:19–23)

Elisha comes up with a performance that is portrayed in equally spectacular terms. Thanks to his intervention, a long-time childless woman from Shunem and her aged husband miraculously produced a son (2 Kings 4:8–17), but a few years later the boy suddenly died and his mother laid the body on the prophet's bed and informed Elisha.

The charismatic healing procedure is described in marvellous detail. First Elisha sent his staff with his servant to touch the face of the child, but the mission failed. So the man of God rushed to the house and delivered a charismatic kiss of life, whereupon seven sneezes marked the departure of the evil spirits responsible for the boy's death.

When Elisha came into the house, he saw the child lying dead on his bed. So he went in and closed the door on the two of them, and prayed to the Lord. Then he got up on the bed and lay upon the child, putting his mouth upon his mouth, his eyes upon his eyes, and his hands upon his hands; and while he lay bent over him, the flesh of the child became warm. He got down, walked once to and fro in the room, then got up again and bent over him; the child sneezed seven times and opened his eyes. (2 Kings 4:32–5)

Charisma was attached even to the dry bones of Elisha, which are reported to have restored to life a corpse that was thrown into the prophet's grave and thus accidentally came into contact with his remains (2 Kings 13:20–21).

Elisha's reputation as a miraculous healer was widespread and persuaded the Syrian general Naaman, stricken with a severe skin disease, to seek his intervention. At the Israelite king's advice Naaman visited the man of God. Elisha, without the courtesy of welcoming the Syrian dignitary, bluntly ordered him through his servant to wash himself seven times in the Jordan (2 Kings 5:10). Outraged, Naaman was on the point of returning home, but his attendants persuaded him to do as the prophet told him. Miraculously 'his flesh was restored like the flesh of a young boy' (2 Kings 5:14).

Miraculous feeding was another charismatic speciality according to the Old Testament. Elijah ensured the survival of his Sidonian bene-factress by a continuous supply of food during the famine (1 Kings 17:8–16), and Elisha, like Jesus was to do in his time, managed to quell the hunger of a hundred people with a few loaves of bread, and there was even some left over (2 Kings 4:42–4).

On the political level, Elisha was venerated as the saviour of his country for compelling the Arameans to end the siege of Samaria by means of the imaginary sound of approaching chariots and horses (2 Kings 7:6) and for giving victory to King Joash of Israel over Aram by symbolically shooting arrows in the direction of the Syrian camp (2 Kings 13:14–19).

With the development of the prophetic movement the popular fea-tures (frenzy and miraculous elements) receded from the foreground of charismatic Judaism and the phenomenon became more intellec-tual and didactic. The task of God's spokesmen was to proclaim a message relevant to contemporary events as well as to forecast the future. Prophets like Isaiah and Jeremiah continued to advise or criti-cize Jewish kings, but on the whole they ceased to be depicted as miracle-workers.

In the eighth and seventh centuries BC some prophets firmly clashed with the priests and were critical of the Temple worship. In their eyes concern with the punctilious performance of the sacrificial cult detracted from the primacy of true religion and morality.

Amos uttered unforgettable words:

> I hate, I despise your festivals,
>> and I take no delight in your solemn assemblies.
> Even though you offer me your burnt offerings and grain-offerings,
>> I will not accept them;
> And the offerings of well being of your fatted animals
>> I will not look upon.
> Take away from me the noise of your songs;
> I will not listen to the melody of your harps.
> But let justice roll down like waters,
>> and righteousness like an ever-flowing stream. (Am. 5:21–4)

8

Isaiah was no less emphatic:

> What to me is the multitude of your sacrifices? says the Lord;
> I have had enough of burnt-offerings of rams
>   and the fat of fed beasts;
> I do not delight in the blood of bulls, or of lambs, or of goats ...
> Trample my courts no more;
> Bringing offerings is futile;
> Incense is an abomination to me.
> New moon and Sabbath and calling of convocation –
>
> I cannot endure solemn assemblies with iniquity ...
> Wash yourselves; make yourselves clean;
> Remove the evil of your doings from before my eyes;
> Cease to do evil, learn to do good;
> Seek justice, rescue the oppressed;
> Defend the orphan, plead for the widow. (Isa. 1:11–17)

Micah, in turn, contrasts the religion of the prophets inspired by God with the Temple cult administered by priests:

> With what shall I come before the Lord,
>   and bow myself before God on high?
> Shall I come before him with burnt-offerings,
>   with calves a year old?
> Will the Lord be pleased with thousands of rams,
>   with tens of thousands of rivers of oil?
> Shall I give my firstborn for my transgression,
>   the fruit of my body for the sin of my soul?
> He has told you, O mortal, what is good;
>   and what does the Lord require of you
> But to do justice, and to love kindness,
>   and to walk humbly with your God? (Mic. 6:6–8)

Some of the messengers of God, like Amos, while claiming divine authority for their message, refused to be called prophets as they were not ecstatics. 'I am no prophet, nor a prophet's son', he told the priest of Bethel (Am. 7:10–15). It took centuries for the popular charismatic colouring of prophecy to wear off. Even as late as the time of

9

Zechariah (about 520–500 BC), messengers of God wished to conceal that they were prophets.

> On that day the prophets will be ashamed, every one, of their visions when they prophesy; they will not put on a hairy mantle in order to deceive, but each of them will say, I am no prophet, I am a tiller of the soil; for the land has been my possession since my youth. (Zech. 13:4–5)

Nevertheless, Isaiah still practised charisma when he cured the mortally sick King Hezekiah by applying a fig cake to his boils and demonstrated his divine call by causing the shadow on the royal sundial to move backwards instead of forwards (2 Kings 20:1–11; Isa. 38:1–8). Ezekiel, too, behaved strangely when he mimed his visions of the future. For example, he enacted the siege of Jerusalem by hitting a brick on which the likeness of a city was scratched, baked barley cakes on human dung to typify the future impure state of his compatriots when exiled to an unclean land, and walked through a hole in the city wall carrying a bag on his back to insinuate the deportation of the Jews to Babylonia (Ezek. 4). Ezekiel's charismatic mimicry was seen as endowed with efficiency: the subsequent events were attributed to his play-acting.

A final point must be made before concluding this sketch of charismatic Judaism in the biblical period. In Jewish thought of the pre-prophetic and prophetic age sickness was understood to be the divine punishment of sin, and conversely, healing was envisaged as God's prerogative. A clear expression of this attitude may be found in the post-exilic account of the end of the Judaean king Asa. While the pre-exilic historiographer was full of his praises (1 Kings 15:11–15), the fourth/third century BC author of 2 Chronicles criticized him for his lack of trust in God, for instead of asking for divine help, he mistakenly put his trust in the doctors (2 Chron. 16:12). The only humans qualified by the Torah to act in a quasi-medical capacity were the priests, whose task was to diagnose the onset and the cessation of 'leprosy', and to administer sundry purificatory rites required in the case of menstruation, childbirth, etc. (Lev. 12–15).

Prophecy, the original home of the charismatic religion, was supposed to have come to an end with the three last representatives of the movement during the period of the restoration of the Temple of Jerusalem under Persian rule (late sixth to fifth century BC). According to an early rabbinic tradition (tSotah 13:2), the death of Haggai, Zechariah and Malachi marked the end of the impact of the Holy Spirit on Israel through prophecy, but not the cessation of direct contact with God: it was maintained through an audible divine pronouncement designated in rabbinic literature as *bat qol* or the daughter of a voice. While the *bat qol* played an important role among the rabbis as well as in the Gospels (see p. 30), history does not support this view about the end of prophecy. In fact, in the final period of the Second Temple era (second century BC to the first century AD) prophets were still expected, as the first Book of the Maccabees (1 Mac. 4:46; 14:41), the Qumran Community Rule (1QS 9:11) and the New Testament (Mt. 11:9; 13:57; 21:11; Mk 6:4; Lk. 4:24; 7:16, 26; 24:19) demonstrate.

Moreover, the Dead Sea Scrolls have disclosed that a new form of prophecy, namely revealed exposition of the ancient predictions, was introduced by the Teacher of Righteousness, the anonymous priestly founder of the Qumran Community, in the middle of the second century BC. He is represented as a charismatic interpreter of biblical prophecy, having been enlightened by God about the true meaning of the obscure auguries recorded in Scripture.

> God told Habakkuk to write down what would happen to the last generation, but he did not make known to him when time would come to an end. And as for that which he said, 'That he who reads may read it speedily' (Hab. 2:2), interpreted, this concerns the Teacher of Righteousness, to whom God made known all the mysteries of the words of his servants, the prophets. (1QpHab. 7:1–5; see also 2:5–10)

Three Essene prophets, dating from the late second century BC to the beginning of the first century AD are mentioned by name in Josephus: Judas, Menahem and Simon (*Ant.* 13.311–13; 15.373–8; 17.345–8).

Charismatic Judaism refused to lie down.

EARLY POST-BIBLICAL LITERATURE

From occasional attestations in the Apocrypha and the pre-Christian Jewish writings known as the Pseudepigrapha, it is apparent that prophetic/popular religion continued in a semi-clandestine form during the last centuries of the Old Testament era. Like in earlier times, its prominent mode of expression was the healing of the sick. Despite the importance of medicine in the ancient Near East, the Hebrew Bible has little to say about Jewish physicians. The Law of Moses mentions Egyptian medical experts (Gen. 50:2), but alludes to their Israelite colleagues only once: in connection with the case of compensation an Israelite had to pay if he had injured someone, he was obliged to pay the bill of the physician who cared for his victim (Exod. 21:19).

At the beginning of the second century BC, Jesus son of Sira, himself a priest from Jerusalem and author of the apocryphal Book of Ecclesiasticus or Wisdom of Ben Sira, attempted to reconcile medicine with religion by turning the physician into a spiritual agent of the Almighty (Ecclus 38:1–14). Pious co-operation between repentant patients (Ecclus 38:9–11) and God-fearing doctors was considered the best recipe for cure in the opinion of Ben Sira. 'There is a time when success lies in their hands, for they too will pray to the Lord that he should grant them success in diagnosis and in healing, for the sake of preserving life' (Ecclus 38:13–14).

In the section of his book known as the Eulogy of the Fathers (Ecclus 44–50), the same sage went on praising the extraordinary power and the miracles of the men of God, Elijah and Elisha. The passage is filled with charismatic associations.

Then the prophet Elijah arose like a fire,
and his word burned like a torch.
He brought a famine upon them,
and by his zeal he made them few in number.
By the word of the Lord he shut up the heavens,
and also three times brought down fire.
How glorious you were, O Elijah, in your wondrous deeds!
And who has the right to boast which you have?
You who raised a corpse from death
and from Hades, by the word of the Most High;
who brought kings down to destruction,
and famous men from their beds;
who heard rebuke at Sinai
and judgments of vengeance at Horeb;
who anointed kings to inflict retribution,
and prophets to succeed you.

You who were taken up by a whirlwind of fire,
in a chariot with horses of fire;
you who are ready at the appointed time, it is written,
to calm the wrath of God before it breaks out in fury,
to turn the heart of the father to the son,
Blessed are those who saw you,
and those who have been adorned in love;
for we also shall surely live.

It was Elijah who was covered by the whirlwind,
and Elisha was filled with his spirit;
in all his days he did not tremble before any ruler,
and no one brought him into subjection.
Nothing was too hard for him,
and when he was dead his body prophesied.
As in his life he did wonders,
so in death his deeds were marvellous. (Ecclus 48:1–14)

These comments of Ben Sira on the two great charismatic prophets of the distant past, recall the summary of the career of Elisha by the first century AD Jewish historian Josephus, who speaks of 'astounding and marvellous deeds' ('*thaumasta gar kai paradoxa erga*', *Ant.* 9.182), performed through his prophetic power, a memorable expression, which recurs in Josephus' portrait of Jesus (see p. 32).

Jesus ben Sira's compromise between religion and medicine turned out to be superfluous and the charismatic-angelic type of healing continued to be popular in Jewish thinking. In post-exilic times illness kept on being linked to evil spirits and control over devils was in the hands of angels, in particular those of Raphael, the healing angel whose name means 'God has cured'. He first appears in the apocryphal Book of Tobit, probably dating from between 400 and 200 BC. In Tobit, Raphael is the God-appointed travelling companion of the young Tobias and his protector against the devil Asmodeus. This evil spirit, infatuated with Tobias's fiancée, the beautiful Sarah, sought to kill him on their wedding night as he had already murdered seven of her previous husbands before they could consummate the marriage. Raphael provided his young protégé with prophylactics, the heart and the liver of a fish, which Tobias had to put on burning incense. Repelled by the smell, the demon ran away, and Raphael pursued the evil spirit to the other end of Egypt and bound him there, thus saving Tobias's life. The same idea of angelic assistance is encountered in the First Book of Enoch, roughly contemporaneous with the Book of Tobit, of which pre-Christian Aramaic fragments have been found at Qumran. It was again the task of Raphael to overpower Azazel, the prince of demons (1 En. 10:1–7).

It is important to remember that the practitioners of charismatic Judaism learned the arcane art of healing from divinely inspired secret books, ascribed to two biblical characters, the patriarch Noah and King Solomon. According to the Book of Jubilees, Noah was taught by an angel how to conquer diseases and master demons through the use of medicinal herbs (Jub. 10:10–14). Solomon was the other source of charismatic wisdom and medicine. Biblical tradition already attributed to him some of the most important sapiential books of Scripture – Proverbs, Ecclesiastes and the Song of Songs – and the author of Ecclesiasticus further enlarged on the scriptural portrait by emphasizing Solomon's international fame (Ecclus 47:15, 17).

Josephus, the near contemporary of Jesus, supplied much additional folkloristic material.

> [Solomon] composed a thousand and five books of odes and songs, and three thousand books of parables and similitudes; for he spoke a parable about every kind of tree, from the hyssop to the cedar; and in like manner also about birds and all kinds of terrestrial creatures, and those that swim and those that fly ... And God granted him knowledge of the art used against demons for the benefit and healing of men. He also composed incantations by which illnesses are relieved and left behind forms of exorcism with which those possessed by demons drive them out, never to return; and this kind of cure is of very great power among us to this day. (*Ant.* 8.42–6)

In addition to general statements about Noah and Solomon regarding healing and exorcism, Jewish literary sources of the age of Jesus have preserved a number of new stories of cure and resuscitation by holy men of the past. The Genesis Apocryphon from Qumran Cave 1, dating from the second century BC, presents the patriarch Abraham as a charismatic controller of demons (1QapGen. 20:16–29). When his wife Sarah was taken to Pharaoh's harem, the patriarch's prayer rendered the king and all his male courtiers impotent to safeguard Sarah's virtue. When Pharaoh offered to release her, Abraham used his charismatic power against the demon: 'So I prayed [for him (Pharaoh)] ... and I laid my hands on his [head]; and the scourge departed from him and the evil [spirit] was expelled [from him], and he lived' (1QapGen. 20:8–29).

The third/second-century BC Hellenistic Jewish historian Artapanus presents Moses too as a miracle-working agent of God. We learn from him that Moses was thrown into prison by Pharaoh when the king heard of his intention to liberate the Jews, but at nightfall a series of miracles happened: the gates of the jail opened; some guards fell asleep while others died, and all their weapons fell to pieces. Thus Moses was able to walk out of the prison and unhindered he entered the royal bedchamber. The angry Pharaoh inquired about his god's name in order to curse it, and the sacrosanct Tetragram was murmured into his ears. He dropped dead at once, but miraculously Moses revived him (Eusebius, *Praep. Ev.* 9.27, 22–6).

A further anecdote of considerable importance comes from a Qumran writing akin to the Book of Daniel and probably dating from the first century BC. The fictional speaker is the last Babylonian king, Nabonidus, who declares that an unnamed Jewish charismatic, probably Daniel, pardoned his sins and simultaneously cured his disease. He is described as a *gazer*. The noun is mentioned in the Book of Daniel (2:27; 4:6; 5:7, 11) next to words signifying magicians, dream interpreters and astrologers. Literally a *gazer* issues decrees or commands; hence it is interpreted as 'exorcist' because the corresponding verb in rabbinic literature is connected to deliverance from demonic possession (see below, p. 24). 'The words of the prayer uttered by Nabunai king of the l[and of Ba]bylon, [the great] king ... I was afflicted [with an evil ulcer] for seven years ... and an exorcist (*gazer*) pardoned my sins. He was a Jew from [among the children of the exile of Judah' (4Q242).

In this Prayer of Nabonidus we have a remarkable anticipation of the Gospels with forgiveness of sins and healing the sick treated as connected notions (cf. Mk 2:8–11). Exorcism and the religious cure of diseases are testified to also in a historical account by Josephus relating to a story belonging to the first Jewish rebellion against Rome (AD 66–70). 'I have seen', Josephus asserts, a certain Eleazar, a countryman of mine, in the presence of Vespasian, his sons, tribunes and a number of other soldiers, free men possessed by demons, and this was the manner of the cure: he put to the nose of the possessed man a ring which had under its seal one of the roots pre-scribed by Solomon, and then, as the man smelled it, drew out the demon through the nostrils, and, when the man at once fell down, adjured the demon never to come back into him, speaking Solomon's name and reciting the incantations which he had composed. (*Ant.* 8.46)

The root in question, the mandrake (*Mandragora officinarum*), grew, according to Josephus, in Transjordan at Baara, not far from Herod the Great's palace at Machaerus. It was believed to be endowed with medicinal and exorcistic qualities (see Joan Taylor, 'Roots, Rem-edies and Properties of Stones', 2009, p. 236), but its collection was considered very dangerous.

Flame-coloured, and in the evening emitting a brilliant light, [the man-drake root] eludes the grasp of persons who approach with the intention of plucking it, as it shrinks up and can only be made to stand still by pouring on it either the urine of a woman or her menstrual blood. Even then to touch it is fatal unless one succeeds in carrying off the root itself, suspended from the hand. Another innocuous mode of capturing it is as follows. They dig all around it, leaving but a minute portion of the root covered; they then tie a dog to it and the animal rushing to follow the person who tied him easily pulls it up, but instantly dies . . . After this none need fear to handle it. With all these attendant risks, it possesses one virtue for which it is praised; for the so called demons . . . are promptly expelled by this root, if merely applied to the patients. (*War* 7.180–85)

Eleazar, like a circus magician, arranged a tangible proof of the departure of the evil spirit for the benefit of his high-ranking Roman spectators, Vespasian and his entourage: '[He] put a cup or foot-basin full of water a little way off and commanded the demon, as it went out of the man, to overturn it and make known to the spectators that he had left the man' (*Ant.* 8.46–8).

The conjecture of scholars that this Eleazar was an Essene broadens the historical perspective. The Essenes together with the Therapeutai, the Egyptian offshoot of the sect, were world-renowned as healers and ascetics. A number of scholars, including myself, link the name 'Essenes' (*Essaioi* in Greek) with the Aramaic *assaya* or 'healers', which is also one of the meanings of the Greek *therapeutai*. Josephus, in his detailed portrayal of the Essene community, emphatically states, 'They apply themselves with extraordinary zeal to the study of the works of the ancients choosing, above all, those which tend to be useful to body and soul. In them they study the healing of diseases, the roots offering protection and the properties of stones' (*War* 2.136).

Philo of Alexandria, in turn, describing the Therapeutai in the opening lines of his book *On the Contemplative Life*, specifies that their name has the double meaning of healers and worshippers of the Deity.

> I have spoken [in *Every good man is free*] of the Essenes who followed with zeal ... the life of action ... I will presently ... say whatever is meet to be said about those that have embraced contemplation ... The purpose and will of the lovers of wisdom is discovered in their very name and title, for they are most fitly called healers, male and female. Either by reason of their professing an art of healing more excellent than that which is found in cities – for this heals men's bodies alone, but theirs souls also ... or because they have been educated by nature and the holy laws to worship the true Being. (*Contemplative Life* 1–2)

Judging both from the New Testament and rabbinic literature, the simplest form of exorcism was through direct command, but it could be made specifically binding by the mention of the devil's name. Jesus once inquired about the identity of the Gadarene demon and learned that it was called 'Legion' (Mk 5:9). In later rabbinic literature we find the early second century AD rabbis Simeon ben Yohai and Eleazar ben Yose exorcising the daughter of a Roman emperor by ordering the devil called Ben Temalion to depart (bMeil. 17b).

Jewish exorcists and healers of the inter-Testamental age were no doubt also equipped with prayers and spells of the Solomonic kind. There exist plenty of magic formulae of a later vintage, but a few incantation texts belonging to the turn of the era are also available. One, found in Cave 4 at Qumran, was part of the Essene teacher's formulary against a variety of evil spirits.

> [God's] dominion is over all the powerful mighty ones
> and by the power of his might all shall be terrified and shall scatter,

and be put to flight by the splendour of the dwelling of his kingly glory.
And I, the Master, proclaim the majesty of his beauty
To frighten and terrify all the spirits of the destroying angels
And the spirits of the bastards, the demons,
Lilith, the howlers and the yelpers ...
They who strike suddenly to lead astray the spirit of understanding
And to appal their hearts. (4Q510, 3–5)

Furthermore, there is a song preserved in Pseudo-Philo's *Book of Biblical Antiquities*, produced in the first century AD. It is attributed to David, whose task was to ensure the well being of King Saul by restraining the evil spirit which was upsetting him.

And in that time the spirit of the Lord was taken away from Saul and an evil spirit was choking him. And Saul sent and brought David and he played a song on his lyre by night. And this was the song he played for Saul in order that the evil spirit might depart from him.

Darkness and silence were before the world was made,
And silence spoke a word and the darkness became light.
Then your name was pronounced ...
And after these was the tribe of your spirits made.
And now do not be troublesome ...
Remember Tartarus [Hell] where you walk
Let the new womb from which I was born rebuke you,
From which after a time one born from my loins will rule over you.
(*LAB* 60.1–3)

By contrast, it is noteworthy that according to the Gospels Jesus used only words of command, and never had recourse to exorcistic formulae.

RABBINIC LITERATURE

To complete the survey of the evidence capable of shedding light on charismatic Judaism, a summary glance must be cast on rabbinic literature's portrayal of prophet-like characters from the age of Jesus (100 BC–AD 100). Two such individuals stand out, Honi-Onias, surnamed 'the circle-drawer', from the time of the conquest of Jerusalem by Pompey in 63 BC, and Hanina ben Dosa, a first-century AD

Galilean holy man. Both resembled the prophet Elijah for their rain-making power; moreover, like Elijah and Elisha, Hanina was also celebrated as a miraculous healer and a general wonder-worker.

The earliest rabbinic version of the Honi anecdote is cast in a humorous mould, suggesting that some rabbis with pedestrian mentalities were not wholehearted admirers of charismatic piety.

> Once they said to Honi the Circle-drawer: 'Pray that it may rain' . . . He prayed but it did not rain. What did he then do? He drew a circle, stood in it, and said to God: 'Lord of the universe, your children have turned to me because I am like a son of the house before you. I swear by the great name that I will not move hence until you be merciful to your children.' It then began to drizzle. 'I have not asked for this,' he said, 'but for rain to fill cisterns, pits and rock cavities.' There came a cloudburst. 'I did not ask for this, but for a rain of grace, blessing and gift.' It then rained gently. (mTaan. 3:8)

Here and elsewhere we encounter a much loved and spoiled son, who is teased by God, his loving father. But the child persists with his demands until the father gives in to his pestering. Conventional rabbis considered Honi's behaviour disrespectful and deserving censure. Indeed, Jewish charismatics, Jesus among them, had a propensity to shock bourgeois sensitivities.

Josephus, writing for both Gentiles and Jews, is wholly reverential. He calls Honi-Onias 'the Righteous'. There is no question of accusing him of irreverence; Josephus depicts him as an admirable personality who, after averting national disaster by ending a disastrous drought, acted as an efficient mediator between God and the Jews. He even becomes a tragic hero who pays with his life for his refusal to take sides in the civil strife in Jerusalem between the Hasmonaean high priests Aristobulus II and Hyrcanus II in the mid-60s BC.

> Now there was a certain Onias, who, being a righteous man and dear to God, had once in a rainless period prayed to God to end the drought and God had heard his prayer, and sent rain; this man hid himself when he saw that the civil war continued to rage but he was taken to the camp of the Jews, and was asked to place a curse on Aristobulus and his fellow rebels, just as he had, by his prayers, put an end to the rainless period. But when in spite of his refusals and excuses he was forced to speak by

the mob, he stood up in their midst and said, 'O God, king of the universe, since these men standing beside me are Thy people, and those who are besieged are also Thy priests, I beseech Thee not to hearken to them against these men, nor to bring to pass what these men ask Thee to do to those others.' And when he prayed in this manner the villains among the Jews who stood round him stoned him to death. (*Ant.* 14.22–4)

Charismatic power ran in the family of Honi and two popular grandsons walked in the footsteps of the venerable grandfather. Abba Hilkiah was apparently a simple farmer, like Elisha before his meeting with Elijah. The title 'Abba' (which means 'Father') worn by both grandsons recalls the style of address of Elijah and Elisha (2 Kings 2:12; 6:21; 13:14). Abba Hilkiah was asked for rain by the rabbis, no doubt when their own formulaic supplications remained ineffective. When the rain arrived, Hilkiah denied that he had anything to do with it – a recurrent feature of modesty in stories told about charismatics, seen through, however, by the shrewd rabbis.

Once when the world was in need of rain the rabbis sent to him two rabbis that he should pray and it should rain. They went to his house, but did not find him. They went to the field and found him ploughing. [Returning to his house he said to his wife] 'I know that these rabbis came to see me for the rain. Let us go up to the roof and pray. The Holy One, blessed be He, will perhaps accept our prayer and there will be rain.' . . . The clouds appeared . . . He came down and asked the rabbis: 'Why did the rabbis come?' 'The rabbis sent us to you, Sir, that you might pray for rain.' He replied, 'Blessed be the Lord who put you beyond the need of Abba Hilkiah's prayer.' But they said, 'We know that this rain has come through you.' (bTaan. 23ab)

Such self-effacement calls to mind Jesus' attribution of healing to the sick person's faith.

Hanan the Shy (literally 'the Hiding'), Honi's other grandson, displayed similar modesty in parallel circumstances. It is worth noting that Hanan called God 'Abba', thus anticipating the terminology used by Jesus (see p. 48).

When the world was in need of rain, the rabbis sent school children to him who pulled the corners of his garment and said to him, 'Abba, Abba, Give us rain!' Hanan said, 'Lord of the universe, Do it for the sake of these who do not distinguish between the Abba who gives rain and the Abba who does not.' And rain came. (bTaan. 23b)

A younger contemporary of Jesus, Hanina ben Dosa, from the Galilean town of Arab (Arava or Gabara), is portrayed as a versatile charismatic; he was not just a rain-maker. He is introduced as the pupil of Yohanan ben Zakkai, the renowned Pharisee teacher active in the period of the first Jewish war. According to the Talmud, Yohanan spent eighteen years in Galilee in Hanina's hometown before moving to Jerusalem as the leader of the Pharisees. Only one peculiar story associates Hanina with rain, which he is depicted as capable of stopping when he was in discomfort, although he then restarted it to ensure that his compatriots would not suffer because of him.

> Hanina ben Dosa was once travelling along the road when it began to rain. He said, 'Lord of the universe, the whole world is in comfort while Hanina is in distress.' The rain stopped. When he reached his house, he said, 'Lord of the universe, the whole world is in distress while Hanina is in comfort.' The rain re-started. (bTaan. 24b)

Most of Hanina's other tales of wonder-working are connected with healing and protecting people from physical harm, but there is also a tale about his encounter with the queen of demons. Two particularly significant healing stories have survived, connected with the cure of the sons of famous rabbis, Yohanan ben Zakkai, Hanina's master, and Rabban Gamaliel, St Paul's presumed teacher.

> It happened when Rabban Hanina ben Dosa went to Rabban Yohanan ben Zakkai to study Torah, the son of Rabban Yohanan ben Zakkai fell ill. He said to him, 'Hanina, my son, pray for him that he may live.' He put his head between his knees and prayed and he lived. (bBer. 34b)

Hanina's charismatic healing was performed by effective prayer. Since the cure immediately followed his intercession, people linked the two and believed that his words actually effected the cure. The curled-up praying posture conducive to absolute concentration, which he adopted when he healed in absentia the son of Yohanan ben Zakkai, recalls Elijah's supplication on Mount Carmel when he bowed down on the ground and pressed his face against his knees (1 Kings 18:42).

A parallel healing narrative, dealing with the miraculous cure of the son of Rabban Gamaliel, has survived in two versions; both resemble the cure of the servant of a Roman centurion in Capernaum by Jesus (Mt. 8:5–13; Lk. 7:1–10).

The shorter one comes from the Palestinian Talmud.

> It happened that Rabban Gamaliel's son fell ill, and he sent two pupils to Rabban Hanina ben Dosa in his town. He said to them, 'Wait until I go to the upper room.' He went to the upper room then he came down. He said to them, 'I am assured that Rabban Gamaliel's son has now recovered from his illness.' They noted the time. In that hour he [the boy] asked for food. (yBer. 9d)

The Babylonian Talmud expands the narrative and inserts an explanation relating to Hanina's awareness concerning the efficacy of his words. For him smooth and spontaneous communication with God indicated success, whereas uninspired, rambling prayer was a bad omen for the patient.

> It happened that when Rabban Gamaliel's son fell ill, he sent two pupils to Rabban Hanina ben Dosa that he might pray for him. When he saw them, he went to the upper room and prayed. When he came down, he said to them, 'Go, for the fever has left him.' They said to him, 'Are you a prophet?' He said to them, 'I am no prophet, nor am I a prophet's son, but this is how I am favoured. If my prayer is fluent in my mouth, I know that he is favoured; if not, I know that the disease is lethal.' They sat down, wrote and noted the hour. When they came to Rabban Gamaliel, he said to them, 'By the worship! You have neither detracted from it, nor added to it, but this is how it happened. It was at that hour that the fever left him and he asked us for water to drink.' (bBer. 34b)

Some New Testament commentators, unhappy about the use of rabbinic anecdotes in the interpretation of the Gospel accounts of Jesus, try to diminish their significance by reducing the status of the leading personality from charismatic healer to that of an ordinary pious Jew praying for the sick. The sick were cured by God and not by them. But this is a present-day pedestrian way of perceiving the issue. In the mind of the contemporaries of Honi and Hanina, the miracle, be it rain or cure, resulted from their words. The case is clearly stated in the Abba Hilkiah episode above. The self-effacing holy man ascribed to God the termination of the drought ('Blessed be the Lord who put you beyond the need of Abba Hilkiah's prayer'), but the judicious rabbis were able to distinguish between an explanation inspired by humility and the real truth: 'We know that this rain has come through you', they tell him (bTaan. 23ab).

In addition to his reputation as healer of the sick, Hanina was also admired, like St Patrick in Ireland, as the protector of his community from poisonous snakes. Apropos of the concentration demanded before prayer, the Mishnah cites the example of the pious men of old who never allowed external circumstances to disturb the mental absorption. They would ignore even the greetings of a king and would fail to notice a snake wound around their foot (mBer. 5:1).

The rabbinic saga about Hanina goes further: he was so lost in prayer that he did not even notice that he was bitten by a reptile. At the end, the story was turned into a proverb.

> They say concerning Rabban Hanina ben Dosa that when he stood and recited the Tefillah, that a poisonous snake/lizard bit him, but he did not interrupt his prayer. His disciples went and found the creature dead at the entry to its hole. They said, 'Woe to the man bitten by a snake, but woe to the snake which has bitten ben Dosa.' (tBer. 3:20)

This basic anecdote developed into a more colourful tale using the imagery of the serpent of Paradise. The reference to Hanina's heel in mBer. 5:1 ('even though a snake wound around his heel') is inspired by Genesis 3:15, where the serpent strikes Adam's heel.

> It happened that there was a place in which there was a snake and it injured people. They went and reported it to Rabban Hanina ben Dosa. He said to them, 'Show me [my children] its hole.' He placed his heel on the opening of the hole. The snake came out, bit him and died. He put it on his shoulder and carried it to the school. He said to them, 'See my children, it is not the snake that kills but sin.' In that hour they said, 'Woe to the man who meets a snake, but woe to the snake that meets Rabban Hanina ben Dosa.' (yBer. 9a)

The anecdote has New Testament resonance and brings to mind Jesus' saying, 'Behold I have given authority to tread upon serpents and scorpions and over all the power of the enemy; and nothing shall hurt you' (Lk. 10:19; see also Mk 16:18). It is worth noting in passing that the charismatic is depicted as unconcerned with contracting ritual uncleanness through touching a dead animal (cf. Lev. 11:29–31).

The confrontation between men of God and the devil, ending with the victory of the former, is also part of the imagery of charismatic Judaism. Jesus is depicted as tempted by Satan; Hanina ben Dosa has an altercation with Agrath the daughter of Mahlath, a story which appropriately ends with expulsion of the queen of the demons. Rabbinic etiquette required people not to walk alone in the street at night, in order to bar gossip and avoid the demons lurking in the dark.

> Do not go out alone at night . . . for Agrath the daughter of Mahlath and eighteen myriads of destroying angels are on the prowl, and each is empowered to strike. In former times she was seen every night. Once she met Rabban Hanina ben Dosa and said to him, 'Had there been no commendation from heaven, "Take heed of Hanina and his teaching", I would have harmed you.' He said to her, 'If I am so highly esteemed in heaven, I decree that you shall never again pass through an inhabited place.' (bPes. 112b)

Hanina's superior status was revealed by a commendation from heaven, no doubt through a divine 'daughter of voice'. Also to effect the exclusion of the demonic queen from areas of human habitation, the Hebrew verb 'I decree' (*'ani gozer*) is used with the same exorcistic meaning as the Aramaic term (*gazer*) that occurs in the Qumran Prayer of Nabonidus (see above, p. 15).

Hanina also enjoyed the reputation of being the performer of a multitude of sundry miracles. For instance, in the Talmud, he enabled his wife to bake bread although there was no flour in the house (bTaan. 24b–25a). He also turned vinegar into oil to correct his daughter's mistake in pouring the wrong liquid into the Sabbath lamp (bTaan. 25a), indirectly recalling Jesus' turning water into wine at Cana (Jn 2:1–11).

Whole-hearted admiration by simple people went hand in hand with suspicion, resentment and jealousy on the part of spokesmen of officialdom, as was also experienced by the prophets of the Old Testament and by Jesus in the Gospels. The filial tone employed by Honi in his commerce with God infuriated Simeon ben Shetah, the chief Pharisee of his age. 'Simeon ben Shetah sent to him a message. "Had you not been Honi, I would have excommunicated you. But what can

I do to you? You importune God, yet he performs your will like a son that importunes his father and he performs his will"' (mTaan. 3:8).

Both Honi and Hanina were criticized for behaving as spoiled children towards their heavenly Father and petty-minded rabbis liked to belittle their achievements, but Yohanan ben Zakkai did not spare Hanina's praises and recognized his superior spiritual power. 'Rabban Yohanan ben Zakkai said, "Even if ben Zakkai had squeezed his head between his knees all day long, no attention would have been paid to him"' (bBer. 34b).

As has been observed, the historian Josephus was fully positive in his judgment of Honi, and considered him a wholly praiseworthy character who deserved the epithet of 'the Righteous'. His esteem was shared by later tradition, too. Thus Honi was compared to the prophet Elijah, both being agents in leading the Jews back to God: 'No man did bring people to the service of the Holy One blessed be He as well as Elijah and Honi the circle-drawer' (Gen. Rabbah 13:7).

Echoing popular admiration, the rabbinic praises of Hanina ben Dosa were no less emphatic. 'When Hanina ben Dosa died, the men of deed ceased' (mSot 9:15). Taking into account the New Testament's use of 'deeds' (*erga*) with reference to Jesus (Mt. 11:2; Lk. 24:19), there are good grounds to identify a 'man of deed' with a miracle-worker. Also, implicitly associated with Elijah, Hanina received the highest acclamation when he was identified as the person for whom the world to come was created (bBer. 61b). According to another legend, Hanina's closeness to God, his sonship of God, was constantly proclaimed by a heavenly voice. 'Every day a *bat qol* was issued [from Mt Horeb] and declared, The whole world is sustained on account of Hanina, my son, but Hanina my son is sustained by one kab of carob from one Sabbath eve to another' (bTaan. 24b). The similar praise of Jesus is recorded at his baptism and transfiguration (Mt. 3:17; Mk 1:11; Lk. 3:22; Mt. 17:5; Mk 9:7; Lk. 9:35).

This survey of over a millennium of Jewish history makes it possible to compile a list of the most notable features of the charismatic religion. Negatively, this type of Judaism had little or nothing to do with priesthood, Torah and Temple worship. The issue of legal observance, so essential for the priests and Levites and for the rabbis of the Mishnah and the Talmud, hardly ever arose in the charismatic context.

The only references to 'proper' conduct were associated with the criticism by conventional rabbis of the nonconformist behaviour of Honi and Hanina ben Dosa. There is only a single case of sacrificial worship: it is connected with the competition between Elijah and the prophets of Baal, introducing a miraculous fire from heaven to prove the superiority of the God of Israel.

Conflict between prophets and priests was endemic. Amaziah ordered Amos out of the royal sanctuary of Bethel (Am. 7:10–13) and the clash between prophets and Temple personnel on the subject of sacrificial worship is apparent in the citations from Amos, Hosea, Isaiah and Micah, and in the famous speech of Jeremiah against the sanctuary in Jerusalem (Jer. 7:1–14). In the first century BC Honi was stoned to death for not supporting either of the two competing high priests.

Turning now to religious activity of mystical character, this is thought to have resulted from the direct influence of the spirit of God, an influence that according to popular tradition was made manifest by charismatic behaviour. Such spirit-produced action is attributed to Moses, to the seventy elders of his council (and in particular, to Eldad and Medad), to Elijah and Elisha, who inherited the double share of Elijah's spirit, and obviously to Jesus. It was characteristic of all the 'men of God' down to the age of the rabbis.

The influence of the divine spirit is often marked by outward signs such as the ecstatic demeanour of the charismatics, the 'sons of prophets', Elijah, Elisha and possibly Ezekiel (as well as the transfiguration of Jesus in the New Testament), and occasionally by heavenly voices speaking to most prophets, including Elijah and Elisha, or giving testimony about Honi or Hanina ben Dosa (and Jesus).

Among the special activities of charismatics figure the ending of famine by the bringing of rain (Elijah, Honi, Hanina ben Dosa), the ability to survive on an insufficient amount of food and drink (Elijah, Hanina ben Dosa), the performance of sundry miracles (Elijah, Elisha, Hanina ben Dosa) and – first and foremost – the healing of the sick or resuscitation of the recently deceased (Moses, Elijah, Elisha, Isaiah, Hanina ben Dosa and Jesus).

The personal impact of the envoy of God plays a paramount role in charismatic Judaism. Contact with him is an essential stepping-stone in the march towards the Deity. In the post-prophetic age the charismatics were publicly proclaimed by heavenly voices (Hanina ben Dosa, Jesus) and their part played in salvation history became the subject of intense religious speculation. In the Old Testament saga Elijah was mysteriously translated to heaven in a fiery chariot drawn by horses of fire. Honi and Hanina ben Dosa were celebrated as protectors of humankind, and the entire Pauline and Johannine literature, not to mention centuries of theological effort deployed by the Christian church, sought to expound Jesus' relation to God and the redeeming character of his life and death.

In short, without a proper grasp of charismatic Judaism it is impossible to understand the rise of Christianity.

2

The Charismatic Religion of Jesus

To define the relationship between Jesus of Nazareth and charismatic Judaism, we have to scrutinize his picture in our earliest sources, the Synoptic Gospels of Mark, Matthew and Luke, with an occasional side glance at the later and historically generally less dependable account of John, the fourth evangelist, who nevertheless occasionally has preserved otherwise unattested historical insights. The apocryphal Gospel of Thomas, which was probably compiled in the first half of the second century AD and displays Gnostic tendencies, yields no trustworthy supplements to the portrait emerging from the canonical Gospels.

No dependable information is available concerning the childhood, youth, education and early adult life of Jesus. The tales about his birth and infancy and the single episode of the twelve-year-old boy's Passover pilgrimage to Jerusalem in the midst of his family constitute an inextricable mixture of legend and popular story-telling. His entry into real history is linked to the ministry of John the Baptist, another character surrounded in the Gospels by an air of mystery and miracle, the staple ingredients of charismatic Judaism.

JOHN THE BAPTIST AND JESUS

John, despite the attempts by the Gospel writers to subordinate him to Jesus, appears in fact as the dominant figure and the spiritual master. His birth is portrayed as miraculous in the infancy narrative of Luke. John was the son of Elizabeth, a relative of the mother of Jesus, a long-time sterile woman, already far beyond childbearing age, and his father was Zechariah, an elderly priest. According to Luke's infancy narrative, John was only a few months older than Jesus. The start of the Baptist's public career is precisely dated to the fifteenth year of the Roman emperor Tiberius, which corresponds to AD 28/9 (Lk. 3:1).

John is depicted in the Synoptic Gospels as a hermit prophet living in the wilderness close to the Jordan and preaching repentance and purification to Jews, whom he encouraged to mark their conversion by a ritual immersion or baptism in view of the imminently expected arrival of the Kingdom of God. A more detached echo is found in the *Jewish Antiquities* of Josephus (*Ant.* 18.117–18). John is called there a good man who encouraged his compatriots to practise piety towards God, justice among themselves and subject themselves to baptism for the purification of the body, their soul having already been cleansed by righteous behaviour. John's furry clothes and leather girdle make him look more like Elijah (see above, p. 5) than his contemporary, the hermit Bannus, young Josephus' spiritual teacher for a short while (Josephus, *Life* 11). Bannus, we learn, covered himself with tree bark rather than with animal skin as John did. Both followed a frugal diet – Bannus living on the produce of the desert, while the Baptist survived more specifically on locusts and wild or field honey (Mk 1:6; Mt. 3:4), the latter being possibly the sweet juice of a plant such as the carob, known also as St John's bread. (For the carob as the staple food of Hanina ben Dosa, see p. 25.)

The connection with Elijah is implicitly alluded to by Mark (1:2) where John is represented as the fulfilment of two prophecies of Malachi: 'See, I am sending my messenger ahead of you, who will prepare your way' (Mal. 3:1) and 'Lo, I will send you the prophet Elijah before the great and terrible day of the Lord comes' (Mal. 4:5 (3:23 in the Hebrew text)). The Baptist's identification with the returning Elijah is expressly attributed to Jesus: 'For all the prophets and the law prophesied until John came ... he is Elijah ...' (Mt. 11:13–14). We learn from words put on the lips of John that the aim of this new Elijah was the proclamation of the impending arrival of God's reign on earth: 'Repent, for the kingdom of heaven is at hand' (Mt. 3:2; Mk 1:15). It is also the implicit message of Luke. They all see in John the realization of the approach of God, the divine King, in the desert as announced in the Book of Isaiah 40:3, 'The voice of one crying out in the wilderness: "Prepare the way of the Lord, make his paths straight"'

(Mk 1:3; Mt. 3:3; Lk. 3:4). The same theme appears in the Dead Sea Scrolls too. Relying on Isaiah 40:3, the Qumran community chose withdrawal to the arid shore of the Dead Sea and return to the divine Law as the ideal condition for preparing the establishment on earth of the Kingdom of God.

John's apparently short career had a violent end when the tetrarch of Galilee, Herod Antipas, ordered his execution. According to the Gospels (Mk 6:17–29; Mt. 14:3–12) the tetrarch was infuriated by John's declaration that his marriage to Herodias, his sister-in-law, was invalid. Josephus, on the other hand, suggests that the eloquence of John appeared a potential threat to Antipas's rule:

> When many others joined the crowds about him, for they were greatly moved on hearing his words, Herod feared that John's great influence over the people would lead to a rebellion (for they seemed ready to do anything he might advise). Herod decided therefore that it would be much better to strike first and be rid of him before his work led to an uprising ... Accordingly John was sent a prisoner to Machaerus ... and was there put to death. (*Ant.* 18.119)

A further feature of charismatic Judaism within the context of an intense eschatological expectation of the Messiah (Lk. 3:15) or 'the one who is to come' (Mt. 11:3) is the testimony of a voice from heaven, accompanying the baptism of Jesus by John (for the *bat qol*, see p. 11). The celestial declaration about Jesus' filial status is given in two forms. In one version the proclamation is addressed to Jesus, and possibly is heard only by him: 'You are my Son, the Beloved; with you I am well pleased' (Mk 1:11; Lk. 3:22). In the other, by contrast, the voice seems to be audible to John and to all the bystanders: 'This is my Son, the Beloved, with whom I am well pleased' (Mt. 3:17). The former version is preferable for, if John heard the divine witness about Jesus, his later doubts as to whether Jesus was the promised Messiah or another was to be expected (Mt. 11:2; Lk. 7:19) are harder to explain.

Jesus entered the public domain as a follower and disciple of John. Mark reveals nothing about John's preaching apart from the general theme of repentance and the exhortation to purificatory immersion (baptism) in the Jordan. Matthew offers a summary statement: 'Repent, for the kingdom of heaven has come near' (Mt. 3:2), together with a reprimand addressed to the Pharisees and Sadducees (or to the multitude according to Luke). He sought to shake their proud conviction that divine favour belonged to them just because they were Jews. Using an Aramaic pun, he threatened them with the loss of their elect status: 'Do not presume to say to yourselves, We have Abraham as our father; for I tell you, God is able from these *stones* [*abnaya*] to raise up *sons* [*bnaya*] to Abraham' (Mt. 3:7–10; Lk. 3:7–9). Aiming at the definition of correct moral behaviour, John advised the multitude to be generous to the needy, the tax collectors to be fair, and the soldiers to be content with their wages and abstain from violence and looting (Lk. 3:10–14).

From this extremely sketchy description it can nevertheless be deduced that John the Baptist was an eschatological prophet from the charismatic lineage of Elijah, who saw himself as entrusted with the task of persuading his fellow Palestinian Jews to revert to a life of justice and benevolence in preparation for the instant approach of God. He was surrounded by a circle of disciples, according to the testimony of the Gospels (Mt. 9:14; Mk 2:18; Lk. 5:33; Jn 3:25). Consequently, if Jesus became one of his pupils, he no doubt inherited from the Baptist his leading ideas – first and foremost, the need for repentance in search of the Kingdom of heaven. If the Fourth Gospel can be relied on, Jesus, already surrounded by his own apostles, began to preach and baptize before John had disappeared from the scene of history. We learn from the Fourth Gospel of John that the original disciples of John complained to their leader about the rival Jesus party, but were silenced by the Baptist (Jn 3:22–30). In fact, Jesus was not competing with John. After the imprisonment of the Baptist by Herod Antipas, Jesus moved to Galilee and continued there the campaign of repentance initiated by the Baptist in the southern region of the Jordan valley (Mk 1:14; Mt. 4:12).

Jesus' original activity was characterized by 'the power of the spirit' (Lk. 4:14) and the essence of his teaching is summarized by Mark: 'The time is fulfilled, and the kingdom of God has come near; repent, and believe in the good news' (Mk 1:15). Matthew in turn expresses the same theme by putting into the mouth of Jesus the words of John's opening message, 'Repent, for the Kingdom of heaven is at hand'

(Mt. 4:17; cf. Mt. 3:2). In the footsteps of John, Jesus appeared as the envoy inaugurating the eagerly awaited onset of the reign of God over Israel and the world.

THE PORTRAIT OF JESUS IN THE GOSPELS

Jesus, the charismatic healer and exorcist

While scholars all agree that the Gospels are not strictly speaking historical documents, the basic depiction of Jesus as a charismatic prophet presents a perfectly credible typological image, that of the 'man of God' of charismatic Judaism. This image is in line with what our analysis of the relevant sources of the Bible, the Apocrypha, the Pseudepigrapha, the Dead Sea Scrolls and rabbinic literature has revealed. To the testimony of the traditional material must be added the authentic part of the *Testimonium Flavianum*, the famous passage of Flavius Josephus (*Ant.* 18.63), where Jesus is described as a 'wise man' and the 'performer of paradoxical deeds' (see G. Vermes, *Jesus in the Jewish World*, 2010, pp. 40–44). The purpose of this chapter is to sketch the portrait of a Galilean holy man, who exclusively addressed, and instructed his disciples to address, Jewish audiences – 'the lost sheep of the house of Israel' (Mt. 10:5; 15:24). Jesus' general contour can be retrieved from the Synoptic Gospels and occasionally from the Gospel of John. At the end of this exercise, the reader will be able to grasp how the evangelists intended their readers to see the historical Jesus, the great prophet from Nazareth in Galilee.

From the New Testament accounts Jesus emerges as a highly popular itinerant spiritual healer, exorcist and preacher. Leaving aside his message to be considered later (see pp. 38–50), let us first concentrate on his charismatic activity. It consisted in the cure of the sick, often also entailing, to use the terminology of the ancients, the expulsion of evil spirits, who were linked in the mind of Jesus' contemporaries to nervous and mental diseases. For the Jews of antiquity sickness, sin and the devil were three interconnected realities (see p. 10 in the previous chapter). Sin, brought about by the devil, was punished by sickness. In consequence, the healing of a disease was tantamount to forgiveness of sin, and both cure and forgiveness were the effects of exorcism.

Charismatic therapy with multiple cures is summarily alluded to in the Synoptic Gospels: 'He healed many who were sick with various diseases' (Mk 1:34; cf. Mk 3:10). The change in the sick persons' physical conditions is sometimes ascribed to their coming into contact with the body of Jesus or only with his garments: 'All who had diseases pressed upon him to touch him' (Mk 3:10), and again, 'And wherever he came ... they laid the sick in the market places and besought him that they might even touch the fringe of his clothes; and as many as touched it were made well' (Mk 6:56).

When resuscitating the young man from Nain, Jesus 'touched the bier' before issuing the command that he should rise (Lk. 7:14). In the case of a woman suffering from a flow of blood, contact with the robe of Jesus resulted in cure, but not without Jesus apparently noticing that power had surged from him (Mk 5:25–33). As has been noted in Chapter 1, charismatics did not feel compelled to protect their ritual purity by keeping themselves at a distance from dead or unclean bodies. Again and again they deliberately reached out towards the patients, either laying their hands on the sick or taking hold of them and raising them up. Thus, when begged by Jairus to touch his dying daughter, Jesus 'took her by the hand' and ordered her to rise from the dead (Mk 5:23, 41) and in the case of the mother-in-law of Simon-Peter, he 'took her by the hand and lifted her up, and the fever left her' (Mk 1:31). The spine of the woman who was humpbacked for eighteen years was straightened when Jesus placed his hands upon her and declared, 'Woman, you are freed from your infirmity' (Lk. 13:12–13).

It is worth pointing out that twice in the Synoptic Gospels and once in the Gospel of John, Jesus is credited with practices of the popular medicine of the age. A deaf-mute was cured after Jesus had put his finger into his ears and transferred his saliva to his tongue while uttering the Aramaic word *Ephphatha*, 'Be opened' (Mk 7:33–4). Likewise he is said to have restored the vision of the blind man from Bethsaida by spitting on his eyes and laying his hands on him. The story reminds one of a rabbinic legend in which the prophet Elijah cured Rabbi Juda ha-Nasi from toothache by touching the bad tooth with his finger (yKet. 35a). Talmudic tradition further holds that human spittle was endowed with therapeutic effect and was especially useful for treating eye troubles. In one of the few healing narratives of the Fourth Gospel, Jesus cured a man who had been blind from birth by smearing on his eyes mud produced from a mixture of dust and his own saliva (Jn 9:6).

The least 'magical-sounding' form of charismatic healing was achieved by a direct word of command: the thaumaturgist spoke and the illness vanished. In Luke's account of the healing of Peter's mother-in-law, Jesus merely 'rebuked the fever' (Lk. 4:39) and she recovered. A leper was cured with the words, 'Be clean' (Mk 1:42) after Jesus had touched him with his outstretched hand. On another occasion ten lepers found themselves restored to health as soon as they obeyed Jesus' injunction, 'Go and show yourselves to the priests' (Lk. 17:14–15). Healing from a distance is referred to in the case of the centurion's servant whose sickness disappeared when Jesus told the officer: 'Go; be it done for you as you have believed' (Mt. 8:13; cf. Jn 4:46–54). The paralysed man from Capernaum was told by Jesus, using the Aramaic idiom *bar nash* as a modest allusion to himself, 'That you may know that the *son of man* has authority to forgive sins . . . I say to you, take up your bed and go home' (Mk 2:10–11; see Vermes, *Jesus in the Jewish World*, pp. 236–55). No longer incapacitated by paralysis he walked away, as did another sick man at the Bethesda pool in Jerusalem (Jn 5:1–9). It is not without interest to note that in one case at least the cure was not instantly successful. The blind man from Bethsaida first regained only partial sight: 'I see men; but they are like trees, walking,' he replied to the question, 'Do you see anything?' A second imposition of hands by Jesus was necessary before full vision was restored (Mk 8:23–5).

The climax of charismatic healing attributed to Jesus is attained through the resuscitation of the dead, or more precisely, of recently deceased persons. Two such cases, recalling the stories of Elijah and Elisha detailed in Chapter 1, are the revival of the daughter of Jairus (Mk 5:21–4, 34–43; Lk. 8:40–42, 48–55; Mt. 9:18–19, 23–6), and that of the son of a widow from Nain (Lk. 7:11–17). Both the twelve-year-old girl and the young man were reawakened by direct command. The Galilean communal leader Jairus' daughter got up when she heard the Aramaic words, '*Talitha qum* . . . Little girl [literally, Little lamb] . . . arise!' (Mk 5:41), and the dead youth from Nain when Jesus declared, 'Young man ... get up' (Lk. 7:14), given only in Greek. (In Aramaic it would have been *Talya qum*.)

The raising of Lazarus in the Fourth Gospel (Jn 11:38–44) substantially differs from the Synoptic revival accounts. The resuscitation takes place not within minutes or hours after death, as in the case of the daughter of Jairus and the young man from Nain, but four days later with the decomposition of Lazarus' body already obvious from the foul smell: 'Lord, by this time he stinketh' (Jn 11:39), we read in the vigorous English of the King James Bible. (The more genteel Revised Standard Version mollifies this to, 'By this time there will be an odour'.) The stress lies on the apologetical value of the event: the raising of a man dead for four days demonstrates to the Jews the supernatural status of Jesus. The account should be regarded as evidence for the developing faith of early Christianity rather than as a testimony suitable for building up the charismatic portrait of Jesus.

Exorcism, or an expulsion order directed towards evil spirits held responsible for sickness, falls into the same category as healing by command. There are no less than ten individual as well as several generic examples mentioned in the Synoptic Gospels. As exorcism was an integral part of charismatic Judaism in the age of the late Second Temple and in the early rabbinic era, Jesus fits into a well-established pattern. Note, however, that not a single exorcism is recorded in the Gospel of John. The silence of the Fourth Gospel is attributable to the evangelist's view that exorcism was beneath the dignity of Jesus, and bodes ill for the general historical reliability of John.

Both exorcism and healing fall into the category of charismatic help. At the beginning of the public career of Jesus in Capernaum, 'they brought to him all who were sick or possessed with demons ... And he healed many who were sick and cast out many demons' (Mk 1:32, 34; cf. Lk. 6:17–18). Jesus' Galilean ministry is summed up as consisting of teaching in synagogues and healing all the sick and the demoniacs by the power that came out of him (Mk 1:39; Mt. 4:23–4; Lk. 6:18–19; cf. Mk 5:30).

Jesus' performance as an exorcist usually included an order given to the evil spirit, such as 'Be silent and come out of him' (Mk 1:25) or 'Come out of the man, you unclean spirit' (Mk 5:8). He probably used the Aramaic imperative *poq!* ('Get out!'), a term associated with exorcism in rabbinic literature. A detailed and definite injunction is found in the story of the epileptic boy whom the disciples of Jesus were unable to heal. 'You dumb and deaf spirit', Jesus declared, 'I command you, come out of him, and never enter him again' (Mk 9:25). The prohibition imposed on the devil from revisiting his former habitat is part of charismatic tradition, as we have seen earlier in the stories of Eleazar in Josephus and Hanina ben Dosa in rabbinic literature (pp. 16, 24). Indeed the human tendency to revert to one's bad old habits is clearly formulated in Jesus' saying:

> When the unclean spirit has gone out of a person, it wanders through waterless regions looking for a resting-place, but it finds none. Then it says, I will return to my house from which I came. When it comes, it finds it empty, swept, and put in order. Then it goes and brings along seven other spirits more evil than itself, and they enter and live there; and the last state of that person is worse than the first. (Mt. 12:43–5; Lk. 11:24–6)

The success of exorcism and of healing depended on a precondition; the possessed or sick person had to have faith in the charismatic ability of Jesus. Without the belief of the patients or of their carers, the exorcist's or healer's charisma was impaired. For instance, few cures were performed in Nazareth because of the unwillingness of the local people to recognize Jesus' special powers. In fact, we are told that even his relatives were incredulous and wanted to put an end to his activity as they thought he was out of his mind (Mk 3:21; 6:5). The words of Jesus' reaction evolved into a proverb, unless he himself was quoting a popular maxim, 'A prophet is without honour only in his home town, and among his own kin, and in his own house' (Mk 6:4; Mt. 13:57). Significantly, his inability or unwillingness to heal in his hometown is associated with the precedent of the prophets Elijah and Elisha, who performed their charismatic deeds for the benefit of foreigners from Sidon and Syria although there were plenty of widows and lepers among the Jewish inhabitants of the kingdom of Israel (Lk. 4:25–7). Also while his disciples, to whom he had delegated his charismatic power, enthusiastically reported, 'Lord, in your name even the demons submit to us!' (Lk. 10:17), for lack of faith now and then, for example in the case of the epileptic boy, they also experienced failures (Mk 9:17–18; Mt. 17:15–16; Lk. 9:38–40).

The Synoptic accounts lay down faith as the prerequisite for the efficacy of the charismatic action. In the episodes of the woman with a flux of blood and of blind Bartimaeus, Jesus directly attributed the cure to their belief. 'Go your way; your faith has made you well' (Mk 10:52); 'Daughter, your faith has made you well' (Mk 5:34; Mt. 9:22; Lk. 8:48). Other sick persons were told, 'Your faith has saved you; go in peace' (Lk. 7:50) and 'Get up and go on your way; your faith has made you well' (Lk. 17:19). The faith in question concerns the charismatic's power to perform the healing act. The story of the two blind men is quite explicit. To Jesus' question, 'Do you believe that I am able to do this?' they reply affirmatively and are told, 'According to your faith let it be done to you' (Mt. 9:28–9). Jesus' apparent denial of his own part in the healing or exorcism is to be ascribed to the customary modesty of the men of God, as we have seen earlier in the case of rabbinic miracle-workers. In other words, Jesus is depicted as conscious of possessing charismatic power. He is said to be aware that such power emanated from him in the course of an efficacious cure (Mk 5:30; Lk. 6:19), not unlike Hanina ben Dosa whose fluency in prayer was the sign of an efficacious cure (mBer. 5:5).

Healing, exorcism and resuscitation are the principal features of the charismatic Jesus, but they do not exhaust all the relevant Gospel material. The story of the miraculous feeding of five thousand with a few loaves and fish and the mention of twelve baskets filled with leftovers (Mk 6:31–44; Mt. 14:15–21; Lk. 9:10–17; see also Mk 8:1–10; Mt. 15:32–9) echo the multiplication of food by Elijah and Elisha (see p. 8). Since the Elisha episode also speaks of leftover food, the detail must conceal a purpose. It is no doubt intended to eliminate the theory that in fact people consumed only a few morsels of food, but were hypnotized to believe that they had a full meal.

Two nature miracles – the stilling of the storm on the Lake of Galilee (Mk 4:35–41; Mt. 8:23–7; Lk. 8:22–5) and the vision of someone (a ghost?) walking on the water (Mk 6:45–52) – belong to the class of legendary folk tales. The transfiguration story associates Jesus with the leading 'men of God' of the Hebrew Bible, Moses and Elijah, and his shining face on a Galilean mountain (Mk 9:2–8; Mt. 17:1–8; Lk. 9:28–36) reminds the reader of Moses' radiant visage on Mount Sinai (Exod. 34:29). The return of the charismatic prophet Elijah as fulfilled in the mission of John the Baptist is also alluded to in the same passage (Mk 9:9–13; Mt. 17:9–13).

In summary, it is worth repeating that the portrayal of Jesus as an exorcist and healer and his link with the figures of Moses, Elijah and Elisha firmly place him in the ideological framework of a charismatic prophet.

Jesus, the charismatic teacher

In addition to his renown as a man of wonders, Jesus was also admired as a powerful and inspiring teacher. We learn from the Gospels that from the outset of his independent mission away from the circle of John the Baptist he taught in local synagogues on Sabbaths, instructed or conversed with individuals or small groups on his journeys across the country, and addressed large gatherings in various places on the hillsides and plains of Galilee. Sometimes, in order to escape the crowds, he delivered his message from a boat, anchored close to the shore of the Sea of Galilee. The audiences found his preaching striking and distinctive. On the very first recorded occasion of Jesus preaching and exorcizing in the synagogue of Capernaum, the listeners expressed their amazement because of the peculiar character of his sermon, which exuded power: 'He taught them as one having authority, and not as the scribes . . . They were all amazed, and they kept on asking one another, "What is this? A new teaching with authority! He commands even the unclean spirits, and they obey him!"' (Mk 1:22, 27; Lk. 4:32, 36).

The elliptic saying – 'a new teaching with authority' – implied that Jesus' message differed from that of the customary synagogue preachers. From rabbinic literature we know that Jewish expositors of that period regularly supported their assertions with suitable Scripture quotations. But in the eyes of the Galilean congregations the confirmation of Jesus' words came, not from proof texts, but from the charismatic events (healings, exorcisms) that habitually accompanied his instruction.

The general Gospel statement that Jesus' preaching differed from that of the scribes is supported by the surprisingly small number of biblical quotations ascribed to him in the Synoptic Gospels. Counting all the examples, they amount to a mere forty-one cases in Mark, Matthew and Luke. This is an unimpressive total compared to the relevant figure in St Paul's Letter to the Romans alone. This single epistle yields twice as many Bible citations as the three Synoptic

Gospels taken together. Moreover, if we discard those quotes that are secondary, being editorial additions intended for clarification or stylistic embellishment, only nine of the original forty-one instances remain directly attributable to Jesus, a definitely unimpressive sum (see G. Vermes, *The Authentic Gospel of Jesus*, 2003, pp. 427–30).

Whole libraries have been written on how to distinguish the genuine teaching of Jesus in the Gospels from what has been added to it by the early church and later Christianity. I have tried to disentangle this highly complex issue in a previous study, negatively by eliminating the sayings which are likely to reflect the ideology, not of Jesus, but of nascent Christianity, and positively by arguing for authenticity from the nature and coherence of the remaining material. The views expressed here almost always rely on the findings of this earlier investigation (*Authentic Gospel*, pp. 376–97; see also Vermes, *Jesus in the Jewish World*, pp. 224–35). I will group the main themes of the teaching of Jesus around three fundamental topics: the Kingdom of God, God the Father and the Son or sons of God.

The Kingdom of God

Few scholars, if any, would dispute that, as far as its substance is concerned, the most essential feature of the religion preached by Jesus concerned the imminent onset of a new age and reality, which he called the Kingdom of heaven or the Kingdom of God. The first words placed on his lips in the Gospels related to the Kingdom and the prologue of the Acts of the Apostles asserts that the last topic he discussed with his inner circle was the same.

> The time is fulfilled, and the Kingdom of God is at hand; repent. (Mk 1:15)

> Repent, for the Kingdom of heaven is at hand. (Mt. 4:17)

> After his suffering he presented himself alive to them by many convincing proofs, appearing to them over the course of forty days and speaking about the Kingdom of God. (Acts 1:3)

The expression 'Kingdom of God' figures about one hundred times in the Synoptic Gospels; it remains important in the letters of Paul too, but almost totally disappears from John, which is written later. Only in a single episode, in Jesus' conversation with Nicodemus, is it mentioned a couple of times in passing (Jn 3:3–5). Not being an abstract thinker, let alone a systematic theologian, Jesus abstained from defining the Kingdom of God, or the Kingdom of heaven as Matthew and the rabbis prefer to call it, and chose rather to delineate it in colourful parables and similitudes. God's Kingdom is compared to this-worldly realities, although, strikingly, never to anything connected with politics or warfare. The conceptual identity of the Kingdom did not obsess Jesus; his fascination focused on the ways and means which would secure admittance into the Kingdom, as will be shown in the section dealing with the religion taught by Jesus. More than a dozen of his parables are Kingdom-centred, among them the parable of the sower (Mk 4:26), the mustard seed (Mk 4:30), the leaven (Mt. 13:33), the hidden treasure, the precious pearl and the net (Mt. 13:44, 45, 47). His teaching was especially concerned with the imminence of the final age, as two well-known sayings demonstrate:

> Truly I tell you, there are some standing here who will not taste death until they see that the Kingdom of God has come with power. (Mk 9:1; Mt. 16:28; Lk. 9:27)

> The Kingdom of God is in the midst of you. (Lk. 17:20)

The nearness of the end is further asserted without the explicit mention of the Kingdom in the eschatological discourse, 'Truly I tell you, this generation will not pass away until all these things have taken place' (Mk 13:30; Mt. 24:34; Lk. 21:32), as well as in the concluding phrase of Jesus' instruction to his twelve apostles concerning the imminence of the final day: 'For truly I tell you, you will not have gone through all the towns of Israel before the Son of Man comes' (Mt. 10:23).

Needless to say, the idea of the Kingdom of God was not invented either by John the Baptist or by Jesus. It grew out of old biblical traditions where it had been developing over centuries. It arose from the combined concepts of God seen as the ruler of Israel, the Israelite nation as God's people, and the Jewish king as ultimately God's lieutenant ruling over all the nations of the earth. Originally confined to God's dominion over the Jews, the idea progressively expanded to a divine rule over the whole of mankind, since God was the Creator of the whole world.

In the Hebrew Bible, God's kingship was expected to be established either through military conquest of the foreign nations by the Jewish king, followed by their religious subjection to the Deity of the victors, or directly by God without the royal or messianic human agency. The first witnesses of this notion were the prophets known as the Second and the Third Isaiah, who flourished in the exilic and early post-exilic age (the sixth century BC) and whose works were attached to the writings of the genuine Isaiah, dating from the eighth century BC.

> The wealth of Egypt and the merchandise of Ethiopia, and the Sabeans, tall of stature, shall come over to you and be yours, they shall follow you; they shall come over in chains and bow down to you. They will make supplication to you, saying, 'God is with you alone, and there is no other; there is no god besides him.' (Isa. 45:14)

> For darkness shall cover the earth, and thick darkness the peoples; but the Lord will arise upon you, and his glory will appear over you. Nations shall come to your light, and kings to the brightness of your dawn. (Isa. 60:2–3)

The Book of Daniel (completed in the 160s BC) and the literature of early post-biblical Judaism, the Apocrypha, Pseudepigrapha and the Dead Sea Scrolls (dating from 200 BC to AD 100) overlaid the Kingdom idea with eschatological traits, including the apocalyptic imagery of a cosmic battle culminating in the triumphal manifestation of the divine King. The religious enthusiasm generated by these ideas again and again developed into political and revolutionary action, as the history of the Jews reveals during the last two centuries of the Second Temple, finishing a generation after the ministry of Jesus with the great uprising against Rome (AD 66–70). During the early period of the rabbinic era (AD 100–300) the Kingdom of God concept with political connotations continued to linger on, notwithstanding a second disastrous rebellion against Roman rule led by Simeon ben Kosiba or Bar Kokhba under the emperor Hadrian (AD 132–5).

The Kingdom of heaven, incorporating the restored earthly kingdom of Israel, was seen as the counterpart of the Roman empire, known as the 'wicked kingdom', although the pious and often apolitical rabbis conceived of the establishment of God's realm, not through the power of the sword, but through total submission to the Law of Moses. This was to happen – to use their own words – through the acceptance of 'the yoke of the Torah'. In the well-known Aramaic prayer the Kaddish, which existed in the earliest rabbinic times and probably originated in the first century AD, God is implored to set up his Kingdom in the present age, 'in your life and in your days ... speedily in a short while'.

Jesus' Kingdom of God is situated between the apocalyptic and the rabbinic images, and on account of its non-bellicose character it rather foreshadows the pacific kingdom dreamed of by the rabbis than brings to fruition the cataclysmic reality of the apocalyptic visionaries, the battle of Armageddon of the author of the New Testament Book of Revelation from the end of the first century AD. It is obvious that Jesus' preaching of the Kingdom of God was not the outcome of ordinary Jewish theological speculation that was keen to discover the moment when God would reveal himself to mankind and outline the portents that signal his approach. The main pattern of this mental exercise is incorporated in the Book of Daniel and is based on the prophecy of Jeremiah 29:10. In it, the Babylonian empire was granted seventy years of domination over the Jews, but in Daniel 9:24 it was reinterpreted as meaning seventy *weeks* of years, i.e. 70 x 7 = 490 years, culminating in the installation of the 'abomination of desolation' in the Temple of Jerusalem, at the end of the present era.

Despite the absence of one out of four time elements, it is reasonable to assume that the eschatological chronology of the Damascus Document from Qumran also embraces the formula of seventy weeks of years. Its author states that 390 years separate Nebuchadnezzar's conquest of Jerusalem from the birth of the Qumran Community. The arrival of the Teacher of Righteousness is set twenty years later. The length of his ministry remains an unspecified X years. Finally, an interval of a further forty years is foreseen from the death of the Teacher until the end of the present era (CD 1:3–11; 20:13–15). Now if we conjecture that the career of the Teacher corresponded to the traditional duration of the leadership of Moses, that is forty years, the figures add up to seventy weeks of years, namely 390 + 20 + [40] + 40 = 490. Likewise an early rabbinic world chronicle, the *Seder 'Olam Rabba* (§30), presents a historically inexact, but theologically correct, time schedule in which the coming of the Messiah would occur 490 years after Nebuchadnezzar's conquest of Judaea. This is broken down into:

Babylonian rule	=	70 years
Persian rule	=	34 years
Greek rule	=	180 years
Hasmonaean rule	=	103 years
Herodian rule	=	103 years
		490 years

Early Christianity inherited a similar calculus, via Jeremiah and Daniel, in the eschatological discourse of Mark 13 and Matthew 24, a literary composition that is more likely attributable to the primitive church than to Jesus. It contains numerous hints borrowed from the eschatological speculations of the Old Testament which indicate that the end time would follow wars and persecutions, and would be preceded by the arrival of false Messiahs. Daniel's 'abomination of desolation', designating a pagan statue placed in the sanctuary, is the climax leading to the destruction of the Temple (Mk 13:5–20; Mt. 24:4–22; Lk. 21:8–24). St Paul, too, devised an amazingly detailed schedule for the final age, the *eschaton*, crowned with the *Parousia*, the Second Coming of Christ.

> As to the coming of our Lord Jesus Christ and our being gathered together to him, we beg you, brothers and sisters, not to be quickly shaken in mind or alarmed, either by spirit or by word or by letter, as though from us, to the effect that the day of the Lord is already here. Let no one deceive you in any way; for that day will not come unless the rebellion comes first and the lawless one is revealed, the one destined for destruction. He opposes and exalts himself above every so-called god or object of worship, so that he takes his seat in the temple of God, declaring himself to be God. Do you not remember that I told you these things when I was still with you? And you know what is now restraining him, so that he may be revealed when his time comes. For the mystery of lawlessness is already at work, but only until the one who now restrains it is removed. And then the lawless one will be revealed, whom the Lord Jesus will destroy with the breath of his mouth, annihilating him by the manifestation of his coming. The coming of the lawless one is apparent in the working of Satan, who uses all power, signs, lying wonders, and every kind of wicked deception for those who are perishing, because they refused to love the truth and so be saved. (2 Thess 2:1–10)

However, such a calculating mentality is irreconcilable with the stance of Jesus, who did not believe in mathematical flights of fancy. Nor was he on the lookout for premonitory give-aways: 'The Kingdom of God is not coming with signs to be observed' (Lk. 17:20; cf. Mk 8:11–13; Mt. 12:38–9; 16:1–4; Lk. 11:16, 29). For Jesus, the date of the arrival of the Kingdom was a mystery with which only God was acquainted: 'But of that day and that hour no one knows, not even the angels of heaven, nor the son, but only the Father' (Mk 13:32; Mt. 24:36). As the eschatological D-day was unpredictable, Jesus advised his followers to be prepared all the time, day or night.

He was indeed convinced from the beginning that the end time coinciding with the manifestation of the Kingdom of God was imminent, and had actually already begun. He did not need forewarnings, and consequently did not look for signs. His approach was not speculative but inspirational, and his charismatic standpoint tolerated no procrastination. The same urgency characterized his order to his apostles when he sent them to announce the instant arrival of the Kingdom of heaven (Mt. 10:7; Lk. 10:9). They were not to waste their time on unresponsive Jews: 'If . . . they refuse to hear you . . . shake off the dust that is on your feet' (Mk 6:11; Mt. 10:14; Lk. 9:5; 10:11), in other words turn your back on them and hurry to the next place which was hoped to be more promising.

In most of the relevant parables, and in all the preserved sayings, the Kingdom is an extant but concealed reality whose presence is, nevertheless, at times palpable and perceptible. According to Jesus, the Kingdom requires, and symbolically results from, the concerted action of the sower, the seed and the field (Mk 4:24–9), or is disclosed by the astonishing growth of the minute mustard seed into a tall shrub (Mk 4:30–32; Mt. 13:31–2; Lk. 13:18–19), or by the transformation of the flour into bread under the mysterious impact of the leaven (Mt. 13:33; Lk. 13:20–21). As good and evil were seen as co-existing, one must conclude that the scene was located in the here and now, at the farthest edge of the present era just before the onset of the new age. Seeds of corn and weeds, edible and inedible fish are still together in the parables of the sower and of the net (Mt. 13:24–43, 47–50). In two parables connected with the marriage feast, wise and foolish bridesmaids are waiting together for the groom and the bride, and worthy and unworthy guests try their best to enter the banquet hall (Mt. 25:1–13; 22:1–14; Lk. 14:16–24). In an anticipatory statement the Jesus of the Synoptic Gospels assured his disciples that the inchoate presence of the Kingdom of God could already be felt; in fact, it was in their midst (Lk. 17:20–21).

According to Jesus, this largely hidden reality of the Kingdom, like water accumulated underground, burst into the open through charismatic phenomena. He announced that victory over evil, the fruit of exorcism performed through the spirit or the finger of God, proved that the Kingdom had already arrived (Mt. 12:28; Lk. 11:20). The proclamation of the Kingdom of God attracted, in fact since the time of John the Baptist, large and tumultuous Jewish crowds elbowing, pushing and shoving their way forward in true Levantine fashion as everyone tried to 'enter by force' (Lk. 16:16; Mt. 11:12). The followers of Jesus were exhorted to believe that the Kingdom of God was just round the corner with its vanguard already almost in sight.

God, the Father

The next step towards the reconstruction of the religion of Jesus will lead to the God whose Kingdom Jesus was announcing and preparing. Jesus did not offer a philosophical or theological definition of God any more than he determined the idea of the divine Kingdom. In the existential and practical thought of Jesus and his disciples, God is what God does. For them, God was first and foremost a caring God, who looked after nature, after the lilies of the field, who provided little birds with nests and foxes with shelter and fed them all. He made the sun shine and the rain fall on each of his creatures. Natural catastrophes, like earthquakes, famine and pestilence, let alone tsunamis, were not encompassed in this vision.

Christians, unfamiliar with post-biblical Jewish religion and the cultural circumstances of first-century Palestine, often entertain an entirely false concept of Jesus' understanding of God and his relation to him. They assume that the contemporaries of Jesus felt distant from God and did not perceive or address him as their Father and the Father of all other creatures. They have also an erroneous appreciation of what the term 'son of God' signified in those days. A well-known New Testament scholar goes so far as to declare that the invocation of God as Father was *unthinkable* (my italics) in the prayer language of the Jews of Jesus' age (Ferdinand Hahn, *The Titles of Jesus in Christology*, 1969, p. 307).

To clarify these issues, one must first focus on the notion of the fatherhood of God in general, and, more precisely, on how God is envisaged in the Gospels as the Father of Jesus and of his followers. The frequency and variety of the phrases used by the evangelists – 'my Father' or 'your Father' (spoken by Jesus or his disciples), and even the all-inclusive 'our Father' – suggest that this nomenclature, together with the vocative use, 'Father!', was in no way peculiar and surprising. On the contrary, the terminology appears to have been common.

As a matter of fact, anyone familiar with Scripture and post-biblical Jewish writings will know that describing God or appealing to him as 'Father' is attested from the earliest times down to the rabbinic era. The personal names in the Bible such as Abi-el ('God is my Father'), Eli-ab ('My God is Father'), Abi-jah ('My Father is Yah [the Lord]', Yeho-ab or Jo-ab ('Yeho [the Lord] is Father') witness from the start a familiarity with the theological concept of divine paternity, and from the exilic period (mid-sixth century BC) the idea is positively formulated. 'For you are our Father, though Abraham does not know us and Israel does not acknowledge us; you, O Lord, are our Father' (Isa. 63:16; see Isa. 64:8; Ps 89:26; 1 Chron. 29:10).

God is spoken of or addressed as 'Father' in the Apocrypha too: 'O Lord, Father and Master of my life, do not abandon me ...' (Ecclus 23:1; see also 4:10; 23:4; 51:10; Tobit 13:4; Wisd. 14:3, etc.). The same is true of the Pseudepigrapha: 'May the Lord God be a Father to you, and may you be the first-born son and a people always' (Jub. 19:29; see also 1:25, 28; Test. of Judah 17:2; 24:2; etc.). Similarly, the Dead Sea Scrolls on various occasions employ the same language: 'My Father and my God, do not abandon me to the hands of the nations' (4Q372 1, 16), and again, 'For you are a Father to the sons of your truth' (1QH 17:35; see also 4Q200 6, 9–10; 4Q502 39, 3; 4Q511 27, 1, etc.).

It goes without saying that in the liturgical language of the public prayer of the Temple and the synagogue, God was usually addressed formally as 'Lord', 'our God' or 'King of the Universe', but one must not overlook the famous supplication, *Avinu, Malkenu* ('Our Father, our King'), a traditional formula associated with Rabbi Akiva already in the early second century AD (bTaan. 25b), and the even more apposite 'our Father who are in heaven' ('*Avinu she-ba-shamayim*'), a customary invocation in rabbinic literature.

Some further early synagogue prayers, too, are directed towards the divine Father: 'Lead us back, our Father, to your Torah . . . Forgive us, our Father, for we have sinned' (Eighteen Benedictions 5–6, Palestinian version) and the Aramaic prayer the Kaddish also mentions 'the Father who is in heaven'. As we have seen in the previous chapter, the ancient Hasidim spent a long period in concentration before directing their prayer towards 'their Father in heaven' (mBer. 5:1). The Galilean Hanina ben Dosa is the outstanding example of this. In brief, it can safely be concluded that calling on God as Father was traditional in Jewish circles; it was not, as has been repeatedly claimed by ill-informed or biased New Testament interpreters, an innovation introduced and practised by Jesus, and handed down only in the circle of his followers.

Arguing this view from a different stance, the renowned German New Testament scholar Joachim Jeremias propounded the thesis that the formula carried a peculiar nuance that linked it exclusively to Jesus (*The Prayers of Jesus*, 1977, pp. 57–65). According to Jeremias, the Aramaic word '*abba* was originally an exclamatory form derived from the babbling of children ('*ab-ba* like da-da, pa-pa, and '*im-ma* like ma-ma). Although addressing God in children's language would have struck conventional Jews as disrespectful, Jesus, conscious according to Jeremias of his unique closeness to the Deity, was brave enough to adopt the puerile '*abba* locution. While Jeremias's odd theory was promptly shown to be misconceived (see G. Vermes, *Jesus and the World of Judaism*, 1983, pp. 41–2; and especially and most powerfully, James Barr, 'Abba isn't Daddy', 1988), nevertheless it continues to be repeated, most recently by Pope Benedict XVI (*Jesus of Nazareth*, 2011, pp. 161–2), despite the fact that it is philologically groundless and from the literary-historical point of view erroneous. '*Abba* is not restricted to children's speech, but appears also in solemn, religious language (e.g. an oath taken on the life of '*abba*). Moreover, the New Testament indicates no awareness of anything being extraordinary in Jesus' use. For instance, the Aramaic term is never rendered in Greek as *papas* or *pappas* ('Dad' or 'Daddy') but is every time formally translated as '(the) Father' (*ho Pater*), once as an invocation spoken by Jesus (Mk 14:36) and twice as a prayer formula used by the Christian communities in the Pauline churches (Gal. 4:6; Rom. 8:15).

The best Aramaic illustration of the twofold significance of 'abba is found in the earlier quoted Talmudic anecdote about Abba Hanan (see Chapter 1, p. 20). Accosted by boys in the street during a period of drought with the request, 'Abba, Abba, give us rain!' the charismatic miracle-worker implored God to listen to the prayer of these children even though they addressed it to the wrong person, being unable to distinguish 'between the 'Abba [God] who gives rain and the other 'Abba [Hanan] who does not' (bTaan. 23b).

The double conclusion one may draw from the foregoing observations is that for Jesus, the almighty Lord of the Creation, the Ruler of the Kingdom of God, was first and foremost a provident and loving Father, and that his disciples too were instructed to adopt the same filial attitude towards their common heavenly Abba. The non-mention of natural catastrophes and of the suffering innocents is typical of Jesus' optimistic outlook regarding the end time. He believed that at the last moment paternal love would eliminate all the miseries of the world and God would be recognized by all as Father. We have to wait until the third century and the great theologian Origen for a firm formulation of this idea (see Chapter 9, p. 222).

As a negative confirmation of the association of Jesus' attitude to God and the address 'Father' it should be pointed out that on the only occasion when his trust appears to have been shaken, namely when the crucified Jesus realized that God was not going to intervene and save him, the invocation *Abba* is replaced by the less filial 'my God', *Eloi, Eloi* (or *Eli, Eli* in the Aramaic version of the opening verse of Psalm 22): '"*Eloi, eloi, lema sabachtani?*" Which means, "My God, my God, why have you forsaken me?"' (Mk 15:34; Mt. 27:46). Less heartrending is the pious prayer of Luke's dying Jesus, 'Father, into your hands I commit my spirit' (Lk. 23:46).

Son of God and sons of God

The concept that is reciprocal to 'God the Father' is 'son of God'. In fact, with apologies – if necessary – for the unavoidable non-inclusive language, any male human being addressing God as Father necessarily imagines himself to be in one way or another his son. However, the matter is not as simple as that. To begin with, the title 'son of God' is employed in the Hebrew Bible in no less than five different ways in relation to humans – not counting a sixth category, that of angels, who are also often designated as 'sons of God'. In the broadest sense, matching the notion of God as the Father of Israel, 'son of God' could be applied to every male member of the Jewish nation. Thus Moses is made to describe God's people to Pharaoh with the phrase, 'Israel is my son, my firstborn' (Exod. 4:22; see Hos. 11:1; Deut. 32:18–19, etc.). However, as time advanced, the sense of the expression became progressively restricted, first to pious Jews (Hebrew Ben Sira 4:10; Wisd. 2:17–18; Jub. 1:24–5, etc.), and later to saintly miracle-workers and charismatic Hasidim or devout men (Chapter 1, pp. 18–27). Close to the summit of the scale, it applies to the kings of Israel, each of whom became a 'son of God' at the moment of his enthronement. Finally, at the top of the pyramid we find the ultimate King, the Messiah son of David (see G. Vermes, *Jesus the Jew*, 1973, pp. 168–73, 180–83).

It is essential, however, to stress that one meaning is never attested because it is incompatible with Jewish monotheism. This is the non-metaphorical, indeed literal, employment of 'Son of God', implying not so much the holder's closeness to God owing to election, but his actual participation in the divine nature. Such a notion, though common in the surrounding Graeco-Roman and Oriental civilizations (see Vermes, *Jesus the Jew*, p. 173), was and has always remained anathema for the Jews of all ages, from biblical times to the present day.

The large majority of the uses of 'son of God' attested both in the singular and the plural in the Synoptic Gospels, reflect the terminology encountered in the Hebrew Bible and in post-biblical Jewish literature. As far as Jesus is concerned, with the exception of a single saying (Mt. 11:27; Lk. 10:22) which will be examined below, he is never recorded calling himself 'son of God' in the Synoptic Gospels. On the other hand, as has been remarked earlier, he is named 'my Son' by a heavenly voice at his baptism by John and by a divine proclamation at the Transfiguration (Mt. 3:17; Mk 1:11; Lk. 3:22; Mk 9:7; Mt. 17:5; Lk. 9:35). He is repeatedly referred to as 'son of God' by demoniacs, by beneficiaries of his healing action, and by his apostles. The phrase is often found on the lips of Jesus in regard to his followers, who were also designated as 'sons of God'. If there is a difference between the applications it is qualitative – Jesus being rated as having a higher degree of entitlement to be called 'son of God' than his disciples.

In the single exception just mentioned (Mt. 11:25–7; Lk.10:21–2), Jesus is identified as pre-eminently '*the* Son' (*ho Huios*). The self-designation occurs in a prayer in which he declares that 'no one knows the Son except the Father and no one knows the Father except the Son'. This dictum, unparalleled anywhere else in the Synoptic Gospels, echoes the theology of the Fourth Gospel and may well be part of a later Christian hymn that found its way into Matthew. The phrase sticks out from the otherwise homogeneous Synoptic terminology. If such a 'high Christology' had been genuinely part of Matthew and Luke (presumably borrowed from the pre-existent hypothetical source known as Q), one would have expected to find it more than once in the Gospels.

Another important saying from Mark and Matthew (Mk 13:32; Mt. 24:36), which states that the precise date of the eschatological D-day is not known to anyone, not even to the angels in heaven or to *the Son*, but only to the Father, places 'the Son' into a lower category than God. In consequence, the use is metaphorical, and conceivably authentic: the divine Father is omniscient while 'the Son' lacks the knowledge of the most crucial chronological detail, the H-hour of D-day. It is worth noting that the textual tradition of this verse is hesitant: the reference to 'the Son' is missing from a number of ancient manuscripts of Matthew and from a few of Mark. As a result, the attempt to eliminate the phrase expressly asserting the ignorance by 'the Son' of the date of the end can be ascribed to later church concern about the enhanced status of Jesus.

In sum, Jesus bore the title 'son of God' on account of his particular closeness to the Father. The choice may be attributed to his recognized status as the Messiah. However, since Jesus never seems to have much cared for the messianic title – as it appears from his usual evasive answer to the question, Are you the Christ? (see Vermes, *Jesus the Jew*, pp. 123–7) – the 'Son of God' epithet should be associated with his dignity as a pre-eminent charismatic prophet and providentially chosen leader of those elected to become the citizens of the Kingdom of heaven.

THE CHARISMATIC RELIGION
PREACHED BY JESUS

In the pursuit of his ultimate aim, the guidance of his followers towards the Kingdom of God, Jesus laid down firm doctrinal directives that his disciples were to embrace. As usual, he did not offer a systematic plan but handed out ad hoc advices, rules and commands. Taken together, they amount to what may be described as the eschatological charismatic religion of Jesus. Does the statement that his message was a 'new teaching' (see above, p. 38) signify that we are faced here with a 'new' religious system, substituted for the old one? Did Jesus launch a new faith? The preliminary question we have therefore to confront is the relationship between the charismatic religion of Jesus and his inherited Judaism.

Whether we judge by the general description of the cultic and cultural context presented by the evangelists, or by the actual teachings ascribed to Jesus, his religious conduct appears to have coincided in all the essentials with that of his Jewish contemporaries in the Holy Land. We are told that he was circumcised when he was eight days old, and his mother presented him in the Temple of Jerusalem and offered the sacrifice prescribed by the Law of Moses forty days after his birth (Lk. 2:22–4; cf. Lev. 12:1–8). According to the Synoptic Gospels, he regularly attended the local synagogue on the Sabbath, where he often taught the assembled gatherings, healed the sick and practised exorcism. He was a popular, much sought-after religious figure who attracted large Jewish crowds and his charismatic nonconformity was criticized by the synagogue and Temple authorities. But during his public career only on one occasion is Jesus said to have actively participated in the public synagogue service, reading the prescribed prophetic portion of the week after the section from the Law, and delivering a sermon on it (Lk. 4:16–22). The Infancy Gospel of Luke ends with the episode of the twelve-year-old, legally adult, Jesus making his pilgrimage to the Temple with other members of his family in conformity with the prescription of the Torah.

Although as a Jew living outside Jerusalem, Jesus was duty-bound to go up to the Holy City only three times a year for the great pilgrim festivals, according to the Synoptic Gospels his contact with the

Temple during his public career was limited to a single visit to the Holy City at the Passover, which turned out to be fatal. The Gospel of John, on the other hand, brings Jesus to Jerusalem during several Passovers, as well as once on the occasion of the autumnal feast of Tabernacles (Jn 7:10–14) and even once at the festival of Dedication (Hanukkah), a feast unlisted in the Torah and consequently not requiring compulsory attendance in the Temple (Jn 10:22–3). On one occasion he is described as paying the annual contribution towards the maintenance of the Temple. The evangelist adds that the money for it did not come from his purse, but was miraculously found in the mouth of a fish caught by Peter (Mt. 17:24–5). Jesus is portrayed as respecting various external observances: for example his cloak had tassels attached to it (Mt. 9:20; Lk. 8:44; Mt. 14:36; Mk 6:56) in conformity with the law of Numbers 15:38. In other words, he behaved and looked as an ordinary Jew of his age.

If Jesus observed the external requirements of the Torah, was he more discriminating in regard to the substance of the Mosaic legislation? There is no hint anywhere in the Gospels that he broke any of the commonly observed rules concerning ownership of property, commerce or agriculture, let alone the laws prohibiting homicide, rape or foreign worship. There are, however, three issues on which his legal observance has been questioned by scholars. It has been argued that Jesus discarded the biblical dietary laws (Mt. 15:10–11; Mk 7:15–20). For the German New Testament specialist Ernst Käsemann, this stance of Jesus amounted to the abandonment of the Jewish religion (*Essays on New Testament Themes*, 1964, p. 101)! But his argument is specious. In his figurative speech, Jesus maintained that the true cause of uncleanness was not external, but internal. Its source was the heart, out of which sprang thoughts leading to fornication, theft, murder, etc. – every breach of the Law. They caused sinfulness much more than food that entered through the mouth and ended up in the latrine. Jesus' words were misinterpreted by a glossator who inserted for the benefit of the later non-Jewish church the phrase 'Thus he declared all foods clean' into Mark 7:19.

No evidence suggests that Jesus intended to annul the distinction between clean and unclean food. If it had been known among his early Jewish followers that he had such an idea in mind, Peter would not have been so shocked by the thought of touching non-kosher meat. Yet when in a vision he was ordered by a heavenly voice to do so, he exclaimed, 'By no means, Lord; for I have never eaten anything that is profane or unclean' (Acts 10:14). Also, Paul's hand would have been strengthened in his rejection of the Jewish ritual law by the knowledge that he was faithfully following the teaching of Jesus.

The second controversial topic concerned forbidden healing activity. No one actually accused Jesus of breaking the relevant law, though one hears occasional indirect grumbles. For instance, the president of a Galilean synagogue is reported remonstrating against those members of the congregation who asked to be cured on the Sabbath. 'There are six days on which work ought to be done; come on those days and be cured, and not on the Sabbath day' (Lk. 13:14). This implies an oblique criticism of Jesus. However the complaint is largely irrelevant. Jesus usually healed by word of mouth and/or by touch, neither of which amounted to 'work' prohibited on the Sabbath, as the carrying or administering of medicines would have. Moreover, according to one of the basic principles of Judaism, the saving of life superseded the Sabbath – and healing definitely fell into the category of saving of life. Of course a pedantic reader could ask whether the illness Jesus treated was serious enough to legitimize healing on the Sabbath, but even according to the punctilious rabbis in case of doubt legal presumption favoured intervention, even when the complaint was no more than a sore throat (mYoma 8:6). The rabbinic dictum, 'The Sabbath is delivered up to you and not you to the Sabbath' (Mekhilta of R. Ishmael on Exod. 31:14) is almost the same as the saying of Jesus, 'The Sabbath was made for man, and not man for the Sabbath' (Mk 2:27).

The third issue concerns the authorization granted by Jewish law to terminate matrimony (Deut. 24:1–4). However, in disapproving of divorce, even at the price of upsetting his own apostles (Mk 10:1–12; Mt. 19:1–12), Jesus intended to lay emphasis on the ideal of life-long union between one man and one woman as it was instituted by God at the beginning (Gen. 1:27). In the final brief interval between his time and the coming of the Kingdom, Jesus proposed to restore the original monogamic form of marriage intended for life.

In addition to these three cases, the so-called 'antitheses', another set of sayings contained in the Sermon on the Mount (Mt. 5:21–48), is sometimes cited by New Testament interpreters as revealing Jesus' hostility to the Jewish Law. In these antitheses various Old Testament commandments are introduced with the words, 'You have heard that it was said to the men of old' or something similar, followed by Jesus' statement: 'But I say to you . . .'

The term 'antitheses' used by modern Gospel specialists to designate the passages in Matthew is probably inspired by the second-century Gnostic author Marcion's lost book, entitled 'Antitheses', in which contradictory Old Testament and New Testament sayings are discussed. Be this as it may; if taken in the strict sense, antitheses, i.e. statements of the opposite or the contrary, is a misnomer for these texts. In none of them does Jesus advocate the opposite of the scriptural saying. The negative commandments of the Decalogue, 'You shall not kill' or 'You shall not commit adultery' were not substituted by Jesus with 'You shall kill', or 'You shall commit adultery'. What he had in mind was to sharpen and underscore the inner significance of the biblical teaching, outlawing not only the sinful act itself (murder, prohibited sex, etc.), but also its inner motivation and root cause (anger, lustful desire). The already criticized Ernst Käsemann also claimed that the antitheses, too, were 'shattering' the framework of Judaism (*Essays on New Testament Themes*, p. 38). His stance reflects an anti-Jewish ideology that by now, fortunately, belongs to the debris of the past.

Did Jesus oppose any of the tenets of the Torah? Some Jews, who disapprove of Jesus, say so, as do some Christians who disapprove of Judaism. However, two statements of Jesus survive in Matthew and Luke that demonstrate that the religion preached by him derived from the Law of Moses and was not a negation of it. For Jesus, Judaism and the Torah were not a passing phase in the divine plan, but a religion destined to remain 'until heaven and earth pass away'. 'Do not think that I have come to abolish the law or the prophets; I have come not to abolish but to fulfil. For truly I tell you, until heaven and earth pass away, not one letter, not one stroke of a letter, will pass from the law' (Mt. 5:17–18).

Some have argued that this is not the voice of Jesus but that of Matthew, buttressing the beliefs of the primitive Judaeo-Christian church as opposed to Pauline Christianity. But the same purpose cannot be ascribed to the non-Jewish Luke, who in many other cases advocated the point of view and catered for the interest of Gentile Christianity (see G. Vermes, *The Changing Faces of Jesus*, 2001, pp. 218–19). Yet he was not less but rather more emphatic than Matthew on the lasting character of the Torah: 'It is easier for heaven and earth to pass away, than for one stroke of a letter in the Law to be dropped' (Lk. 16:17).

Therefore, let it be restated that if it had been known in the early church that Jesus was ready to discard at least part of the Torah, Paul would have had no difficulty in exempting his Gentile converts from the observance of the Jewish ceremonial law and circumcision.

Jesus was definitely not an antinomian; he was not against the Mosaic Law. Rather he tried, like other Jewish teachers before and after him, to summarize and abridge the Torah and help his disciples to concentrate their minds on the essentials. He selected the Ten Commandments as the kernel of Judaism (Mk 10:17–19; Mt. 19: 16–19; Lk. 18:18–20) as did his contemporary, Philo of Alexandria (*Special Laws* 1.1). Like Philo (*Hypothetica* 7.6) and the famous rabbi Hillel (bShab. 31a) among others, Jesus also proposed the so-called Golden Rule as his one-article code of morality: 'Whatever you wish that men would do to you, do so to them; for this is the Law and the Prophets' (Mt. 7:12). That Jesus used the positive form of the precept instead of the negative formula attested in Jewish sources makes no qualitative difference. In fact, the earliest Christian citation of the Golden Rule in the Didache follows the negative Jewish form (see Chapter 6, pp. 137–8). Finally to an honest seeker, who was 'not far from the Kingdom of God', Jesus disclosed the great commandment, the combination of two fundamental precepts of the Torah, 'Hear O Israel, the Lord our God, the Lord is one and you shall love the Lord your God with all your heart' (Deut. 6:4–5), and 'You shall love your neighbour as yourself' (Lev. 19:18, both quoted in Mk 12:28–34). Nothing stands closer to the heart of Judaism.

In short, the religion of Jesus was the religion of Moses and the biblical prophets, but a religion adapted for the requirements of the final age in which he and his generation believed they found themselves. All we need now is to sum up the disparate sayings that Jesus issued during his brief teaching career and ordered his followers to obey while they were awaiting the approaching Kingdom of God.

In the religion of Jesus customary priorities were reversed. Not only did he embrace prophetic preferences, placing the poor, the orphans, the widows and the prisoners before the conventionally devout, but he offered privileged treatment to the sick and to the pariahs of society. In his view, God preferred the prodigal son, the repentant tax collector and whore to the always well-behaved bourgeois conformist. The sayings abound. The preacher, nicknamed 'the friend of tax collectors and sinners' (Mt. 11:19; Lk. 7:34), did not appeal to the righteous (Mk 2:17; Mt. 9:13; Lk. 5:32), but to 'the lost sheep of the house of Israel' (Mt. 15:24; see also Mt. 10:6). Like the shepherd who forsakes his flock to find the one stray lamb and his joy overflows on retrieving it, so does according to Jesus the heavenly Father. His delight over one repentant sinner is greater than over ninety-nine just (Lk. 15:4–7).

In the hierarchy of access to the Kingdom of God, those animated by the simplicity, trust and intense desire of a child, those inspired by absolute reliance on a loving and caring heavenly Father are as highly valued as the truly repentant sinners: 'Unless you turn and become like children, you will never enter the Kingdom of heaven' (Mt. 18:3; Mk 10:15; Lk. 18:17). As has been remarked in connection with charismatic healing, faith/trust is the dominating virtue in the religion of Jesus. A hungry son trusts that his father would not give him a stone to eat when he has asked for bread, or a snake instead of fish (Mt. 7:9–10; Lk. 11:11–12). Also the hopeful gaze of a small child impresses God more than the self-assurance of a sage (Mt. 11:25; Lk. 10:21).

This stress laid on a childlike attitude towards God is peculiar to Jesus. Neither biblical nor post-biblical Judaism make of the young an object of admiration. The elderly wise man is the biblical ideal. Even St Paul, who proclaims himself an imitator of Christ (1 Cor. 11:1), still considered the child's behaviour inferior to that of an adult. 'When I was a child, I spoke like a child, I thought like a child, I reasoned like a child; when I became a man, I gave up childish ways' (1 Cor. 13:11). And again, 'Do not be children in your thinking ... in thinking be mature' (1 Cor. 14:20). Set against such a sensible statement of a grown-up, Jesus' advice and prayer strikes as an astonishing novelty.

> Whoever does not receive the Kingdom of God like a child shall not enter it. (Mk 10:15; Lk. 18:17)

> I thank you, Father, Lord of heaven and earth, because you have hidden these things from the wise and the intelligent and have revealed them to infants. (Mt. 11:25; Lk. 10:21)

The same sentiment of confidence is at the heart of Jesus' attitude to prayer. Limitless trust in God is its primary characteristic. Without trust, supplications to the heavenly Father are meaningless words; with it, everything moves to the sphere of the possible. 'Ask and it will be given you; seek and you will find; knock and it will be opened to you' (Mt. 7:7; Lk. 11:9). Inclined to emphasize and even to exaggerate, Jesus assured his followers that faith as small as a mustard seed could move mountains (Mk 11:23–4; Mt. 21:21–2). He best phrased his total reliance on God in the brief but memorable formula, 'Your will be done', the striking and unforgettable third petition of the Lord's Prayer.

Privacy was another prominent feature among the instructions of Jesus on prayer. He himself is repeatedly depicted as choosing solitude for communicating with God: he prays in the desert (Mk 1:35; Lk. 5:15), on a mountain close to Bethsaida (Mk 6:46; Mt. 14:23; Lk. 6:12), or in the garden of Gethsemane at some distance from his apostles (Mk 14:35; Mt. 26:39; Lk. 22:41). He disapproved of pompous or ostentatious prayer and advised his followers to perform good deeds and speak to God unwitnessed and without presenting him with a lengthy shopping list:

> Whenever you pray, go into your room and shut the door and pray to your Father who is in secret. When you are praying, do not heap up empty phrases as the Gentiles do; for they think that they will be heard because of their many words. Do not be like them, for your Father knows what you need before you ask him. (Mt. 6:6–8)

With the exception of the words of 'Our Father', which are in the first person plural, Jesus formulated all the other prayers to fit not communal but individual worship; eschatological piety appears to be essentially personal.

For Jesus, citizenship of the Kingdom depended on total devotion to the cause. To use the imagery of his parables, whoever wished to acquire a precious pearl or a treasure hidden in a field had to be ready to pay the price and sacrifice everything he had (Mt. 13:44–6). He placed next to the image of the infant that of the poverty-stricken widow who put her last two coppers into the Temple treasury. She was prepared to hand over 'everything she had, her whole life' (Mk 12:44; Lk. 21:3–4). Finally, using grim imagery, the Jesus of the

Synoptic Gospels asserted that a man had to castrate himself or get rid of an eye or a limb if that was the price to pay for entry into the Kingdom of God (Mk 9:45–7; Mt. 18:9; 19:12). As we shall see in Chapter 9, taking literally the hyperbolic counsel of Jesus, in his youthful but foolish enthusiasm the great Origen made a eunuch of himself.

Filial trust and readiness to sacrifice the entirety of what one possessed had to be followed up, in Jesus' thinking, by immediate and wholehearted action. 'Repent and believe' (Mk 1:15; Mt. 4:17) was a command which had to be implemented at once. Attention had to be fixed on the present time, on today: 'Do not be anxious about tomorrow . . . Let the day's own trouble be sufficient for the day' (Mt. 6:34; Lk. 12:22–31). One had to pray for the day's bread (Mt. 6:11; Lk. 11:3) and not for the availability of supplies for weeks or months ahead. The march towards the Kingdom was not permitted to be held up, not even, speaking by exaggeration, for the time needed to bury one's father (Lk. 9:60; Mt. 8:22). And once on the way, the new recruit was forbidden to hesitate about the future or dream nostalgically about the past: 'No one who puts his hand to the plough and looks back is fit for the Kingdom of God' (Lk. 9:62).

The eschatological religion laid out by Jesus before his followers was a reformulation of traditional Judaism in the framework of charismatic eschatology. It did not include a vision of a lasting future. Animated by pressing urgency, it demanded readiness to sacrifice all for the ultimate cause. When the end was expected at any instant, the present completely obliterated the morrow and sagacious planning for the future appeared to be fatuous. First personal property was to go overboard: in the urgency imposed by the imminent end, there was no time simultaneously to serve God and Mammon (Mt. 6:24). Also, one had to be prepared, as forewarned in biblical prophecy, for rifts in the family in the age leading to the manifestation of the Kingdom of God. The words of Micah (7:6), quoted in Matthew – 'For I have come to set a man against his father, and a daughter against her mother, and a daughter-in-law against her mother-in-law; and one's foes will be members of one's own household' (Mt. 10:35–6) – were believed to be approaching realization. The same idea recurs without Bible quotation in Mark 13:12: 'Brother will betray brother to death, and a father his child, and children will rise against parents and have them put to death.' Hence, in Jesus' mind, if duties towards one's family hampered progress in the advancement towards God, parents, spouses, siblings and children had to be sacrificed. The interest of the Kingdom of God overshadowed all other considerations. 'Truly I tell you, there is no one who has left house or wife or brothers or parents or children, for the sake of the kingdom of God, who will not get back very much more in this age, and in the age to come eternal life' (Lk. 18:29–30).

Finally, following the extreme hyperbole of Luke, to become a follower of Jesus, the disciple had to be ready to abandon his nearest and dearest and even sacrifice his own life, if necessary. 'Whoever comes to me and does not hate father and mother, wife and children, brothers and sisters, yes, and even life itself, cannot be my disciple' (Lk. 14:26).

In fact, in the particular circumstances of the final age ordinary family bonds, if they turned out to be an obstacle, had to be cut and fellow seekers of the Kingdom were to become one's new family. 'Whoever does the will of God is my brother, and sister, and mother' (Mk 3:35).

In sum, the Judaism preached by Jesus focused on the disciple's striving for God's impending Kingdom, and within it for the encounter with the loving and solicitous divine King and Father. It is remarkable to note that the concept of the church as an institution intended to continue the mission of Jesus, or the ceremony of baptism as a gateway into the community are completely absent from the Gospels of Mark and Luke, and appear only on three odd occasions in Matthew.

> On this rock I will build my church, and the powers of Hades shall not prevail against it. (Mt. 16:18)

> If [your brother] refuses to listen to [two or three people who try to correct him], tell it to the church; and if he refuses to listen even to the church, let him be to you as a Gentile or a tax collector. (Mt. 18:17)

> Make disciples of all the nations, baptizing them. (Mt. 28:19)

Neither is the institutional character of the Lord's Supper mentioned in Mark and Matthew. It is hinted at only in Luke, probably under Pauline influence, with the added command, 'Do this in remembrance of me' (Lk. 22:19; 1 Cor. 11:24–5).

The religion proclaimed by Jesus was a wholly theocentric one in which he played the role of the man of God par excellence, the prophet of prophets, the shepherd of the flock, the leader, revealer and teacher without being himself in any sense the object of worship as he later became in the fully fledged Christianity created by Paul and John, and especially from the second century onwards. In the Synoptic Gospels, unlike in the rest of the New Testament, the focal point of reflection and teaching is God, and not Jesus or Christ. It is towards God, the heavenly Father, that prayers and worship are directed without mediators. It is the Father himself who listens to supplications, offers a helping hand, and acts as protector, comforter and saviour. Surrounded by an aura of charisma, the religion practised and preached by Jesus was meant to be a passport allowing the holder without let or hindrance and without the need for other go-betweens to enter directly into the Kingdom of God. Christocentricity does not stem from the historical Jesus.

3

Nascent Charismatic Christianity

Nascent Christianity is defined here as the religion preached and organized by the apostles of Jesus and their associates during the first few decades of the new movement, from AD 30 to 70, and even as far as the end of the first century. Did it differ from the religion of Jesus and his Palestinian contemporaries? In other words, was their faith and practice still Judaism or was it already developing into something recognizably new? Also, what sort of evidence enables a researcher of today to come to grips with these problems?

To begin with an answer to the last question, the state of play relative to the religious conduct of the first generation of Jesus' disciples in Palestine can be reconstructed from the first twelve chapters of the Acts of the Apostles, and indirectly from some of the letters of Paul, especially 1 Corinthians, Galatians and Thessalonians. To a lesser extent, the epistles of James and John, and 'The Teaching of the Twelve Apostles' or Didache, the first manual of Christian practice dating to before AD 100, may also serve as sources. The original Palestinian branch of the church was first led by Peter, but fairly soon he was replaced by James, the brother of Jesus, as the dominant figure in the Jerusalem church. The relevant information about the creation and organization of the non-Jewish churches in the Diaspora is contained in the second half of Acts from chapter 13 onwards and especially in the letters of Paul, which will be discussed in Chapter 4.

The image of budding Christianity, mirrored in the missives of Paul and dating to the mid-first century AD, is older than the corresponding picture supplied by the Acts of the Apostles. The latter most probably reached its final form of composition sometime during the last two decades of the first century. Therefore we must allow here for the possibility of the further development of religious ideas concerning, for example, the Kingdom of God and the second coming or *Parousia* of Christ. Thus in Acts the expectation of the returning Jesus is less acute than in 1 Thessalonians (see pp. 79–81, and pp. 103–6), in conformity with Luke's tendency, two generations after the crucifixion, to water down the eschatological urgency characteristic of the mentality of Jesus and his immediate Palestinian followers. Luke for instance repeatedly leaves out the mention of the imminent arrival of the Kingdom of God, firmly stated in Mark and Matthew (Mk 1:15; Mt. 3:2; 4:17; 10:7). He is also silent on the return of the Son of Man with or on the clouds (see Mk 14:62; Mt. 26:64; Lk. 22:69).

The Acts of the Apostles, which is assumed to have been written by the same author as the Third Gospel, also incorporates editorial manipulations. It seeks to harmonize with the later, more sedate outlook of the church the early enthusiastic *Parousia* expectation, and modifies also other concepts such as the presentation of Peter, whom it turns into a champion of the Gentiles, and the portrayal of Paul as a miracle-working Palestinian charismatic. Such revisions apart, Acts offers a genuine insight into the life, thought and aspirations of the first generations of Jewish Christians. The picture it hands down, especially concerning the communities of the Holy Land, is closer to the religion of Jesus than to the Christianity of Paul and John.

THE PRIMITIVE JEWISH-CHRISTIAN CHURCH

How did the religious practices of the primitive church relate to those of Jesus and his Palestinian co-religionists? The short answer is that they were identical in substance. At the start, all the members of the Jesus confraternity were Jews, and they continued their traditional Jewish way of life, cultic practice included. Only when the question of the acceptance of non-Jews into the church first arose was the new movement confronted with an apparently unforeseen issue – the attitude they should adopt to pagans who wished to become Christians. The only notable difference compared with the public career of Jesus concerned the geographical setting of the Jewish-Christian community. Although Acts 9:31 speaks of the church in Galilee and Samaria, and mentions also Christian congregations in the coastal plain in

Lydda, Joppa, Ptolemais and Caesarea (Acts 9:32; 10:23; 21:7, 16), the centre point of Christian activity was by then no longer the Galilean homeland of Jesus, but Jerusalem, the religious centre of Judaism, and the south. Acts places the leading apostles, Peter, John and James, the brother of Jesus, in the capital of Judaea during the early days of the church. It was also in Jerusalem that the council of the apostles was convened (*c.* AD 49), when in the wake of Paul's first fruitful missionary expedition among pagans the problem of the admissibility of Gentiles into the Jesus fellowship was officially resolved. It was achieved by a compromise which exempted them from the preliminary duty of full embracement of Judaism. The Judaean location of the centre is confirmed by Paul's personal account in his letter to the Galatians, where he refers to two visits to Jerusalem, the first occurring three years after his so-called conversion, when he went to visit Peter and James in the Holy City, and a second fourteen years later, at the council of the apostles in Jerusalem, where he met with the approval of the 'pillars' of the church, James, Peter ('Cephas') and John (Gal. 1:18–19; 2:1, 9). Paul paid his respects once more to James, but not to Peter, on the occasion of his last sojourn in Jerusalem in AD 58 (Acts 21:18), by which time Peter must have left Jerusalem.

Again it is the Jerusalem church that is presented as the model community, to a limited extent similar in aspiration and organization to the Essene-Qumran sect. In order to finance life in common, its members were encouraged to sell their possessions to help their poorer brethren and put the proceeds into a common purse administered by the apostles (Acts 2:44; 4:34–5). They mainly differed from the Dead Sea sectaries in that their parting with property was voluntary, whereas at Qumran religious communism was obligatory. Nevertheless, the Ananias-Sapphira episode (see below, p. 71) reveals that a considerable moral pressure was exerted on members to place their wealth into the hands of the apostles. Apropos the centrality of Jerusalem, one should note that even the mother and brothers of Jesus are said to have left Nazareth and joined the community in the capital (Acts 1:14). This is the last reference to Mary in the New Testament, but Paul mentions the married siblings of Jesus as ministers of the Gospel (1 Cor. 9:5), and his brother James rose to prominence and replaced Peter as the head of the church of Jerusalem.

The genuine Jewishness of the confraternity is revealed by its attitude to the Temple, the spiritual centre of Judaism prior to AD 70. It was there that the daily and festive sacrificial worship was offered by the priests, accompanied by the prescribed prayers and followed at the appropriate time by the blessing of the worshippers. The Jewish sanctuary continued to be frequented even by Paul, up to the time of his last visit to Jerusalem in AD 58, and no doubt by all the followers of Jesus until its destruction twelve years later. The apostles visited the Temple not only because its courtyard was the normal place for open-air teaching (Acts 5:12, 20, 25, 42), but also to pray privately and publicly as other Jews did.

Peter and John are reported to have attended prayer in the Temple at three o'clock in the afternoon, the moment of the evening sacrifice, and healed a beggar who approached them at the so-called 'Beautiful Gate' (Acts 3:1–10). They performed a cure on another occasion in Solomon's Portico (Acts 5:12–16). The Temple was also the regular venue for prayer for all the members of the Jerusalem church, who spent much time in the sanctuary every day (Acts 2:46).

The religious activity of Paul in the Temple is also depicted in great detail. During his trip to Jerusalem after he had joined the Jesus movement, he had a trance while praying in the sacred precincts (Acts 22:17). On his last visit to the Holy City, he underwent the prescribed ritual cleansing, including the shaving of his head, thus preparing himself for the sacrifice the priests were to offer on his behalf (Acts 21:24–6). Finally, in his speech before the Roman governor Felix, Paul reasserted that he had come to Judaea to complete the obligatory rites of purification and offer sacrifices (Acts 24:17–18).

ENTRY INTO THE CHURCH

At the beginning, while in conformity with Jesus' command not to approach Gentiles (Mt. 10:5), all the potential candidates were Jews and the process of entry was simple. They continued to live in conformity with the Law of Moses and the ancestral customs, but also accepted the proclamation of the apostles about Jesus – namely that he was the promised Messiah, famous for his charismatic deeds, who was recently crucified, resurrected and taken up to heaven, and whose return would inaugurate God's everlasting Kingdom.

According to the Acts of the Apostles, entry into the new religious community was originally marked by a charismatic event, the reception of the Holy Spirit, which was followed by baptism. Thus initiated, the new adherents to the church placed themselves under the authority of the apostles of Jesus. Charismatic behaviour under the influence of the Holy Spirit was the identifying mark of the faithful. The phrase 'Holy Spirit', which occurs no less than seventy times, is the hallmark of the Acts of the Apostles. The author of Acts reports that the apostles were promised by Jesus the power of the Holy Ghost (Acts 1:8) and on the feast of Pentecost the twelve, or possibly the whole original assembly of 120 disciples (Acts 1:15), were filled with the fiery sparks of the Spirit (Acts 2:3–4). They went into a state of frenzy, 'speaking in tongues', like their Old Testament forerunners (p. 4). Seen from the point of view of outsiders, the frantic conduct of the spirit-possessed apostles resembled drunkenness, as reflected by the onlookers' remark, 'They are filled with new wine' (Acts 2:13). However, Peter attributed his and his colleagues' behaviour, not to the influence of alcohol, but to the fulfilment of a prediction by the prophet Joel about God pouring out his Spirit on the sons and daughters of Israel to make them prophesy, see visions and dream dreams (Acts 2:14–21).

The cultic entry into the Christian movement took the form of baptism. It was administered in the name of Jesus and was thus distinguished from the immersion ritual associated with John the Baptist. We are told that baptism preceded the descent of the Spirit on the occasion of the 3,000 Jews who, moved by Peter's speech at Pentecost, joined the original company of disciples. As usual with ancient storytellers, the figure may be inflated, for how could such a large group have been immersed in a pool in the middle of Jerusalem (Acts 2:38–41)? Sometimes, however, like in the case of Saul-Paul (Acts 9:17–18) and of the family of the Roman centurion Cornelius (Acts 10:44–5), possession by the Spirit preceded baptism. Later on the imparting of the Holy Spirit became formalized and followed the imposition of the apostles' hands, the rite previously used for healing. This was performed by Peter and John for Samaritan converts (Acts 8:16–17) and by Paul for the twelve Jewish disciples in Ephesus who had previously undergone only the baptism of John. After Paul had laid his hands on their heads, 'the Holy Spirit came upon them and they spoke in tongues and prophesied' (Acts 19:2–7).

The Holy Spirit is claimed also to have governed the activity of the prophets and teachers of the early church. One of them, Agabus, who travelled from Jerusalem to Antioch, predicted 'by the Spirit' a famine that was to devastate many countries during the reign of the emperor Claudius (AD 41–54). Josephus reports that it actually hit Judaea between AD 46 and 48, during the governorship of Tiberius Julius Alexander (*Ant.* 20.101). On a later occasion, the same prophet acted as a mime, tying up his feet and hands with Paul's girdle, and declaring in the name of the Holy Spirit: 'This is the way the Jews of Jerusalem will bind the man who owns this belt and will hand him over to the Gentiles' (Acts 21:10–11). To the Holy Spirit was attributed also the choice and dispatch of Paul and Barnabas on their first missionary journey (Acts 13:1–4), as well as major practical or disciplinary decisions such as whether Paul should preach in the provinces of Asia, Bithynia and Macedonia (Acts 16:6–7; 19:21) or, most important, whether the Gentile converts should be excused from the bulk of duties laid on the Jews by the Law of Moses. The decree of the council of the apostles asserted: 'It has seemed good to the Holy Spirit and to us to impose on you no further burden than the essentials' (Acts 15:28).

THE ADMISSIBILITY OF NON-JEWS INTO THE JESUS MOVEMENT

The case of the family of the Gentile Cornelius raises the most crucial problem the original disciples of Jesus had to confront: the handling of non-Jews who wished to join their community. This question gained particular intensity in the wake of the missionary activity of Barnabas and Paul in Antioch and Asia Minor, though no doubt unhistorically Acts antedates it to Peter's ministry in the Holy Land. The instinctive Judaeo-Christian answer was that if Gentiles desired to become fully fledged members of their community, they had first to convert to Judaism – through circumcision in the case of male aspirants – and that both men and women had to take on themselves all the moral, cultic and dietary obligations of the Mosaic Law.

The apostles possessed no ready-made answer, which means that there existed no tradition originating with Jesus relative to the treatment of Gentiles who declared willingness to accept the Gospel.

Indeed, no authentic command to bring the good news to all the nations of the world can be traced to Jesus. The issue did not truly arise before the success of St Paul's mission among non-Jews in the Graeco-Roman world.

The Acts of the Apostles offers a twofold solution to the dilemma of the Gentiles' admission to the church. The first is exceptional, theological and possibly fictional. Its leading actor is Peter and the action focuses on the fate of Cornelius, a Roman centurion stationed in Caesarea. The whole miracle-filled story smacks of legend. The pious Cornelius, renowned as a God-fearing sympathizer of Judaism and admired for his generosity towards the members of the local synagogue, was instructed in a heavenly vision to invite Peter to his home. Simultaneously Peter, while at Joppa, fell into a trance as he prayed on a housetop in the midday sun. He saw a sheet descending three times from heaven, holding a mixture of ritually clean and unclean creatures and heard a command: Slaughter and eat! He instinctively refused, protesting that being an observant Jew he had never tasted forbidden food in his life. However the heavenly voice rebuffed him: 'What God has cleansed, you must not call profane' (Acts 10:1–16).

This dream vision was immediately followed by the arrival of Cornelius' envoys, who asked Peter to accompany them to Caesarea. In the light of the heavenly cancellation of all distinction between clean and unclean (understood to apply also to clean Jews and unclean Gentiles), Peter felt authorized to preach the story of Jesus to Cornelius, his family and friends. Then out of the blue, the Holy Spirit fell on the non-Jews. They, like the apostles at Pentecost, became ecstatic and began to speak in tongues and praise God. So they all were baptized without further ado in the name of Jesus (Acts 10:17–48).

Despite this purported divine approval of the admission of Gentiles into the Christian fold without passing through Judaism, the conventional Jewish members of the Jerusalem church, 'the men of James' sarcastically described as the 'circumcision party' (Acts 11:2; Gal. 2:12), continued with their refusal either to accept uncircumcised pagans as brethren or to associate themselves with them in a common table fellowship.

As the Cornelius episode in Acts is the only conversion recorded there of a non-Jew to Christianity in the Holy Land, the enthusiastic part assigned to Peter who, as the later clash between him and Paul in

Antioch reveals, was only a half-hearted champion of the Gentile mission, makes one wonder whether the role attributed to him here and in the council of the apostles is 'politically' motivated. It is likely to reflect a growing rivalry between Peter and James, the brother of Jesus, regarding the leadership of the Jewish-Christian branch of the new church. Both Acts and Paul consider Peter as the apostle entrusted with the gospel for the Jews, while Paul was in charge of the Gentiles – as he bluntly put it, he was preaching 'the gospel for the foreskin' (Gal. 2:7).

It should be observed that the author of Acts paints an incoherent picture of Peter. On the one hand, he is made out to be a strict observer of the Mosaic Law who has never in his life consumed non-kosher food. On the other hand he is portrayed as a champion of the acceptance of the Gentiles into the church and calls the Torah an intolerable burden: 'a yoke that neither our ancestors nor we have been able to bear' (Acts 15:10). The moral cowardice attributed to him by Paul (see p. 69) tallies with the faint-hearted behaviour that Peter displayed after the arrest of Jesus according to the report of all the four Gospels (Mk 14:66–72; Mt. 26:69–75; Lk. 22:56–62; Jn 18:17, 25–7).

The real battlefield on which the acceptance of the Gentiles into the Jesus fellowship was fought lay outside Palestine, in Antioch in northern Syria in the first instance, and the chief actors were Paul and Barnabas representing the interest of Gentile converts on the one hand, and on the other James with his associates from Jerusalem, some of them formerly of Pharisee persuasion, who argued the case of the Judaeo-Christians firmly attached to Jewish ancestral traditions. The inconsistent Peter played an equivocal part in the conflict. The author of the Acts of the Apostles tried to sweep under the carpet the open row between Peter and Paul, but Paul in his own account stands up for his convictions, portraying Peter as gutless and two-faced.

The mission in Antioch began with Palestinian refugee members of the Christian movement preaching the message about Jesus exclusively to the Jews of the city, but some Jewish brothers from Cyprus and Cyrene ventured to proclaim the Gospel also to the Greeks, many of whom showed interest. Barnabas, dispatched from Jerusalem to lead the new community, went to fetch Paul from Tarsus in Cilicia to assist him (Acts 11:19–26). The two branches of the Christian community, the Jewish and the Gentile, peacefully mingled for a while and had meals together, and Peter, visiting Antioch, did not hesitate to eat at the same table as the Gentile Christians. However, as we learn from Paul, when emissaries of James's 'circumcision party' turned up in Antioch, Peter, together with all the other Jewish Christians (including even Barnabas), withdrew from the common table, and the furious Paul openly accused Peter and the rest of the Jews of hypocrisy (Gal. 2:11–14).

The obligation of Gentile Christians to embrace Judaism before being baptized continued to be maintained in Jerusalem, while Paul toured the cities of Asia Minor, making little or no impact on Jews in synagogues, but winning over many pagans, thanks to his liberal policy that did not force them to 'judaize'. A decision concerning their status could no longer be postponed. A meeting of the apostles and elders was called in Jerusalem to hear Paul and Barnabas. The ex-Pharisee Christians of James's entourage still wanted to impose on non-Jewish candidates for baptism the whole Law of Moses, including circumcision for males, but after the intervention of Paul and Barnabas a compromise formula was proposed, not by Peter, but by James who chaired the council (Acts 15:19–21). Gentiles ready to enter the church had to abstain from food sacrificed to idols, from the consumption of blood, from eating non-ritually slaughtered meat and from fornication, comprising all the various shapes and forms of sexual prohibitions among Jews. The selection of these rules appears to have been inspired by the so-called laws of the children of Noah that the resident aliens, i.e. Gentiles permanently settled in the land of Israel, were expected to observe. The decree of the council of the apostles settled the strife in principle, though local upheavals persisted, as is shown by Paul's report regarding the efforts of judaizers who sought to compel his Gentile converts in Galatia to submit themselves to circumcision and observe the whole Torah (Gal. 2:4, 12–13; 6:12). Notwithstanding this rearguard action, Paul's liberal policy towards non-Jews prevailed and considerably facilitated the spread of Christianity among the Gentiles of the Graeco-Roman world.

THE PLACE OF THE CHRISTIAN CONFRATERNITY IN JEWISH SOCIETY

The membership of the Jesus movement is designated by three different terms in the New Testament. Insiders of the group often allude to themselves as members of an *ekklesia*, 'congregation' or 'church'. The meaning of this term was still loose in Acts, where it could appear without connoting exclusive group identity. For instance, *ekklesia* is used in connection with the community of the biblical Israel in the wilderness after the exodus from Egypt in the speech of the deacon Stephen (Acts 7:38), and in relation to the assembly of the pagan citizens of Ephesus (Acts 19:32, 39, 41). The notion 'church' merely points to a segment of society, applicable either to a local unit like the church of Jerusalem, Antioch or Ephesus on the one hand, or on the other hand to a regional group such as the church of Syria or Cilicia (Acts 8:1; 11:26; 15:41; 20:17). It could also designate the Christian movement as a whole (Acts 12:1; 15:22; 20:28).

The Greek title 'Christian' (Messianist), first forged in Antioch according to the Acts of the Apostles (Acts 11:26), is the second designation. It occurs only on two further occasions in the New Testament: once used semi-mockingly by King Agrippa II (Acts 26:28) and finally by the writer of 1 Peter (4:16), who employs it as an honorific epithet: 'If any of you suffers as a Christian . . . glorify God because you bear this name.'

'The Way' is the third specific self-description of the movement. It comprises the entire ideology followed by the group. Short for 'the Way of the Lord' in which the Christian preacher Apollos is said to have been instructed (Acts 18:24–5), the phrase recalls a prophecy from the Book of Isaiah which is also applied to John the Baptist in the Gospel: 'The voice of one crying out in the wilderness: Prepare *the way of the Lord*' (Isa. 40:3 in Mk 1:3). In the light of this prophecy, the '*way* of *the Lord*' became identical, not with the way of Jesus, but with the way of God, as is obvious also from the use of the same Isaiah quotation in the Community Rule of Qumran where the words are linked to the establishment of the Dead Sea sect:

> They shall separate from the habitation of unjust men and shall go to the wilderness to prepare the way of Him; as it is written, *Prepare in the wilderness the way of* . . . . [the four dots stand for the divine name YHWH], *make straight in the desert a path for our God.* (1QS 8:13–14)

The followers of Jesus, like the Dead Sea sectaries, have 'chosen the Way' in order to walk in its perfection (1QS 9:5, 18). The concept of the Way in the Acts is not directly connected with the Qumran and Judaeo-Christian metaphor of the two ways, the way of truth and that of falsehood as later used in the Didache and in the Epistle of Barnabas, but more appropriately recalls the rabbinic notion of *halakhah*, derived from the verb *halakh* 'to walk' and signifying correct conduct. This correct conduct was determined in Palestinian Jewish-Christianity by the Torah, the Law of Moses, as it was, as far as the theological and moral laws were concerned, even in St Paul's non-Jewish churches.

Right behaviour was enforced with great severity in the Jesus movement. A dishonest couple belonging to the Jerusalem church, Ananias and Sapphira, who pretended to hand over to the apostles the entire proceeds of the sale of their property while secretly they kept part of the money for themselves, were severely reprimanded by Peter ('Why has Satan filled your heart to lie to the Holy Spirit? You did not lie to men but to God'), and one after the other they both were struck dead (Acts 5:3–4, 9–10). In a like manner, as we learn from Paul, a member of the church in Corinth, who scandalized the faithful and even the pagans by having an affair with his stepmother, was sentenced by Paul and the church to be handed over to Satan 'for the destruction of the flesh' (1 Cor. 5:1–5).

As in mainstream Judaism and in the Qumran community, a breach of the essential rules carried with it definitive and irrevocable excommunication. The severity of the legislation is bound up with the expectation of the imminent return of Christ (see pp. 79–81). A worldview with no future prospect justifies and to some extent demands rigorous asceticism. For instance, Paul, who was unmarried, advised the faithful to follow his example without, however, making celibacy compulsory (1 Cor. 7:8–9).

> I think that, in view of the impending crisis, it is well for you to remain as you are. Are you bound to a wife? Do not seek to be free. Are you free from a wife? Do not seek a wife . . . The appointed time has grown short: from now on let even those who have wives be as though they had none . . . For the present form of this world is passing away. (1 Cor. 7:26–31)

The Acts of the Apostles includes several designations of the Christians used by outsiders. Their opponents, like the attorney Tertullus, hired by the Temple authorities to plead before the Roman governor

Felix their case against Paul, described the followers of Jesus as representatives of the sect (*hairesis*) of the Nazarenes (*Nazoraioi*), no doubt after the Nazarene (*Nazoraios*) Jesus (Acts 24:5, 14). In later patristic literature the heretical Judaeo-Christians were also called Ebionites or 'the Poor' (see pp. 85–6 below). The leaders of the Jewish community of Rome also describe the Jesus party as a Jewish sect, a sect allegedly opposed by Jews everywhere (Acts 28:22). The common feature in both these passages is that the Christian brotherhood was seen as a separatist group within the body politic of Judaism, and not something alien to it. Josephus, too, refers to the three main Jewish religious parties, the Pharisees, Sadducees and Essenes, as sects (*Ant.* 13.171). The use of this terminology further confirms that the nascent church not only considered itself, but was also acknowledged as a genuine part of Jewish society. If the final sentence of the Jesus notice of Josephus is accepted as genuine, Josephus speaks of the Christians of his time as a tribe (*phylon*), that is a separate segment of the Jewish nation still existent in the Holy Land at about the end of the first century (*Ant.* 18.64).

CHARACTERISTIC PHENOMENA IN THE RELIGION OF THE EARLY CHURCH

Faith healing

How did the original Jesus movement distinguish itself from the Judaism of the mainstream? The frequent healing of the sick and exorcism, the most prominent features in the life of the newly born community led by the apostles, were in direct continuity with the activity of Jesus. Both functions had already been delegated by Jesus to his disciples, who performed them with varying degrees of success (see pp. 35–7). The same phenomenon characterized the early church, according to the Acts of the Apostles. For the followers of Jesus, successful spiritual healing was the proof of the continued presence in their midst of their crucified master, a tangible sign that he went on acting on their behalf – in short, that he had risen from the dead. Peter and Paul imitated Jesus in their therapeutic activity, but there was one difference: Jesus healed the sick directly without reference to anyone else, whereas

the apostles had to invoke their master when they cured and performed exorcisms. It was in the name of Jesus of Nazareth that Peter
made a lame man stand up and walk in the Temple (Acts 3:6) and
Paul exorcized a fortune-telling slave girl thought to be possessed by
a spirit (Acts 16:18). Peter is further reported to have successfully
treated in Lydda a paralytic, stricken by the disease for eight years,
and raised from the dead a woman from Joppa called Tabitha (in
Greek Dorcas, 'Gazelle') with the words, 'Tabitha, get up' (Acts 9:33–
41). Rabbinic literature, too, alludes to a Jewish-Christian, Jacob of
Kfar Sama or Kfar Sekhaniah, who healed the sick in the name of
Jesus (tHullin 2:22–4). The author of Acts speaks of itinerant Jewish
exorcists, unconnected with the community of the apostles. They
usurped the name of Jesus in their attempts to expel demons, but their
efforts proved unsuccessful (Acts 19:13–15).

The miraculous quality of the apostles' healing power is so greatly
emphasized in Acts that it appears almost to exceed that of Jesus.
While in the Gospels sick people had to touch the garment, or at least
the fringes of the robe of Jesus, in order to regain health (Mk 5:28;
6:56; Mt. 9:20; 14:36; Lk. 8:44), according to the Acts of the Apostles
the shadow of Peter was enough to achieve the same result (Acts
5:15–16). As for Paul, the narrator asserts, wishing to show him no
less powerful than Peter, even without his presence an object belonging to him, his handkerchief or apron, sufficed to cure a disease (Acts
19:11–12).

On the communal level, without requiring the attendance of the
apostles, the prayer of the church elders in the name of Jesus and
their anointing the sick with oil were believed to ensure recovery. The
efficacy of the church leaders' intervention is expressly associated
with the miracle-working power of the prophet Elijah, the chief
representative of charismatic Judaism in the Hebrew Bible (James
5:14–18).

Manifestations of the Spirit in the Acts of the Apostles

Charismatic conduct was the identifying mark of the faithful in the
Acts of the Apostles. The presence of the Holy Spirit, like the state of
prophecy in the Old Testament, revealed itself through perceptible
external signs. The state of ecstasy expressed itself in rapturous talk

called *glossolalia* or 'the speaking in tongues'. Glossolalia is attributed in Acts to Peter and his companions who declared 'God's deeds of power' at Pentecost (Acts 2:4, 11), to Cornelius and his family who 'extolled God' (Acts 10:46), and to the twelve disciples who 'prophesied' after Paul had baptized them in Ephesus (Acts 19:6–7). Apart from Acts, the chief New Testament passages dealing with glossolalia are chapters 12 and 14 of the first letter to the Corinthians. But what Paul means by speaking in tongues – spiritual gibberish – seems to be very different from the glossolalia of Acts. The ecstatic phenomenon, witnessed by the Jews assembled from the four corners of the earth in Jerusalem on one of the three pilgrimage festivals, was extraordinary but not unintelligible. A group of 'uneducated and common' Galilean men (Acts 4:13) were listened to by Jewish pilgrims from all over the ancient near eastern world, from Iran to Egypt and Rome, as they proclaimed God's mighty acts (Acts 2:7–12).

Where did the miracle lie: in the speakers or in the listeners? All we are told was that the message was understood and the bystanders were amazed and impressed. Did the apostles use their everyday vernacular Aramaic which the members of the audience grasped in their own languages, or were the ecstatic Galilean fishermen talking in other tongues? In the absence of a recording the problem remains unresolved. Nevertheless an anecdote surviving in rabbinic literature may open a fresh perspective.

In the biblical account of the choosing of seventy elders to assist Moses in the government of Israel in the wilderness of Sinai (Num. 11:24–30), two of them, Eldad and Medad, were seized by the Spirit of God and began to prophesy in the camp (see Chapter 1, p. 4). One of the Palestinian Aramaic paraphrases of this passage, Targum Pseudo-Jonathan, reproduces five of the words of their ecstatic utterances: **Kiris etimos** *lehon besha'at* **aniki**. The words printed in italics ('to them in the hour of') are in Aramaic, but the three appearing in bold characters are in Greek (*Kyrios etoimos* and *anankê* meaning 'The Lord is ready' and 'distress'). The sentence given in this *macédoine* of Greek and Aramaic may be translated, 'The Lord is ready for them in their hour of distress.' Now if the apostles mixed some Greek with their own Galilean Aramaic, the assembled Jewish crowd, all of whom were supposed to speak either Greek or Aramaic, would have realized that at least part of the speech represented their native tongue.

Examples of prophecy and healing have already been given and countless miraculous events and angelic appearances are recorded in the Acts of the Apostles. We gain the impression that charismatic experiences are envisaged as everyday happenings in the Palestinian church and, as will be seen, in Paul's Corinthian community too. Even the election of a replacement for Judas in the college of the apostles was decided by casting lots, thus allowing the Spirit of God to decide (Acts 1:26). Such occurrences ascribed to the Holy Spirit were used as an instrument of publicity for the benefit of non-believers.

The breaking of the bread

In addition to their traditional Jewish religious practices (observance of the Torah and participation in Temple worship) and the initiation rite of baptism (inherited from John the Baptist and Jesus), the first Palestinian members of the Jesus movement observed also a ritual of their own: a communal meal partaken in private houses and called the 'breaking of the bread' (Acts 2:42, 46). From Acts, we learn that Paul too broke bread in Troas at the assembly of the local believers (Acts 20:7, 11). The custom was associated in the Gospels with Jesus, and in particular, under Pauline influence, with the ceremony of the Last Supper (Mt. 14:19; Mk 8:6, 19; Mt. 15:36; Mk 14:22; Mt. 26:26; Lk. 22:19; 24:30, 35; 1 Cor. 10:16). A similar meal reserved for fully initiated members was part of the daily routine of the Qumran sectaries according to the Community Rule (1QS 6:4–6), a routine they expected to continue even in the messianic age (1QSa 2:17–22).

The frequency of these dinners (referred to also as 'love-feasts', Jude 12) is not determined in the New Testament. Their celebration on Sunday ('the first day of the week') is mentioned in the Troas episode in Acts 20:7, but there the date (Sunday) may be merely accidental. However, by the end of the first century AD, 'The Teaching of the Twelve Apostles' envisages a specifically Christian feast when it issues the following command: 'Assembling on every Lord's day, break bread and give thanks' (Did. 14.1) The corresponding practice in the Pauline churches will be described in Chapter 4 (see pp. 91–2).

THE PRINCIPAL BELIEFS OF EARLY CHRISTIANITY

Set against mainstream Judaism, three distinctive teachings secured recognizable identity for the Christian movement: the Kingdom of God; the crucified, risen and exalted Messiah; and the *Parousia* or second coming of Christ.

The Kingdom of God

The doctrine of the approaching Kingdom of God constituted the kernel of the message delivered by the apostles in continuity with the central theme of the preaching of Jesus during his public career. The nature of the Kingdom remained the main topic of the instruction attributed to the risen Jesus (Acts 1:3) and the time of its arrival, or more precisely, the arrival of its synonym, the Kingdom of Israel, was according to the Acts of the Apostles the last question the disciples put to their master immediately before his disappearance in the direction of heaven (Acts 1:6). Though, curiously, the Kingdom of God is absent from Peter's speeches in Jerusalem, it is the subject of the message of the deacon Philip in Samaria (Acts 8:12) and of the preaching attributed to Paul during his missionary tour, notably in Pisidian Antioch, Ephesus, Miletus and Rome (Acts 14:22; 19:8; 20:25; 28:23, 31). In the apostolic teaching the coming of the Kingdom is identified with the return of Christ and will be considered in the section about the *Parousia*.

The crucified, risen and glorified Messiah

To the specifically Christian or church content of the apostolic proclamation, as distinct from the message of the Gospel, belong the themes of the identity, suffering and resurrection of the Messiah. These topics figure already in the Gospels where they were inserted under the impact of early church tradition. We know that Jesus did not greatly care about being called the Messiah, and neither his death nor his resurrection and second coming were announced by him or corresponded to the expectation of his apostles and disciples. Instead they caused surprise, shock and astonishment (see G. Vermes, *The Changing Faces of Jesus*, 2001, pp. 171–2, 180–83).

In his first speech in the Acts of the Apostles, Peter proclaimed Jesus, before the Jewish crowd on the day of Pentecost, as 'Lord and Messiah' who was 'crucified, killed and raised' (Acts 2:36). The apostles continued to deliver the same message in the Temple and in various homes where believers met in Jerusalem (Acts 5:42). The deacon Philip did likewise in Samaria (Acts 8:5) – in apparent ignorance of Jesus' command, 'Enter no town of the Samaritans' (Mt. 10:5). Peter declares Christ to be 'the Lord of all' and 'the judge of the living and the dead' (Acts 10:36, 42). In a vision the deacon Stephen saw Jesus 'standing at the right hand of God' (Acts 7:55) and dying he prayed, 'Lord Jesus, receive my spirit' (Acts 7:59).

Likewise Paul proclaimed to the Jews of Thessalonica and Corinth that Jesus was the Messiah and had to suffer and rise (Acts 17:3; 18:5), and made an identical assertion when he spoke in Caesarea before the procurator Festus and King Agrippa II (Acts 26:23). The Alexandrian Apollos delivered the same teaching to the Jews in Achaia (Acts 18:28). Jesus' death and resurrection are also the constant theme of Paul's message throughout his letters. In general, the nomenclature applied to Jesus in Acts signals, not a superhuman being, but a chosen man of God, the hero prefigured in the charismatic Judaism of the Old Testament.

The suffering, death and resurrection of Jesus, the Messiah, as well as his exaltation are argued in the earliest addresses of Peter to Jews in Jerusalem with the help of a technique well attested in the Dead Sea Scrolls too. The Qumran *pesher*, a term literally meaning 'interpretation', refers in practice to a biblical prophecy perceived as foretelling the life of a leader, who actually fulfilled the predictions. In Acts the prognostications relating to Jesus are selected from the Psalms, considered as prophecies written by David under the influence of the spirit of prophecy (see 11QPs 27:11). In Peter's view Jesus was crucified in order to realize symbolically the words of Psalm 118:22, 'The stone that was rejected by you, the builders, has become the cornerstone' (Acts 4:10–11). In turn, Psalm 2:1–2, 'Why did the Gentiles rage ... The kings of the earth took their stand and the rulers have gathered together against the Lord and against his Messiah', is understood by the apostles as alluding to the condemnation of Jesus by

Herod Antipas, Pontius Pilate and the Romans in cahoots with the priestly leaders of the Jewish people (Acts 4:25–7). In a previous speech, at Pentecost, Peter presented the resurrection as the fulfilment of the words of David in Psalm 16:10: 'For you will not abandon my soul in Hades, or let your Holy One experience corruption' (Acts 2:24–8). As for the ascension of Jesus to heaven, it is claimed to be the realization of Psalm 110:1, 'The Lord said to my Lord, sit at my right hand' (Acts 2:34).

It should be observed that the biblical prophecy which modern interpreters consider most convincing as regards the suffering and death of the Messiah, namely the song of the Suffering Servant of the Lord (Isa. 53), is hardly ever used in the New Testament. Accidentally, it happened to be read by a high-ranking Ethiopian proselyte in his chariot on his homeward journey from Jerusalem, and expounded to him by the deacon Philip as applying to Jesus (Acts 8:27–35). The only other New Testament writing that implicitly refers to Isaiah 53 is the not particularly influential first letter of Peter (2:21–5). On the whole, the New Testament *pesher* is no more convincing than its Qumran equivalent.

Model sermons aimed at Jews and presenting the Messiah Jesus as the fulfilment of Israel's history from Abraham to the speaker's day are included in the proto-martyr deacon Stephen's rambling speech before the Sanhedrin (Acts 7:2–53) and in Paul's lengthy homily in the synagogue of Antioch in Pisidia (Acts 13:16–41). Both addresses failed to convince the audience. The first resulted in Stephen being stoned to death by an enraged Jewish mob, and the second provoked a violent disagreement among the members of the local Jewish community. Most of the non-Jews who were impressed by the Christian preaching were God-fearing pagan sympathizers of Judaism, who frequented the synagogue on every Sabbath. The sole attempt to persuade educated Gentiles is associated with an oratorical performance of Paul in Athens, preaching the unknown God, the creator of people and things, and exhorting his Greek listeners to repent before facing judgment by a man who was raised by God from the dead. This reference to resurrection alienated his audience, which comprised Epicurean and Stoic philosophers, resulted in a complete fiasco and made no impact on educated Greeks, who had had no previous contact with the Jewish religion.

The Second Coming of Christ

The most influential religious idea in the early church, affecting both thinking and behaviour, was the *Parousia*, the expectation of the imminent or delayed return of Christ. This concept is familiar in Paul, in the letters of James and 1 John, and is placed on the lips of the two angels after the ascension of Jesus in the opening chapter of the Acts: '[He] will come in the same way as you saw him go to heaven' (Acts 1:11). In his address to the Jews assembled in the Temple, Peter likewise asserts that God will send again the Messiah from heaven at the moment of the time of universal restoration (Acts 3:20–21). He also refers indirectly to the Second Coming when he presents Jesus to the household of Cornelius in Caesarea as the one whom God will dispatch to judge the living and the dead (Acts 10:42).

The urgency and the timetable of the *Parousia* are set out in different ways in the New Testament, reflecting the changing attitudes of the primitive church towards the great event. Acts, though not fully explicit in the passages just quoted, seems to imply that Jesus' contemporaries will witness his return – in other words, that it will happen during the lifetime of the same generation. In effect, Jesus' expectation of the instant arrival of the Kingdom of God was immediately replaced by the prospect of his impending Second Coming. The most colourful picture of this eschatological frenzy is offered by St Paul in his Second Letter to the Thessalonians written in the early 50s, barely more than twenty years after the crucifixion (see Chapter 4, p. 104). The first epistle of John also mentions the imminence of the *Parousia*: 'Children, it is the last hour! As you have heard that the antichrist is coming, so now many antichrists have come. From this we know that this is the last hour' (1 Jn 2:18). However later, with the time of expectation getting longer and longer, perseverance became the key virtue in the eyes of the leaders of the church. The author of the letter of James in the late first century AD exhorts his addressees:

> Be patient, beloved, until the coming of the Lord. The farmer waits for the precious crop from the earth, being patient with it until he receives the early and the late rain. You also must be patient. Strengthen your hearts, for the coming of the Lord is near ... See, the Judge is standing at the door. (Jas 5:7-9)

At about the same time, the earliest church manual, 'The Teaching of the Twelve Apostles', propounds the same firm message (see Chapter 6, p. 145).

The pseudonymous author of the second letter of Peter, probably writing in the first half of the second century AD, was faced with open scepticism among some of his readers, whom he calls 'scoffers', people tired of waiting, disenchanted and grumpy: 'Where is the promise of his coming? For ever since our ancestors died, all things continue as they were from the beginning of creation!' (2 Pet. 3:3–4). Pseudo-Peter comforted them by pointing out that the divine perception of time is not the same as theirs. For God, 'one day is like a thousand years and a thousand years like one day'. Also what struck them as slowness and delay was in fact divine long-suffering, which provided more time for repentance (2 Pet. 3:8–9). In adopting such explanatory tactics, the New Testament writer simply imitated his Qumran predecessor, author of the Commentary on Habakkuk, who also found the waiting time much longer than had been foreseen. Indeed, the prophets had no idea 'when time would come to an end'. As an ultimate evasive explanation, he laid emphasis on the inscrutability of the mysterious divine plans (1QpHab. 7:1–9).

Eschatological enthusiasm could not be maintained for too long. It is therefore normal that the calming down of unbridled hopes became an essential part of all apocalyptically inspired ideology in early Christianity. Demand for patience was also introduced, as it were by the backdoor, into the eschatological discourse attributed to Jesus by the final redactors of the Gospels and, without the use of the term *Parousia*, into some of the church-made or church-edited parables of the New Testament. Believers were encouraged to constant vigilance as it was impossible to know when the thief would break in or the master return (Mt. 24:42–4; Lk. 12:39; Mk 13:33–7; Mt. 24:45–51; Lk. 12:42–6). The head of a household having gone on a long journey, his servants had to be prepared to settle accounts with him at any time, even if his homecoming would be sudden (Mt. 25:14–30; Lk. 19:11–27). The bridesmaids waiting at the home of the bridegroom had to carry a good supply of oil for their lamps so that they would not run out of fuel, even if the nuptial procession arrived late. The foolish virgins who lacked foresight had to pay a heavy penalty (Mt. 25:1–13).

In brief, the disciples had to be constantly ready for the *Parousia*, an event expected to be as sudden and quick as 'the lightning that comes from the east and flashes as far as the west' (Mt. 24:26–7; Lk. 17:22–4). Protected by these cautionary advices, the hope of an impending or not far away Second Coming stayed alive for over a hundred years until the middle of the second century, by which time the progressive cooling down of the expectation removed the *Parousia* from all practical impact on the life of the Christian community.

AN OUTLINE OF FIRST-CENTURY CHRISTIANITY

Let us repeat the questions asked at the start of this chapter: how does the religion preached by the apostles relate to the Judaism of the period? And how does it compare with the religion proclaimed by Jesus?

As has been asserted more than once, the leaders of the Jesus movement thought as Jews, lived as Jews, and shared the aspirations of their fellow Jews. They remained subconsciously attached to the Law of Moses and when in Jerusalem, they went on participating in Temple ceremonies, and also used the forecourt of the sanctuary for preaching. They considered themselves, a small chosen unit within the large body of the Jewish people, the biblical 'remnant' entrusted with the correct understanding of Judaism, thanks to the instruction received from God's special envoy, Jesus. Baptism, a rite of repentance and purification, and the regular participation in a communal meal assured their group identity. They were also recognizable, at least during the first phase of the movement in Jerusalem, by a freely undertaken practice of religious communism.

While the members of the church did not feel cut off from the rest of their co-religionists, the leaders of the Jewish people treated those who called themselves 'believers' as a distinct faction, alluded to as a sect, one among many that co-existed in late Second Temple Judaism. The Christians had two distinguishing features compared with ordinary Jews of the age. They believed that the Messiah promised by the prophets had already revealed himself in the person of Jesus of Nazareth and that this Messiah, contrary to the ideas of mainstream Jews, suffered, died, rose from the dead, was exalted to heaven and would soon return to inaugurate the eschatological Kingdom of God. This return of Christ, intensely awaited in the course of the second half of the first century AD, lay at the heart of apostolic Christianity.

The second distinguishing feature of the primitive Jesus movement was an all-embracing manifestation, indeed overflow, of charisma. A kind of contagious ecstatic behaviour characterized the life of the community, which started with the Pentecost display and continued with the persistent manifestation of spiritual healing, exorcism and the 'descent of the Holy Spirit' on the members of the church both in the Holy Land and in the Diaspora.

The activity of Jesus already witnessed the abundance of charisma, but the question of a separate community did not arise as the number of the regular followers of Jesus was far too small – with 70 or 72 or 120 as the maximum mentioned (Lk. 10:1, 17) – to appear as a distinct religious party. There was no need for a hierarchical structure either, Jesus being their uncontested leader. He had no deputy, but there existed a trio closest to him: Peter and the two sons of Zebedee, James and John. In the early Palestinian church, James, son of Zebedee, failed to keep his leading position. He was beheaded at the order of King Herod Agrippa I (AD 41–4). John, his brother, continued to share the leadership with Peter in Jerusalem and in Samaria, but they were soon joined by the other James, who received from Paul the epithet, 'the brother of the Lord' (Gal. 1:19), and was also referred to as the brother of Jude (Jude 1). Both James and Jude or Judas are listed as the brothers of Jesus in the Gospels (Mk 6:3; Mt. 13:55). The remaining members of the inner circle of twelve remain inconspicuous. The deacon Philip is portrayed as an active propagator of the Gospel. His colleague Stephen was less fortunate and got himself stoned to death for his hot-headedness at an early stage of his ministry. It should be noted that according to Acts (6:1–6), the seven deacons, all with Greek names, were initially charity workers, entrusted with the care of the impoverished widows of the Hellenist followers of Jesus, resident in Jerusalem.

Paul, in turn, claimed to be in charge of the mission to the Gentiles as Peter was the apostle of the circumcised (Gal. 2:7). His field of activity was the Diaspora because the Palestinian church itself belonged to James. The latter's rise to prominence is demonstrated by his presidential role at the council of the apostles and by Paul's reverential attitude towards him on two separate visits to Jerusalem. The family connection of James is emphasized by Josephus, too, when he identifies him as 'the brother of Jesus surnamed Christ' in his account of James's execution by stoning, decreed by the high priest Ananus, son of Ananus, in AD 62, an event unrecorded in the Acts of the Apostles. According to Josephus, Ananus' act was found so scandalous by the most fair-minded citizens of Jerusalem that they denounced the high priest before King Agrippa II and the new Roman procurator, Albinus, and obtained his dismissal (*Ant.* 20.200–201). This account of Josephus suggests that James the brother of Jesus himself, and possibly the Jewish-Christian community as a whole, were still not seen as complete outsiders by the leading Jerusalem circles as late as AD 62.

Eusebius of Caesarea (*c.* AD 260–339), citing the second-century historian Hegesippus, grants James the honorific title 'the Righteous', and sees in the war against the Jews led by Vespasian divine revenge for the crime committed by Ananus and his cronies against the brother of the Lord (*EH* 2.23, 17). Early Christian tradition implies that James's choice as leader of the Palestinian Christian community owed a great deal to his family link with Jesus. The election of Symeon son of Clopas, James's (and Jesus') cousin, as the next head of the mother church followed the same trend. Thirteen more bishops of Jerusalem came from 'the circumcision', their list terminating in AD 135 with the end of the second war of the Jews against Rome (*EH* 4.3, 5). Apparently, according to the Christian writer Julius Africanus (*c.* AD 160–*c.* 240), cited by Eusebius, the descendants of the family of Jesus in Nazareth and in Cocheba continued to boast about their genealogy and were known as *Desposynoi* or 'the Lord's people' (*EH* 1.17, 14). From these data it would appear that the Jerusalem church and Judaeo-Christianity, originally led by members of the family of Jesus, survived institutionally until Hadrian and sporadically continued in pockets until the third or fourth century.

In anticipation of the study of Pauline Christianity, it may be useful briefly to note that Paul kept in his own hands the overall government and care of the churches established by him, but being a far-sighted and practical organizer, he delegated the day-to-day oversight of the new communities to trusted associates. At a somewhat later stage, probably after the death of Paul, we learn from the so-called Pastoral epistles (1 and 2 Timothy and Titus) that the Pauline churches were administered by a series of appointed officials.

A final question concerns the place of Jesus in the teaching of early Judaeo-Christianity. His position in the Pauline and Johannine church will be considered in the next two chapters. Relying mostly on the Acts of the Apostles, one notes that Jesus bears many titles in the terminology of his immediate followers. However, one observes with surprise that the title 'Son of God', frequently employed in the Gospels (see Chapter 2, pp. 48–9) is nowhere used in Peter's addresses and occurs only twice in Acts – once on the lips of Paul speaking to Jews after his Damascus experience, and again in his sermon in the synagogue of Pisidian Antioch, where Psalm 2:7, 'You are my Son, today I have begotten you', is somewhat inappropriately quoted to prove the resurrection of Jesus (Acts 13:33).

Jesus is labelled 'the Servant' or 'holy Servant of God' (Acts 3:26; 4:27, 30). This is the lowliest epithet applied to him, which soon vanished from further Christian usage. He is also designated as 'Leader' (*archêgos*) and 'the Righteous One' (Acts 7:52; 22:14). None of these is a particularly exceptional title. Once he is also referred to by the distinguished name of 'a prophet like Moses' (Acts 3:22). The first and most telling definition of Jesus contained in Acts is found in the speech of Peter in Jerusalem on the feast of Pentecost, where he is called 'a man attested by God with deeds of power, wonders and signs' (Acts 2:22) – the typical definition of a charismatic prophet. This description recalls Josephus' phrase 'wise man and performer of paradoxical deeds' found in the *Testimonium Flavianum* (see Chapter 2, p. 32).

There are only two passages in Acts with a potentially more elevated meaning. Both occur in the account of the martyrdom of Stephen. The first is the vision in which Jesus is seen 'standing at the right of God' (Acts 7:55). However this image, associated with Jesus' ascension to heaven, does not imply divine status. Enoch and Elijah in the Bible, and Moses and the prophet Isaiah in post-biblical Jewish tradition, also enjoy the privilege of such exaltation, the first two without dying, and Moses and Isaiah after their deaths. The second reference that might suggest Jesus' elevation to divine status is connected with the dying Stephen's prayer, 'Lord Jesus, receive my spirit'

(Acts 7:59). Although as a rule Jewish prayer is directed to God, we must bear in mind that Stephen's supplication echoes the request of the repentant criminal crucified on Golgotha, asking the innocent and righteous Jesus to remember him when he enters God's Kingdom (Lk. 23:42). Treating these words as amounting to a deification of Jesus would be a serious misjudgment.

In sum, all the titles of Jesus in the Acts of the Apostles are those of a man of God, a man of high spiritual dignity, and by no stretch of imagination can we see in them a hint at a divine being. It is also worth noting that despite the presumed common authorship of the Gospel of Luke and Acts, the latter includes no mention of the miraculous conception and birth of Jesus, reported in the Nativity story of the Third Gospel.

In respect of the Jesus image of the Acts of the Apostles, light may be obtained from traditions stemming from the Judaeo-Christians called Ebionites (the Poor) or Nazarenes (followers of Jesus of *Nazareth*) and preserved in patristic literature (see E. K. Broadhead, *Jewish Ways of Following Jesus*, 2010). The chief sources, ranging between the second and the early fifth centuries AD, are Irenaeus (*c.* 130–*c.* 200), Origen (*c.* 185–*c.* 254), Eusebius (*c.* 260–*c.* 340) and Jerome (*c.* 342–420). The Jewish Christians had the unpleasant experience of falling between two stools, or as St Jerome's sharp pen puts it in his Letter 89 to St Augustine: '*Dum volunt et Iudaei esse et Christiani, nec Iudaeai sunt, nec Christiani*' ('While they wish to be both Jews and Christians, they are neither Jews, nor Christians').

The more lenient view, expressed by the Church Fathers, states that the Ebionites-Nazarenes were Jewish followers of Jesus who remained faithful observers of the Mosaic Law, but believed in the miraculous birth of the Messiah. The more rigorous form of Ebionism denied both the virginal conception and the divinity of Christ. Moreover, they all rejected the letters of Paul, whom they considered an apostate, and Eusebius further specifies that they held only the now lost Aramaic Gospel according to the Hebrews as authentic. The sarcastic explanation of the name Ebionites in patristic literature linking the concept of poverty to the quality of their understanding of Christ is totally baseless. The term, 'the Poor', was used as an honorific title in the Hebrew Old Testament, and the devout members of the Dead

Sea Sect were also known as *Ebyonim*, the Poor (1QpHab. 12:3, 6, 10, etc.).

To sum up, the earliest Christianity, both in its Palestinian charismatic and Gentile missionary forms, reflects traditional Judaism in the light of faith in the Messianic status of the crucified and exalted Jesus, combined with an ardent expectation of his triumphant and not too distant reappearance from heaven.

4

The Christianity of Paul

PAUL'S MINISTRY AMONG JEWS AND GENTILES

To understand the nature of the Pauline church, a good grasp of its genesis is essential. How did Paul, the Jew from Tarsus, envisage his vocation as the chosen messenger of Jesus Christ? The Acts of the Apostles (chapters 9–28) and the autobiographical references in Paul's letters (Gal. 1:13–2:14; 2 Cor. 11:21–9) provide sundry and sometimes contradictory information. We learn from Acts that Paul originated from and at various times resided in the city of Tarsus in Cilicia (southern Turkey); he was a Jew who for some unspecified reason had Roman citizenship from birth (see A. N. Sherwin-White, *Roman Society and Roman Law*, 1963, pp. 151–3); and he is said to have been educated in Jerusalem 'at the feet of Gamaliel', the famous rabbinic teacher who flourished in the first half of the first century AD (Acts 9:30; 11:25; 22:3, 25–8). While none of the claims made by the writer of Acts is intrinsically impossible, it is rather odd that Paul never alludes to any of them in his letters, although mention of his Jewish academic pedigree and his enviable Roman legal status might have been advantageous for him in his dealings with Jewish and Gentile officials.

Again according to Acts, Paul proclaimed the gospel both to Jews and to Gentiles. His preaching to Jews in Damascus nearly cost him his life (Acts 9:20–25). In Pisidian Antioch, Iconium, Beroea, Corinth and Rome he approached Jews with limited success. In general, he was given short shrift by the synagogue leaders, for whom he was a troublemaker who threatened communal peace. Paul's preaching met with greater interest among the Gentile sympathizers in synagogues and among pagans with no prior connection with Judaism.

Paul saw himself as chosen by God to announce the good news to the foreign nations of the world, as 'a minister of Christ Jesus to the Gentiles in the priestly service of the gospel of God' (Rom. 5:16), or simply 'a teacher of the Gentiles', an apostle 'entrusted with the gospel for the uncircumcised' (Gal. 1:16; 2:7; 1 Tim. 2:7). The evangelization of the Jews was the assignment of Peter, who proclaimed 'the gospel for the circumcised' (Gal. 2:7). While Paul never contemplated preaching to the Jews as his direct duty, his intention to bring them to Christ is expressed indirectly. His spreading the gospel to the entire Gentile world would be accompanied by a divine act of mercy towards the children of Abraham and salvation would be granted to all of them. 'I want you to understand this mystery: a hardening has come upon part of Israel, until the full number of the Gentiles has come in and so all Israel will be saved' (Rom. 11:25–6).

According to the Acts of the Apostles, Paul's teaching activity outside the Holy Land regularly started in synagogues, where the local Jewish community and a number of God-fearing Gentiles listened to his speeches. Indeed, he once declared that his vocation consisted in being a servant to all men, Gentiles as well as Jews:

> To the Jews, I became as a Jew, in order to win Jews ... To those outside the law I became as one outside the law ... so that I might win those outside the law ... I have become all things to all people ... I try to please everyone in everything. (1 Cor. 9:20–22; 10:33)

His missionary work among Diaspora Jews was conflict-prone and resulted in an impressive series of punishments inflicted on him by synagogue authorities: 'Five times I have received from the Jews the forty lashes minus one [the severest corporal chastisement permitted in Jewish law according to mMakkot 3:10]. Three times I was beaten with rods. Once I received stoning' (2 Cor. 11:24–5).

In the light of a critical assessment of the data contained in Acts, the most likely scenario may have been this. In the course of their journeys, Paul and his travelling companions regularly sought and found hospitality in the local Jewish communities. He then availed himself of the first opportunity to address the congregation, no doubt during their Sabbath service. He was sometimes even invited to preach a second time. At the end some Jews and usually a larger number of Gentile 'God-fearers' followed Paul and sought further instruction.

The majority of the Jews, however, remained unmoved, and the hostile synagogue leaders, who saw in Paul an enemy of communal peace, tried as a rule to persuade his converts to rejoin the fold (see Acts 13:45; 17:13). On such occasions, Paul and his colleagues turned their backs on the Jewish community and entirely devoted their efforts to the instruction of Judaizing Gentiles and other interested pagans. Scolding the unsympathetic Jews, they declared: 'It was necessary that the word of God should be spoken first to you. Since you reject it ... we are now turning to the Gentiles' (Acts 13:46). Such non-Jewish converts formed the nucleus of the new Pauline congregations. Their members foregathered in house-churches, that is, in the larger homes of wealthier members of the community. This is how Gentile Christianity began to expand in the Hellenic world.

THE VISIBLE FEATURES OF PAULINE CHRISTIANITY

These visible features will be examined first. They comprise baptism, the breaking of the bread, charismatic phenomena, the Christian way of life and the hierarchical organization of the church.

Baptism

How were Paul's Gentile listeners persuaded to embrace his message and become Christians? As their Palestinian counterparts had to, they were required to believe in the Redeemer as preached by Paul, the crucified and risen Jesus Christ (see below, pp. 100–103), and be baptized in his name. When the Corinthian church was split into factions, each rival group claiming to belong to a different leader – some to Paul, some to Apollos and others to Cephas – Paul resolved the dispute with a rhetorical question: 'Were you baptized in the name of Paul?' (1 Cor. 1:12–13). The answer was of course that people were baptized in the name of Jesus Christ, not in the name of church leaders. In fact Paul stressed that he was not sent by Christ to baptize but to announce the gospel (1 Cor. 1:17) and that, with three exceptions (1 Cor. 1:14–16), the baptismal ritual was delegated to his assistants.

Although Paul had a great deal to say about charismatic gifts of the Spirit, unlike the author of Acts (see Chapter 3, p. 65), he never associated them with baptism. His contribution to the initiation ritual was doctrinal and consisted in the exposition of the underlying spiritual significance. In the context of his teaching about redemption (see pp. 100–103), Paul envisaged baptism as a mythical re-enactment of the mystery of the death, burial and resurrection of Jesus by the person undergoing Christian initiation. He gave an unexpected twist to the imagery of an ordinary Jewish purification ritual.

In Judaism, immersion into water was intended to wash away the ritual impurity caused by certain bodily functions (sex, menstruation, childbearing) and by dermatological and genital diseases or by contact with a dead body. In a more spiritual sense, the baptism of repentance, administered by John the Baptist, symbolized the removal of the pollution caused by sinful conduct. The fundamental cleansing significance survived even in rituals performed only once, like the baptism of proselytes which marked their admission into the Jewish fold. The immersion associated with the entry into the Covenant of the new members of the Qumran community also remained essentially an act of purification: 'When his flesh ... is sanctified by cleansing water, it shall be made clean by the humble submission of his soul to all the precepts of God' (1QS 3:9).

For Paul, the baptismal pool had a deep allegorical meaning. It symbolized the tomb in which the crucified body of Jesus was laid to rest and where it remained until the resurrection on the third day. Baptism for Paul is a myth-drama. Being dipped into and lifted from the baptismal pool meant an allegorical identification with the death, burial and resurrection of Jesus. Through the baptismal ritual, the effects of the cult drama were transferred onto the new Christian. Baptism seen through believing eyes was a sacramental rebirth.

> Do you not know that all of us who have been baptized into Christ Jesus were baptized into his death? Therefore we have been buried with him by baptism into death, so that, just as Christ was raised from the dead by the glory of the Father, so we too might walk in newness of life. (Rom. 6:3–4)

Paul's understanding of baptism is closer to the ideas of the Greek, Egyptian, Syrian and Persian mystery cults that flourished in the

Roman Empire in the age of Jesus than to the traditional Jewish and Judaeo-Christian purification ritual.

The Lord's Supper

In addition to baptism, the first and unrepeatable Christian rite, Paul inherited from his predecessors a second great cult practice, the communal meal, referred to as the 'breaking of the bread' as well as 'thanksgiving' or *eucharist* in Greek. As in the case of baptism, Paul supplied a new meaning to the community meal and turned it into an imitation and repetition of the 'Lord's Supper' – Jesus' last Passover dinner with his apostles on the evening before his crucifixion.

Paul implies that the mythical significance of this meal was revealed to him directly by Christ: 'I received from the Lord what I also handed on to you' (1 Cor. 11:23). He does not say that it came to him through apostolic tradition as the story of the death, burial and resurrection of the Saviour: 'I handed over to you what I in turn had received' (1 Cor. 15:3). If my understanding is correct, the mystical significance of the Last Supper must not be attributed to the Synoptic evangelists composing their accounts between AD 70 and 100, but to Paul writing in the early 50s. It seems that the idea entered the tradition of the Gospels of Mark and Matthew through Luke, Paul's disciple, whose Last Supper account mirrors that of his teacher. Only Paul and Luke mention Jesus' command relating to the repetition of the ritual. For Paul the rite comprised a twofold allegory: the participation of the believers in the redemptive acts of the death and resurrection of Christ, and their assimilation into the mystical body of Jesus and the church.

In Paul's view, those who partook of the bread and drank from the cup were in the first instance united, mystically and sacramentally, with the redeeming death of Christ.

> The Lord Jesus on the night when he was betrayed took a loaf of bread, and when he had given thanks, he broke it and said, 'This is my body that is for you. Do this in remembrance of me.' In the same way he took the cup also, after supper, saying, 'This cup is the new covenant in my blood. Do this, as often as you drink it, in remembrance of me.' For as often as you eat this bread and drink the cup, you proclaim the Lord's death until he comes. (1 Cor. 11:23–6)

Moreover, as the bread was the symbol of Jesus' flesh, the many who consumed it were in addition spiritually transformed into a single body, that of the church: 'The bread that we break, is it not a sharing in the body of Christ? Because there is one bread, we who are many are one body, for we all partake in the same bread' (1 Cor. 10:16–17; Rom. 12:4–5).

Having invested the communal meal with such superhuman qualities, it is not surprising that Paul's plebeian followers in Corinth fell short of the required standard both in thought and in behaviour. He complained that the members of the congregation, far from being united, were split into factions along social lines (1 Cor. 11:18; see 1:12) and they behaved in a disorderly fashion during the ceremony itself. Instead of all sharing the same meal, each family brought along their own food, and while the less well off felt humiliated and remained hungry, the wealthy gorged themselves on delicacies and got drunk (1 Cor. 11:21–2, 33–4). Paul paints an odd portrait of the company making up the Corinthian church when he prohibits table fellowship with drunkards, idolaters, revilers and robbers and with the sexually immoral and greedy (1 Cor. 5:11).

Be this as it may, the breaking of the bread or the 'Lord's Supper', as perceived through Paul's eyes, became the cornerstone of the cultic edifice of Gentile Christianity in his day and has remained so ever since.

Charismatic manifestations

Charismatic religion, which characterized the activity of Jesus and the life of the Palestinian apostolic church (speaking in tongues and healing as well as angelic appearances in the Acts of the Apostles), was common in the Pauline communities, too, if the picture of the Corinthian church may be taken as typical of Gentile Christianity as a whole. Paul distinguishes nine varieties of spiritual gifts intended for the common good.

> To one is given through the Spirit the utterance of *wisdom*, and to another the utterance of *knowledge* . . . to another *faith* . . . to another gifts of *healing* . . . to another the working of *miracles*, to another *prophecy*, to another the *discernment of spirits*, to another various

kinds of *tongues*, to another the *interpretation of tongues*. (1 Cor.
12:8–10)

Of these, healing, miracle-working, prophecy and speaking in
tongues have already been listed in the early chapters of Acts and the
reader gains the impression that charismatic experience was a daily
occurrence in the Palestinian as well as in the Pauline churches. However, whereas the miraculous aura of the charismatic events was seen
as the manifestation of divine approval in Palestinian Jewish circles,
Paul judged some of them, in particular glossolalia or speaking in
tongues, potentially counterproductive during the religious services of
his Gentile-Christian congregations.

Whereas the apostles' speech in tongues at Pentecost was said to
have been comprehensible to the crowd of bystanders (Acts 2:6), the
Corinthian glossolalia is best described as unintelligible ecstatic bab-
ble. It was attributed to the inspiration of the Holy Spirit but was,
according to Paul, beneficial only to the speakers themselves. (To male
speakers, that is, as Paul did not allow women to open their mouths
in the church – 1 Cor. 14:34; cf. 1 Tim. 2:11–12.) However, such
meaningless noise distracted and confused rather than edified the
congregation; hence Paul only tolerated it at church meetings if a
charismatic language interpreter was present (1 Cor. 14:9–11). In
their absence speakers in tongues were ordered to convey silently 'the
mysteries of the Spirit' to God, for without interpreters nobody in the
congregation would be able to understand them (1 Cor. 14:2). Paul
added, no doubt without intending to be boastful, that he could speak
in tongues much better than all the Corinthians taken together, but he
preferred to instruct them in a comprehensible fashion and not in
some kind of holy gibberish: 'In church I would rather speak five
words with my mind ... than ten thousand words in tongues' (1 Cor.
14:18–19). His favourite kind of spiritual gift, the one he warmly
commended to his followers, was prophecy: 'One who prophesies is
greater than one who speaks in tongues, unless someone interprets, so
that the church may be built up' (1 Cor. 14:5). In the interest of orderly
worship, Paul was determined to keep under control, if not the Holy
Spirit, at least its ebullient spokesmen. Only two or three persons
were authorized to perform glossolalia or prophetic revelations per
service (1 Cor. 14:27–9). As I once said addressing members of the

Society of Friends, the worship in the community of Corinth resembled a Quaker meeting enlivened by the chanting and shouts of a Pentecostal service.

Christian way of life

As far as their outward conduct was concerned, Paul's Gentile Christians were exempted from the ceremonial and dietary regulations of the Mosaic Law. Chief among these was compulsory male circumcision, an obligation that would have considerably diminished for non-Jewish men the attractiveness of Pauline Christianity. Apart from a few practices set out in the decree of the council of the apostles as particularly abhorrent to Jews and Jewish Christians, such as eating meat deriving from pagan sacrifices, the flesh of animals killed by strangulation, the consumption of blood, and certain prohibited sexual activities (Acts 15:19–21; see Chapter 3, p. 69), Paul, following the decree of the apostolic council, excused his Gentile followers from the rest of the cultic obligations imposed by the Torah. Pagan sacrificial meat, part of which was offered for sale in butchers' shops, raised a special problem among Gentile Christians. Some of them, having embraced the Jewish view that the gods of other nations were nonexistent, could consider themselves free to partake of any food, even of meat offered to 'idols'. 'Eat whatever is sold in the meat market without raising any question on the ground of conscience', was Paul's instruction to them (1 Cor. 10:25). But others, lacking such clear judgment or believing that the pagan gods were evil, would have been scandalized by fellow Christians eating food originating from 'the table of demons'. Hence Paul advised the strong: 'Take care that this liberty of yours does not somehow become a stumbling-block to the weak' (1 Cor. 8:1–10; 10:19–21, 26–9; cf. Rom. 14:13–21).

None of the letters of Paul include a general code of behaviour for members of his churches. As a rule, he offered them, in the concluding part of several of his letters, a long or short list of moral rules inspired by, and reflecting, the Jewish ethics of the age. His most detailed register is contained in the epistle to the Romans, chapters 12–15, furnishing an amalgam of varied precepts: Do not have an exaggerated esteem of yourselves. Embrace each other with mutual affection. Be patient in suffering. Extend hospitality to strangers. Live in harmony with one another. If your enemies are hungry, feed them. Obey the governing authorities and pay your taxes. In short, love your neighbour as yourself.

Elsewhere Paul instructed the Corinthians to set aside a sum of money for the poor on the first day of each week, the day of the Christian cultic gathering for the 'breaking of the bread' (1 Cor. 16:2; see Acts 20:7; Did. 14.1 and compare with CD 14:12–16). In the letter to the Galatians (5:19–23) the works of the flesh (fornication, impurity, licentiousness, idolatry, sorcery, drunkenness, etc.) are contrasted with the fruits of the Spirit (love, joy, peace, patience, kindness, generosity, self-control, etc.). Repeatedly he encouraged peaceful harmony: husbands were to love their wives, wives to be obedient to their husbands, children to honour their parents, fathers not to provoke their sons, slaves to respect their masters.

In addition to these general exhortations, we find specific commandments, which, Paul says, are traceable to Jesus. Apart from that relating to the Lord's Supper (1 Cor. 11:23; see above, p. 91), he lists two further commandments of the Lord, which he does not expressly claim to have personally received from Jesus, but presumably from apostolic tradition: the absolute prohibition of divorce (1 Cor. 7:10–11; no reference is made to the Matthean exception clause of fornication in Mt. 5:32; 19:9) and the entitlement of the preachers of the gospel to be maintained by the churches (1 Cor. 9:14).

Distinct from the commandments of biblical origin and those coming from the Lord are the precepts promulgated by Paul on his own authority. He urged the faithful not to change their marital status in the eschatological age, but to devote themselves wholeheartedly to seeking entry into the Kingdom of God.

> I think that, in view of the impending crisis, it is well for you to remain as you are. Are you bound to a wife? Do not seek to be free. Are you free from a wife? Do not seek a wife . . . The appointed time has grown short: from now on let even those who have wives be as though they had none . . . For the present form of this world is passing away. (1 Cor. 7:26–31)

Paul, who was unmarried, encouraged the faithful to follow his example, but unlike the Essene ascetics he did not make celibacy compulsory. Those who found bachelor existence unbearable were permitted to marry (1 Cor. 7:8–9), though Paul warned them that because of the cataclysmic conditions of the impending end time, the married would experience more distress than those who were single (1 Cor. 7:28). He even provided a permissive solution for a particular marital problem. Should one of the partners of a married pagan couple convert to Christianity, if the pagan husband or wife was willing to live with the Christian spouse, they were to stay together. However, if the non-Christian party decided to quit or was making married life unbearable, Paul allowed the Christian consort to remarry (1 Cor. 7:12–15). This so-called Pauline privilege is still part of canons 1143–4 of the *Codex Iuris Canonici*, the law code of the Roman Catholic Church.

There is also the debated case of 'virgin spouses', namely couples committed to long-lasting or permanent sexual abstinence. If the husband felt unable to keep his vow, Paul half-heartedly permitted him to consummate the marriage: 'If his passions are too strong, and so it has to be, let him marry as he wishes; it is no sin' (1 Cor. 7:36–8). Finally, equally half-heartedly, he authorized the remarriage of a widow to a Christian man, but considered her more praiseworthy if she remained single (1 Cor. 7:40).

The ministers of the Pauline church

As the early Jewish-Christian church of Palestine was geographically limited and numerically restricted, its leadership comprised primarily Peter and the eleven apostles, James the brother of the Lord and probably other members of Jesus' family (1 Cor. 9:5). To these one should add a small number of other disciples chosen by the leaders: the seven deacons, Judas Barsabbas, Silas and Barnabas, the latter two being colleagues of Paul, together with Barnabas's nephew John Mark, companion of both Paul and Peter (1 Pet. 5:13), and supposedly the author of the oldest Gospel.

While in the Holy Land the apostles were able to exercise leadership and supervise the local churches, which were within relatively easy reach of Jerusalem, the diversity and geographic spread of the Pauline communities in Syria, Asia Minor, mainland Greece and Italy prevented Paul from personally looking after the many local congregations founded during his several missionary journeys. He occasionally revisited his churches or sent his special envoys, Timothy, Titus and Silas, to oversee the developing communities, but from an early stage he realized that without a solid administrative structure the new churches would disintegrate. Paul's neophytes, largely made up of lower-class, unsophisticated Greeks plus a few more opulent merchants and craftsmen, were not ready for religious self-government. Paul therefore devised for them a special administrative regime based not on a council of elders, as was the case in the Jewish synagogal communities in Palestine and the Diaspora, but on single bishops, assisted by presbyters and male and female charity workers, called deacons and deaconesses or widows. The organization of the community of the Dead Sea Scrolls, with a priestly overseer at the head of each community, offers the best parallel for the Gentile church and may have been the source of inspiration for Paul. According to church tradition, Paul's two close assistants, the half-Jewish Timothy (son of a Jewish mother and a Gentile father) and the Gentile Titus, were appointed as bishops of Ephesus and Crete.

The function of the bishop and the attributes required of candidates to be selected for the office are listed in the Pastoral Epistles (1 and 2 Timothy and Titus), which are generally held to be deutero-Pauline, that is, produced by Paul's disciples but sailing under the flag of Paul's name. The qualities demanded of a bishop mirror the society from which members of the Pauline church were recruited. They also reflect the stage when the eschatological enthusiasm generated by Jesus and displayed by Paul in the earlier part of his ministry was already on the wane.

The Pastoral Epistles and the Teaching of the Twelve Apostles furnish a picture of the intellectual and moral qualifications of a bishop (1 Tim. 3:2–7; Titus 1:7–13; Did. 15.1). He was to be a good teacher and a gifted debater, possessing a firm grasp of sound doctrine and an ability to defend it against purveyors of falsehood, especially the propagators of 'Jewish myths' that no doubt entailed the imposition on Gentile candidates of circumcision and the remainder of the Mosaic Law. The bishop was not to be a recent convert as quick promotion might fill him with pride. Beside teaching and defending the faith, the bishop as 'God's steward' had also pastoral duties. Here again the Damascus Document among the Dead Sea Scrolls may supply a useful parallel, with the guardian or overseer being depicted as a father and shepherd who loved and protected his children (CD 13:7–10). Thirdly, he was to be chiefly responsible for the administration of the church funds; hence he was not be known as a greedy man or a lover of money.

Above all, the bishop had to be a living example of virtue. He had to be blameless, prudent, temperate, not addicted to wine, gentle and self-controlled, and having a good reputation among non-Christians. It may surprise Roman Catholics, accustomed to the idea of a celibate clergy, that lack of marital experience was considered in the Pauline church a disqualification from the office of bishop. Candidates had to be once married men, i.e. if widowed, they were forbidden to remarry. Their ability to manage their families and bring up their children was considered proof that they would be capable of looking after their flock. Oddly enough, Paul, the self-confessed bachelor, and for that matter even Jesus, would have failed the test for the noble and difficult role of bishop.

The presbyters or priests were the principal assistants of the bishop, sharing his duties of preaching, teaching and pastoral care of the faithful. They too had to be once married heads of pious families and, like bishops, they were entitled to be maintained by their congregations (1 Tim. 5:17–18; Titus 1:6).

It is remarkable that neither the Pastoral Epistles nor the Teaching of the Twelve Apostles assign any particular role to the bishops and presbyters in the conduct of the Lord's Supper. Their duties were exclusively didactic and pastoral. The Eucharist was a communal ceremony and the other principal rite, baptism, also could be administered by anyone.

The task of the deacons remains undefined in 1 Timothy 3:8–13, but the Acts of the Apostles presents them as social workers (Acts 6:2). They were tested for the excellence of their faith and had to be once married, good fathers of family and endowed with the same moral qualities as the bishops.

Women, like Phoebe in Cenchreae (Rom. 16:1), were allowed to serve as deaconesses, whose job was to care for church members who needed help. The office was open to once married devout women above the age of sixty, who in addition to being model mothers and grandmothers, had excelled in charitable work throughout their lives, showing hospitality, 'washing the feet of the saints', helping the afflicted and performing all kinds of good deed. Younger widows, under the age of sixty, were expressly excluded as they could easily change their mind and decide to remarry, as well as become gossips and busybodies (1 Tim. 5:3–13).

The structure of church hierarchy described in the Pastoral Epistles clearly reflects the changed circumstances of the post-apostolic age. Bishops, presbyters, deacons and deaconesses represented a world view no longer focused on the imminent arrival of the Kingdom of God or the return of Christ, but envisaged a long-term normal future in which concern for the Christian community replaced Jesus' and Paul's expectation of the *Parousia*. The eschatological age was giving way to a church firmly rooted in time, space and history.

THE INVISIBLE FEATURES OF PAULINE CHRISTIANITY

The difference between the Jesus of the Gospels and the Jesus of Paul is that the former is understood to be a teacher divinely appointed to deliver a message, whereas Paul's Christ is the very object of this message. Paul was not concerned with the concrete details of the life and activities of the historical personality called Jesus. He had nothing to say about Nazareth, or Galilee, about the parents of Jesus, the high priests Annas and Caiaphas or even Herod Antipas or Pontius Pilate. Ignoring the historical context, Paul had his eyes fixed only on the three-day period that started with the night of Jesus' betrayal (1 Cor. 11:23), without naming the traitor Judas, and finished with his resurrection.

The invisible features that underlie Pauline Christianity consist in an elaborate doctrinal construct developed by Paul's fertile mind on the subject of the death and resurrection of the Lord Jesus Christ. Compared to his vision, the theology of the Synoptic Gospels and of the Acts of the Apostles appears primitive, but Paul finds his match in John's superb mystical portrait of the superhuman Christ. Deep familiarity with Judaism and at least a superficial acquaintance with classical culture, linked to a powerful spiritual imagination, enabled Paul to re-use the Jewish religious concepts of Messianism and of the merit gained by the self-sacrifice of martyrs, and create out of these elements an impressive doctrinal synthesis in which Christ was depicted as the final Saviour.

The symbolism of Christ's death and resurrection

While taking on board and applying to Jesus the biblical notion of the royal Messiah, the expected final liberator of the Jews and restorer of justice and virtue on earth, Paul went beyond the technique of the Qumran fulfilment *pesher* (see pp. 77–8) and the rabbinic-type of scriptural exegesis. He created a majestic cult drama on the theme of the myth of the dying and rising Son of God. The leading *dramatis personae* are the first Adam, the father of mankind, and Jesus Christ, the second or last Adam. Important supporting roles are played by Abraham and Isaac, the prototypes of faith and self-sacrifice. The main theme of the redemption mystery is the atonement achieved by the death and resurrection of the last Adam that compensated for the loss of immortality inflicted by the sin of the first man on his whole posterity.

Instead of enjoying perpetual life in the paradise of Eden, the first Adam allowed himself to be seduced by the devil-serpent with the help of Eve. Thus a single act of disobedience, the 'original sin' as St Augustine was later to call it, brought about the loss of immortality, and the sentence of death affected not only the first couple guilty of disobedience, but also their entire posterity. Satan's envy (Wisd. 2:24) and his tempting of Eve's foolishness (Ecclus 25:24) implanted in every member of the human race an evil inclination (the *yetser ra'* of the rabbis) or a wicked heart (*cor malignum* of 2 Esdr. 3:20–22), and thus inflicted death on them all as the consequence of the sin of the proto-parents of mankind.

Paul believed that Adam's transgression in a mysterious way affected the nature of the human race. This primeval sin, a Pauline creation with no biblical or post-biblical Jewish precedent, was irreparable by ordinary human effort. Not even God's direct saving act in favour of the Jews after the exodus from Egypt could change this situation. On the contrary, the Covenant concluded at Sinai was associated with the gift of the Torah, a code of precepts, which by emphasizing what was prohibited revealed sin to the Jews. In Paul's psychological understanding of the Law, the knowledge of what was sinful provided a stimulus to experiment with what was prohibited and simultaneously brought condemnation down on the ensuing rebellious deeds:

If it had not been for the Law, I would not have known sin. I would not have known what it is to covet, if the Law had not said, 'You shall not covet.' But sin, seizing an opportunity in the commandment, produced in me all kinds of covetousness . . . Apart from the Law sin lies dead . . . When the commandment came, sin revived and I died, and the very commandment that promised life proved to be death to me. (Rom. 7:7–10)

In the Pauline perspective, before the great event of redemption achieved by the death and resurrection of Jesus, righteousness or spiritual health was obtainable by faith and not by the performance of precepts, first those given to the children of Noah and then, after the exodus from Egypt, to the Jews by Moses. This faith, a trustful self-surrender to God, was first and foremost exemplified in Abraham. The patriarch was not reckoned righteous for the observance of a precept such as the acceptance of the painful rite of circumcision, but on account of his heroic faith. At the age of ninety-nine years he believed that the Almighty would enable him to render his hitherto sterile ninety-year-old wife pregnant and produce a male heir. Even more so, Abraham received justification for his willingness to sacrifice the miraculously born son in obedience to a capricious divine command. In fact, the post-biblical Jewish notion of the 'Binding of Isaac', combining the biblical idea of the epic subservience of Abraham with positive co-operation by Isaac, the victim in the sacrifice, seems to have provided the inspiration for Paul's discovery of the redeeming character of the death and resurrection of Christ. For half a century I have argued that the Pauline theology of the atoning virtue of Jesus' self-offering is inspired by the story of Abraham and Isaac (G. Vermes, *Scripture and Tradition in Judaism*, 1961, pp. 193–227). One needs only to compare Romans 8:31–2, 'He who did not withhold his own Son, but gave him up for all of us, will he not with him also give us everything else?', with Genesis 22:16–17: 'By myself I have sworn, said the Lord: Because you have done this, and have not withheld your son, your only son, I will indeed bless you.'

Genesis 22 may well be the unnamed biblical passage envisaged by Paul when he wrote, 'Christ died for our sins in accordance with the Scriptures' (1 Cor. 15:3), the passage that accounts for the proneness of the Church Fathers to see Isaac as the prototype of Jesus the

Redeemer. It should also be borne in mind that since the mid-second century BC in a layer of Jewish tradition, first attested in the Book of Jubilees, the date of the binding of Isaac coincides with that of the feast of Passover, the time when Jesus' suffering and death took place.

Considering the issue as a whole, the underlying logic of Paul's reasoning is clear. Each human being has sinned and deserves punishment. This punishment is death, 'the final enemy' (1 Cor. 15:26), that constitutes 'the wages of sin' (Rom. 6:23). However, this state of affairs, that followed the first Adam's foolish act, underwent a complete change when Christ, the sinless Son of God, was 'made to be sin' (2 Cor. 5:21), to atone through his death on the cross for all the transgressions of mankind. In the tortured body of the crucified Christ, God the Father punished 'sin in the flesh' (Rom. 8:3). In Paul's thought, when Christians believe in the redeeming virtue of the death and resurrection of Christ, mythically/mystically they die to sin and are reborn to a new life. 'We are convinced that one [Jesus] has died for all; therefore all have died. And he died for all so that those who live might live ... for him who died and was raised for them' (2 Cor. 5:14–15).

In the religious synthesis devised by Paul, the death of Christ is the fulcrum and Calvary is the centre of world history: hence Paul's claim that he has preached nothing 'except Jesus Christ, and him crucified' (1 Cor. 2:2). For him, the cross comes first and the resurrection is a straightforward corollary of it. The two saving acts of Jesus potentially redeem and revivify the believers. However, potentiality cannot be converted into reality without faith. Ultimately, belief in the sacramental virtue of baptism, the Pauline symbol of Christ's death and resurrection, passes on to the individual the saving virtue of the cross and the rising from the grave. This is why the baptism of the catechumens, the candidates under instruction in the mysteries of Christianity, was reserved for the vigil of Easter in the early church.

Conditioned by this Jewish mode of thought, Pauline Christianity recognized in the blood of the crucifixion the ultimate fulfilment of all the typological animal slaughters in the Temple: for Paul and his school as for the rabbis, without blood there was no atonement (bYoma 5a; Heb. 9:22). Justification was gained 'through ... Christ Jesus whom God put forward as a sacrifice of atonement by his blood, effective through faith' (Rom. 3:24–5). The crescendo of this teaching and the mixing of ancestral Judaism and Paul's newly formulated faith were reached when the new Isaac, the new Passover victim, was nailed to the cross: 'Christ, our paschal lamb, has been sacrificed' (1 Cor. 5:7). The image of the self-oblation of Isaac, dated in early post-biblical Jewish tradition to Passover day on 15 Nisan, must have been lurking in Paul's subconscious.

In the Pauline religion salvation from sin and re-awakening to a new life due to the death and resurrection of the Redeemer are inter-changeable aspects of the same spiritual reality. The cross comes first, but it is vindicated by the resurrection in its incandescent glory. The death of Jesus is the focal point of Paul's preaching, but without belief in resurrection, Christianity would collapse. 'Now if Christ is pro-claimed as raised from the dead, how can some of you say there is no resurrection from the dead? If there is no resurrection of the dead, then Christ has not been raised . . . your faith has been in vain' (1 Cor. 15:12–14; see G. Vermes, *Jesus: Nativity – Passion – Resurrection*, 2010, pp. 413–22).

In summary, the invisible features of Pauline Christianity during the pre-*Parousia* era may be summarized as a belief in liberation from sin and entitlement to resurrection, both obtainable through faith in the atoning and revivifying power of Jesus' death and rising from the tomb. But in Paul's view, the present era was nearly at its end, and for this reason the concept of the new age inaugurated by the Second Coming of Christ had to be integrated into the all-encompassing fresco he painted for his followers. The *Parousia* was the ultimate act of the religious drama in Pauline Christianity.

The return of Christ

The Christianity taught by Paul, like the religion preached by Jesus, was driven by an overpowering eschatological ardour. Jesus repeat-edly asserted that the Kingdom of heaven would be revealed to his generation (see Chapter 2, pp. 39–40). Paul was perhaps even more emphatic about the immediacy of the return of Christ and the inaugu-ration of the reign of God.

A fully developed form of Pauline eschatology is attested already in the initial phases of his preaching, in the First Letter to the Thessalo-nians, probably written in AD 51, and in 1 Corinthians, dating from a couple of years later. Paul exhorted the Thessalonians to wait eagerly for the reappearance of Jesus, who would abruptly arrive from heaven 'like a thief in the night' (1 Thess 5:2). Throwing all caution to the winds, he boldly asserted – as a certainty based on Christ's promise – that he and his flock would participate in the great encounter, which he sketched with masterly strokes.

> For the Lord himself, with a cry of command, with the archangel's call and with the sound of God's trumpet, will descend from heaven ... Then we who are alive, who are left [without experiencing death], will be caught up in the clouds together with them to meet the Lord in the air; and so we will be with the Lord for ever. (1 Thess 4:15–17)

Such a firm announcement of the imminence of the Second Coming, which continued to be ardently expected until as late as the end of the first century AD, turned out to be dangerous as it clearly unsettled some of the faithful. On the one hand, rumours began to spread that the *Parousia* was not just fast approaching, but had already happened. Members of the Thessalonian community referred to an alleged oral message of Paul, or to a letter sent by him, which announced that Christ had already made his return in some unspecified place and that his arrival in Thessalonica could happen at any moment (2 Thess 2:1–2). As a result, the normal life routine was upset. Some church members imagined that the final holiday had already begun and they stopped working (2 Thess 3:6–13). The unfettered frenzy needed some cooling down and Paul, convinced that the day of the Lord, though near, was still some way ahead, presented the Thessalonians with a precise sequence, a detailed timetable of preliminary happenings.

> Let no one deceive you in any way; for that day will not come unless the rebellion comes first and the lawless one is revealed, the one destined for destruction. He opposes and exalts himself above every so-called god or object of worship, so that he takes his seat in the temple of God, declaring himself to be God. Do you not remember that I told you these things when I was still with you? And you know what is now restraining him, so that he may be revealed when his time comes. For the mystery of lawlessness is already at work, but only until the one who now restrains it is removed. And then the lawless one will be

revealed, whom the Lord Jesus will destroy with the breath of his mouth, annihilating him by the manifestation of his coming. The coming of the lawless one is apparent in the working of Satan, who uses all power, signs, lying wonders, and every kind of wicked deception for those who are perishing, because they refused to love the truth and so be saved. (2 Thess 2:3–10)

By the time Paul wrote his Letter to the Romans, some time between AD 55 and 58, he was still hopeful, but had learned to be less exuberant and watch his words: 'Salvation is nearer to us now than when we became believers; the night is far gone, the day is near' (Rom. 13:11–12).

Obsession with the idea of the Second Coming created additional problems and provoked further anxiety in the Pauline churches, notably in Thessalonica and Corinth. They found it reassuring that at the approach of the triumphant Lord the living Christians would be miraculously lifted up towards the clouds, but what would happen to those church members who had died before the great day of the Lord? Though united to Christ through baptism, had they in fact missed the boat and lost their chance to meet him at the *Parousia*? Paul issued words of comfort to the apprehensive. At the moment of the *Parousia*, the deceased members of the church will be awakened by God's trumpet and will rise to join the living Christians to pay homage to the returning Lord (1 Thess 4:15–16). Concerned Corinthians tried to include even those friends and relations who had never heard about the Gospel and for this reason invented, without incurring Paul's disapproval, a vicarious baptism ritual for the dead (1 Cor. 15:29).

Combining the features separately laid out in the letters to the Thessalonians, Corinthians and Romans, Pauline Christianity's majestic canvas of the end may now be sketched. Eschatological D-day will dawn when the preaching of the Gospel has reached the westernmost extremity of the Gentile world – as far as Spain (Rom. 15:24). The sight of the entry of the full number of the pagans into the church will then kindle the jealousy of the Jews and they too will come along in droves so that 'all Israel will be saved' (Rom. 11:11–12, 25–6) together with all the non-Jews.

On the final day the assembled living Jewish and Gentile disciples of Jesus will witness the resurrection of 'the dead in Christ', the deceased Christians, and they all will mysteriously encounter the returning Lord somewhere between earth and heaven, and will abide with him for ever (1 Thess 4:15–17). With this majestic scenario will be combined the victory of Christ over all the enemies of God, over 'every ruler and every authority and power', the last enemy to be destroyed being Death. At that moment the Son, to whom everything has been subjected, will hand over the Kingdom to the Father and will subject himself to him (1 Cor. 15:24–8).

Pauline Christianity's perception of the end culminates in this magnificent vision. Yet despite the miracles of modern technology that have brought the Gospel to the ends of the world, no premonitory signs of the *Parousia* can be detected on the spiritual radar screen.

THE STATUS OF CHRIST IN THE PAULINE RELIGION

If all the letters of Paul are taken into consideration, that is to say, in addition to the authentic ones (1 and 2 Thessalonians, 1 and 2 Corinthians, Galatians, Romans, Philippians and Philemon) also those usually ascribed to Paul's disciples (Ephesians, Colossians, Timothy, Titus and Hebrews), the status of Christ will still not be firmly established, though the curve will appear to be rising. So let us be brave and ask whether a literary, historical and critical analysis of the Pauline corpus can confirm the view of the later tradition of the church and state that Jesus Christ was divine?

The titles 'Son of God' and 'Son of the Father' were incontestably part of Paul's language and conceptual world. However, one must not overvalue the phrases and, ignoring their meaning in the religious language of the Jews of the age, turn 'Son of God' into a synonym for God. In fact, Paul never envisaged Jesus as fully sharing the nature of the Deity. When compared to God the Father, 'the Son' always occupies an inferior position in Pauline thought, although he stands far above ordinary humans. The co-equality of the divine persons is a concept that is still centuries away.

The superiority of God over Christ is manifest in Paul's religious imagery. Just as he gave man a dominating role over woman in the context of marriage, he placed Christ above the humans, but below

God. Woman, man, Christ, God is Paul's ascending hierarchical order. 'I want you to understand that the head of every man is Christ, the head of a woman is her husband, and the head of Christ is God' (1 Cor. 11:3).

The situation is made clear in the Pauline sketch of the denouement of the eschatological drama. After the defeat of all the hostile powers by God through the Messiah, it will be the turn of Christ, the Son, to bow and subject himself to God the Father. Paul argues his thesis from a Midrashic fulfilment interpretation of Psalm 8:6.

> But when it [the Psalm] says, 'All things are put in subjection', it is plain that this does not include the one [God] who put all things in subjection under him. When all things are subjected to him, then the Son himself will also be subjected to the one who put all things in subjection under him, so that God may be all in all. (1 Cor. 15:27–8)

The two extracts quoted from 1 Corinthians clearly indicate that in the genuinely Jewish conceptual world of Paul, no one had the same dignity or possessed the same power as God; no one, not even Christ, was his equal. 'The Son' stood head and shoulders above the other 'sons of God' whose dignity derived from the fact that they were 'predestined to be conformed to the image of the Son ... the firstborn among many brethren' (Rom. 8:29). How did, then, Jesus the Christ acquire this peerless dignity? Was he born with it? The answer is no. First of all, Paul shows no interest in the life story of Jesus before his betrayal and crucifixion. All we learn from him about Jesus the man is that he was 'born of a woman ... under the Law' (Gal. 4:4), i.e. that he was the son of an unnamed Jewish mother and that as the Christ/Messiah he belonged to the family of King David (Rom. 1:3). His elevation to divine sonship was posthumous: he was 'designated Son of God in power ... *by his resurrection from the dead*' (Rom. 1:4). In other words, Jesus was granted the status of Son of God in the full sense, not from his birth, let alone from eternity, nor during his lifetime, but by virtue of his rising from the tomb. In plain words, in Paul's thought expressed in his most influential writings (1 Corinthians, Galatians and Romans), Jesus' elevation to the dignity of 'Son of God' postdated his earthly existence.

However, there are two passages in the authentic Pauline corpus and three statements in the deutero-Pauline literature that appear to raise Christ to higher spheres. The first of the genuine texts is Romans 9:4–5. It comes after Paul's passionate praise of the election of the Jews, to whom belong sonship, glory, covenants, the gift of the Law, worship, patriarchs and, ultimately, the Messiah. The eulogy ends with an unclearly worded blessing. Its precise meaning could be easily clarified by the use of punctuation, a facility unfortunately not yet in use in ancient Greek manuscripts. Without commas and dots, the extract written in capitals reads: 'AND OF THEIR RACE ACCORDING TO THE FLESH IS CHRIST THE ONE OVER ALL GOD BLESSED FOR EVER AMEN' (Rom. 9:5). The million-pound question is this: Is the blessing attached to Christ or to God? Now if the benediction formula is linked to Christ, as it is in the translation of the King James Bible, one reads 'Of their race . . . is the Christ, the one over all God, blessed for ever. Amen'. If so, Paul hails Jesus as a divine being. But the alternative punctuation, adopted by most contemporary translators and interpreters of the verse, results in a very different understanding: 'Of their race . . . is the Christ. The one over all, God, be blessed for ever. Amen.' Here Christ and God appear in separate categories. Our forthcoming survey of Paul's doxologies and prayer addresses will help to decide which punctuation should be preferred.

The second passage is a hymn to Christ found in chapter 2 of the Letter to the Philippians. It is important to note that the poem's aim is to inculcate humility by encouraging the faithful to imitate Christ's attitude to God.

> Have this mind among yourselves, which you have in Christ Jesus,
> Who, though he was in the form of God,
> Did not count equality with God a thing to be grasped,
> But emptied himself, taking the form of a servant,
> Being born in the likeness of men.
> And being found in human form, he humbled himself
> And became obedient unto death, even death on a cross.
> Therefore God has highly exalted him
> And bestowed on him the name which is above every name,
> That at the name of Jesus every knee should bow,
> In heaven and on earth and under the earth,
> And every tongue confess that Jesus Christ is Lord
> To the glory of God the Father. (Phil. 2:6–11)

Put simply, relinquishing his equality with God, Christ lowered himself by taking human nature to redeem mankind. Now, if this poem is authentically from Paul, it is unique in the genuine corpus of his letters. However, questions may be raised about its Pauline character on two grounds. Some of the key terms – being in the form of God, grasping equality and emptying oneself – are unparalleled in Paul's writings. Furthermore, the theme of the hymn, Christ's total abandonment of his former self, does not correspond to the purpose of his message which is to encourage the Philippians to live in harmony with one another. I feel justified therefore to repeat my earlier judgment and assert that the hymn is not an integral part of the original chapter 2 of Philippians. In fact, it could be excised from it without anyone noticing that something is missing (Vermes, *The Changing Faces of Jesus*, 2001, pp. 78–9). Both the terminology and the style seem to point to the ideology of early second century AD. Ancient church tradition connects the Fourth Gospel, filled with similar ideas, to Ephesus. We also know from Pliny the Younger, governor of Bithynia in AD 110, that Christians from Asia Minor were in the habit of 'singing alternately a hymn to Christ as to a god' (*Letters* 10.96: '... *carmenque Christo quasi deo dicere secum invicem*'). My critics complained that I rejected the authenticity of the passage from Philippians because its Christ picture did not agree with my theory. As a matter of fact, I argue against its Pauline origin on the grounds that it does not fit into *Paul's understanding* of Jesus, as reflected throughout all his genuine letters and in particular in his numerous prayer formulas and doxologies (see pp. 111–12). In consequence, I continue to maintain that the poem was inserted into the Letter to the Philippians by a later editor.

An ideology echoing Philippians 2:6–11 inspired the poetic piece incorporated in the deutero-Pauline Letter to the Colossians, which celebrates the eternal Creator and Saviour Son of God.

> He is the image of the invisible God,
> the first-born of all creation;
> for in him all things were created
> in heaven and on earth, visible or invisible,
> whether thrones or dominions
> or principalities or authorities –

all things were created through him and for him.
He is before all things and in him all things hold together.
He is the head of the body, the church;
He is the beginning, the first-born from the dead,
that in everything he may be pre-eminent.
For in him all the fullness of God was pleased to dwell,
and through him to reconcile to himself all things,
whether on earth or in heaven,
making peace by the blood of his cross. (Col. 1:15–20)

In reading these theologically charged lines, it is impossible not to recall, in addition to Philippians, the Prologue of the Fourth Gospel. This Prologue, as we shall see, is an impressive synopsis of the dominating ideas of the Gospel (the divine Word who is the Son of God contains and reveals the fullness of the Father), probably written by a hand other than the evangelist's, in the early second century AD.

The deutero-Pauline epistle addressed to the Hebrews is introduced by the same imagery implying the quasi-divinity of Christ the Son, instrument of the creation and mirror-image of God.

> In many and various ways spoke God of old to our fathers by the prophets; but in these last days he has spoken to us by a Son, whom he appointed the heir of all things, through whom also he created the world. He reflects the glory of God and bears the very stamp of his nature, upholding the universe by his word of power. (Heb. 1:1–3)

A passing hint at the secondary instrumentality of Christ in God the Father's creative action may be found in 1 Corinthians 8:5–6. The statements of the Epistle to the Hebrews are all very close to the boundary separating the human from the divine and leave only a slight element of equivocation. The notions of the image or icon and the stamp of God, used by Paul in 2 Corinthians 4:4 before Philippians 2:6, and by the author of Hebrews 1:3 are inspired by Genesis 1:26–7 where God is said to have created Adam in his own image and likeness. If Genesis 1:26–7 is the basic inspiration, Paul may envisage similarity rather than identity when he compares Christ to God.

There is finally an ambiguous formula of the deutero-Pauline Letter to Titus 2:13, referring to the expectation of 'the appearing of the glory of our great God and Saviour Jesus Christ'. It is taken by some as asserting the divine status of Christ. But another rendering, separating in the sentence God from Jesus, is equally possible. The Revised Standard Version, the New English Bible, the Jerusalem Bible, etc., propose in footnotes an alternative reading: 'the appearing of the glory of the great God and our Saviour Jesus Christ'. Here divinity applies where it belongs: to God, not to Christ.

The examination of a collection of texts, which by their nature reveal Paul's true mentality, will clarify the ambivalence of the two quotations from Romans and Philippians and the three deutero-Pauline passages. They unquestionably show to whom prayers and blessings are regularly addressed in Pauline literature. I trust readers will forgive me for presenting them with such a long list of examples. Their purpose is to demonstrate that the five passages discussed above conflict with Paul's thought and should therefore be judged inauthentic.

Prayer formulas

'We cry Abba! Father!' (Rom. 8:15)

'May the God of steadfastness and encouragement grant you to live in such harmony with one another, in accord with Jesus Christ, that together you may with one voice glorify the God and Father of our Lord Jesus Christ.' (Rom. 15:5–6)

'I appeal to you, brethren, by our Lord Jesus Christ . . . to strive together with me in your prayers to God on my behalf.' (Rom. 15:30)

'I give thanks to God always for you.' (1 Cor. 1:4)

'I thank God that I speak in tongues more than you all.' (1 Cor. 14:18)

'He will worship God and declare that God is really among you.' (1 Cor. 14:25)

'Thanks be to God who gives us the victory through our Lord Jesus Christ.' (1 Cor. 15:57)

'Thanks be to God who in our Lord Jesus Christ always leads us in triumph.' (2 Cor. 2:14)

'Thanks be to God who puts the same earnest care for you into the heart of Titus.' (2 Cor. 8:16)

'Thanks be to God for his inexpressible gift.' (2 Cor. 9:15)

'We pray God that you may not do wrong.' (2 Cor. 13:7)

'Because you are sons, God has sent the spirit of his Son into your hearts, crying, Abba! Father!' (Gal. 4:6)

'I thank my God in all my remembrance of you.' (Phil. 1:3)

'We give thanks to God always for you all . . . remembering before God our Father all your work.' (1 Thess 1:2–3)

'For what thanksgiving can we render to God for you?' (1 Thess 3:9)

'May the God of peace himself sanctify you.' (1 Thess 5:23)

'We are bound to give thanks to God always for you.' (2 Thess 1:3)

Benedictions and doxologies

'From him [God] and through him and to him are all things. To him be glory for ever. Amen.' (Rom. 11:36)

'To the only wise God be glory for evermore through Jesus Christ. Amen.' (Rom. 16:27)

'Blessed be the God and Father of our Lord Jesus Christ.' (2 Cor. 1:3)

'The God and Father of our Lord Jesus Christ, he who is blessed for ever.' (2 Cor. 11:31)

'To our God and Father be glory for ever and ever. Amen.' (Phil. 4:20)

These examples demonstrate that Paul directed his prayers, thanksgivings and benedictions to God alone, and never to Christ. Jesus Christ appears as the mediator through whom God is approached and not the addressee of the prayers. These citations furnish a practical, and as it were experimental proof of the distinction in Paul's thought between the role of the Father and that of the Son. Father and Son are not, to use the later theological definition, co-equal.

A final element of proof derives from the deutero-Pauline sources.

In spite of their near equation of God and Christ, they still abstain from worshipping the latter and continue to address, in the old Pauline and Jewish mode, prayer and thanksgiving to God or to God the Father.

'Blessed be the God and Father of our Lord Jesus Christ.' (Eph. 1:3)

'Always and in everything giving thanks in the name of our Lord Jesus Christ to God the Father.' (Eph. 5:20)

'We always thank God, the Father of our Lord Jesus Christ, when we pray for you.' (Col. 1:3)

'To the King of ages, immortal, invisible, the only God, be honour and glory for ever and ever. Amen.' (1 Tim. 1:17)

'Now may the God of peace who brought again from the dead our Lord Jesus ... equip you with everything good that you may do his will ... through Jesus Christ; to whom [viz. to God] be glory for ever and ever. Amen.' (Heb. 13:20–21)

PAUL'S PART IN THE FORMATION OF CHRISTIANITY

Compared with the charismatic-eschatological religion of Jesus and the charismatic-eschatological messianic doctrine of the early Jewish-Christian church, Pauline Christianity appears as a significant new departure. It is not surprising therefore that Paul is often presented as the true founder of the religion centred on Jesus, not only by iconoclastic New Testament scholars like Gerd Lüdemann (*Paul, The Founder of Christianity*, 2002), but even by as authoritative a textbook as *The Oxford Dictionary of the Christian Church*, 3rd rev. edn, 1997), which states that 'Paul came widely to be regarded as the creator of the whole doctrinal and ecclesiastical system presupposed in his Epistles' (p. 1048).

Acting as God's special envoy during his ministry, Jesus sought to persuade his Palestinian Jewish disciples to repent and make ready for entry into the Kingdom of heaven. He was heading an eschatological movement which was meant to absorb the whole Palestinian Jewish society. The Jewish-Christian church of the apostles of Jesus carried on preaching the coming of the Kingdom that would be brought about – the crucified, risen and triumphant Messiah Jesus still seen as an essentially Jewish entity, but envisaging even before Paul's arrival a modest opening for Gentile proselytes and sympathizers.

With Paul proclaiming himself and being accepted with varying degrees of willingness by the other leaders of the church as an apostle, the situation underwent a notable change. While the envoy to the Gentiles showed interest also in the Jews in the Greek Diaspora, their general unresponsiveness increased his keenness to convert the Gentiles. So Pauline Christianity focused on preaching the crucified and resurrected Christ to the wider human community. At the same time Paul became the explorer of the depths of the Christian message concerning the death and resurrection of the Son of God, and the consequent atonement for sin and universal salvation.

The outward expression of Christianity changed, too, and the communities of enthusiasts progressively gave way to hierarchically organized and firmly governed churches.

The status of Christ was also changing. From a seemingly unsuccessful prophetic Messiah he was metamorphosed into a triumphant heavenly Son of God, whose day of glory was expected to dawn in the very near future. Paul's Christ truly became the Lord of the universe, standing somewhat below the Father. However, the final New Testament stage of doctrinal advancement was still to be reached in the Johannine Christology.

5

Johannine Christianity

Johannine Christianity, that is the religion reflected by the Fourth Gospel and the letters attributed to John, represents a monumental advance on the religion of the early charismatic church. Its doctrinal contribution is as substantial as that of Paul but is formulated along very different lines. Whereas the Pauline writings transmit the extensive reflections of Paul on the significance of the divine mission of Jesus and rules regulating the conduct of the religious communities founded by the apostle of the Gentiles, the Fourth Gospel is a theological life story based on lengthy reflections attributed to Jesus on the fundamentals of the supernatural relationship between himself and the everlasting Deity. The Jesus figure of the Fourth Gospel greatly differs from the portrait drawn by the Synoptic evangelists. Rituals are not directly treated and the religious activity of the disciples is restricted to the fostering of belief in Christ and fraternal love among themselves.

THE JOHANNINE LITERATURE AND ITS AUTHORS

The doctrinal message is expounded in the many rambling, self-descriptive monologues of the Johannine Jesus. Compared to the teaching conveyed in the Synoptic Gospels, they are best understood as reformulations by the evangelist under, as he would say, the influence of the Holy Spirit, of words expressing the message of the Master.

Johannine Christology permeates the whole Gospel and bursts into the open in many places, but is most magnificently concentrated in the eighteen verses of the Prologue (Jn 1:1–18), a mystical digest prefixed to John's Gospel, the origin and nature of which will be investigated later. The first epistle of John supplies some further information, but the other two letters are insignificant.

The First Epistle of John, which is so identified by tradition without in fact being ascribed to any named writer in the text itself, stresses that Jesus is the promised Christ, who is once referred to, using the language of the Prologue, as the eternal 'Word (*Logos*) of God' whose earthly manifestation in a human body is denied by some heretical contemporaries of the writer. The two 'mini' letters, known as 2 and 3 John, come from an anonymous author called 'the Elder' or Presbyter. Surprisingly, the third letter names three otherwise unknown individuals: Gaius, the addressee; Demetrius, 'the postman' who delivers the missive and is commended by the writer; and Diotrephes, a communal leader, who refuses to accept the authority of the Elder. It seems that love, peace and harmony did not always triumph in the Johannine communities. The heresy denying the reality of the incarnation of the Word/*Logos* is attested already in this early age.

The last writing of the Johannine corpus, the Book of Revelation or Apocalypse, is attributed to a visionary by the name of John who lived in exile on the Aegean island of Patmos. From there he sent letters to seven churches in the great cities of the Roman Province of Asia. For a long time, church leaders hesitated about the canonicity and the authorship of the Apocalypse, but by the fourth century it was admitted into the New Testament and the visionary John was conflated with the apostle bearing the same name. Whereas some common elements exist between the Fourth Gospel and Revelation, for instance in the latter, as in the Prologue, Jesus is once called 'the Word of God' (Rev. 19:13), and is also referred to symbolically as 'the Lamb', an image familiar from the Gospel, the two works are poles apart from the point of view of language and must come from different writers. In fact, Revelation, unlike the Gospel, is a typical Jewish apocalypse in which a belligerent Christ, wearing the warrior's bloodstained robe, exterminates all the enemies of God before being transformed into the heavenly bridegroom. He is seen as descending from above together with the celestial Jerusalem to celebrate his wedding feast with his bride, the church.

It is impossible to determine the identity of the fourth evangelist. The date and place of origin of the Johannine literature can only be surmised from circumstantial evidence. Since the Fourth Gospel's religious message is much more advanced than that of the Synoptic Gospels, which are commonly assigned to the last three decades of the first century AD, its most likely origin must fall somewhat later. It obviously precedes the earliest Johannine papyrus fragments, which belong to the period between AD 125 and 150. The first mentions of John by the Church Fathers also date from the middle or the second half of the second century. Hence the most reasonable surmise dates the fully redacted Gospel of John from the first decade of the second century, from between AD 100 and 110. Tradition associates it with the city of Ephesus on the Aegean coast of Asia Minor.

The suggested dating makes it highly unlikely that the evangelist was a contemporary of Jesus such as the apostle John. The document itself nowhere discloses the name of the author and the traditional title, 'The Gospel according to John', comes from later scribes and copyists of the work. The only attempt in the Gospel, in chapter 21:20, to point out the author ascribes the work to the nameless 'disciple whom Jesus loved' (see Jn 13:23, 25). Church tradition presumes that the phrase refers to the apostle John, son of Zebedee. However, this chapter 21 is not part of the genuine Gospel; it is an appendix attached to the original conclusion of the work and must represent a second thought: 'Now Jesus did many other signs in the presence of his disciples, which are not written in this book; but these are written that you may believe that Jesus is the Christ, the Son of God, and that believing you may have life in his name' (Jn 20:30–31).

That the identification of the author was produced by a hand other than the evangelist's is manifest from the gloss written by a third person and given in chapter 21, verse 24: 'This is the disciple who is bearing witness to these things, and who has written these things and we know that his testimony is true.' This comment precedes the second conclusion, 'But there are also many other things which Jesus did; were every one of them to be written, I suppose that the world itself could not contain the books that would be written' (Jn 21:25).

The chief early authority identifying the author of the Fourth Gospel is St Irenaeus, bishop of Lyons, a native of Asia Minor (see Chapter 8, p. 193). He reported around AD 180 that the apostle John spent the final period of his life in Ephesus in Asiatic Turkey, where he also wrote his Gospel. But no New Testament source connects John with Ephesus. The Acts of the Apostles (8:14) mentions him as one who evangelized Samaria, and according to Paul, John, together with Peter and James the brother of the Lord, formed the three pillars of the Jerusalem church (Gal. 2:9). What is more to the point, in his letter to the Ephesians, Ignatius of Antioch in AD 110 describes the inhabitants of Ephesus as the people of Paul, who spent two years there before his last journey to Jerusalem (Acts 19:10), and not of John, presumed to have lived and died in Ephesus (on Ignatius, see Chapter 7, p. 166). It may also be useful to recall, against the identification of the evangelist with the apostle John, that Papias, bishop of Hierapolis (c. AD 60–130), mentions John the Elder among his teachers, whom he explicitly distinguishes from John, son of Zebedee. Such a person of Greek culture, whether a Jew brought up in a Hellenized setting or a native Greek convert to Judaism, is more likely to be the author of the Fourth Gospel – imbued with Greek ideas and mysticism – than the Galilean fisherman John, characterized by the high priests Caiaphas and Annas as an 'illiterate (*agrammatos*) and common (*idiōtēs*)' man (Acts 4:13). Whoever the fourth evangelist was, he was active in, and most likely came from, Ephesus or its neighbourhood. The non-Jewish character of his audience may be deduced from the need to translate into Greek the commonest Jewish religious terms like Rabbi as 'Teacher' or Messiah as 'Christ'. Its non-Jewish orientation gives the Gospel an entirely distinct colouring.

THE JOHANNINE JESUS

The Jesus of the Fourth Gospel has little in common with the popular preacher familiar from the Synoptic Gospel tradition, 'the prophet Jesus from Nazareth of Galilee', the guide appointed by God to lead his repentant contemporaries to the 'Kingdom of heaven' (Mt. 21:11; cf. Lk. 7:16; 24:19). With the exception of Jesus' nocturnal encounter with the Jewish teacher Nicodemus in chapter 3 of John, where he twice alludes to the divine Kingdom, this fundamental teaching topic of the Synoptic Gospels is absent from the Fourth Gospel. So too are Jesus' parables with their popularly picturesque style of instruction, which form a substantial part of his teaching in Mark, Matthew and Luke. The lordly, transcendent and authoritarian Johannine Jesus expects instant acceptance and approval of his words without spending any effort to make himself understood. He is far above all others and his superiority is displayed not only towards people from outside his familiar circle like Nicodemus (Jn 3), the Samaritan woman at Sychar (Jn 4) or the unfriendly Galilean crowd, outraged by the imagery of the sermon about eating the flesh and drinking the blood of Jesus (Jn 6), but even towards the closed circle of his apostles and disciples; when they grumble about the cannibalistic words concerning the consumption of Jesus' flesh and blood – 'This is a hard saying; who can listen to it?' – they are not offered an explanation. In fact, Jesus further confuses them by the blank announcement of his return to heaven from whence he came (Jn 6:60–62). Elsewhere he simply rebukes even an intimate disciple like Philip for his lack of understanding: 'Have I been with you so long, yet you do not know me?' (Jn 14:9). The Johannine Jesus does not waste his time on didactic finery.

Jesus the Christ

The meaning of the titles or qualification of Jesus is never expounded in the Fourth Gospel. Even the term 'Messiah' remains a vague concept, which, as has been noted, needs to be translated into Greek as 'Christ' and is never given any further elucidation. Not surprisingly, some of Jesus' compatriots openly wondered whether the designation could apply to him at all and others were convinced that he could not be the Messiah because he was known to be from Galilee, whereas the Messiah had to be a Judaean: 'Has not the scripture said that the Christ . . . comes from Bethlehem, the village where David was?' (Jn 7:42). Yet another group argued against his messianic status on the grounds that the Messiah's place of origin was concealed, whereas Jesus' connection with Nazareth was common knowledge (Jn 7:27).

The so-called messianic secrecy characteristic of the Gospel of Mark, namely the duty imposed on the apostles to keep quiet that Jesus was the Christ, is an idea alien to John. His Jesus never hesitates to proclaim his dignity. After meeting him, the future apostle Andrew unhesitatingly declared to his brother Peter, 'We have found the Messiah' (Jn 1:41). Neither did the Jesus of John, when asked whether he was the Christ, give non-committal answers such as 'You say so' or 'This is what you say', as did the Jesus of the Synoptic Gospels. On the contrary, the modesty of the Jewish holy man had disappeared. He was either clearly affirmative, as in the case of the Samaritan woman whom he solemnly informed when she was speaking of the Messiah, 'I who speak to you am he' (Jn 4:26), or he complained of being tired of repeating again and again the clear statement which his listeners had refused to believe on the earlier occasions. His despondent reply to a group of Jews in the Temple of Jerusalem is typical. Asked to tell plainly whether or not he was the Messiah, he answered: 'I told you, and you do not believe' (Jn 10:24–5).

Jesus the Son or the Son of God

It is the title 'Son' not that of 'Messiah' that most suitably defines the Johannine Jesus. The idea is indirectly derived from the combination of the expression Christ / Son of God / King of Israel (Jn 1:41, 45, 49). But whereas in common Jewish parlance, 'son of God' indicated the holiness of a person, the particular closeness of a human being to the Almighty (see Chapter 1, p. 25), for John's Jesus it amounted to a more elevated and intimate relationship. Since most of the references to Jesus in the Fourth Gospel are self-descriptive, they would suggest that we are reading an autobiography narrated in the third person. Bearing in mind, however, the fundamental differences between this portrait and the Jesus we find in the earlier Synoptic Gospels, it is more reasonable to conclude that the Johannine characterization of Jesus is the work of the fourth evangelist, a high level pondering on the Jesus figure inherited from earlier church tradition.

John's 'Son of God' is not an ordinary earthly human being, but a mysterious otherworldly personality. He stands, as has been observed, at a substantial distance from his disciples, let alone from ordinary Jews or other members of the human family. 'You are from below, I am from above', Jesus declares in John 8:23. He came down from heaven, and will return there after his transient passage on earth to prepare places for his followers in the Father's abode. 'No one has ascended into heaven but he who descended from heaven' (Jn 3:13). A re-descent to earth, corresponding to the idea of the 'Second Coming', will follow with a view to leading the faithful up to their celestial home. In short, a double return journey is envisaged: descent and ascent and again descent and ascent. For the Jesus of the Synoptic

Gospels, the *Parousia* was not part of his original schedule but the consequence of the unexpected interruption of his mission by the cross. For the Christ of John, it was an intrinsic part of the eternal plan. The Jesus who came from above proclaims:

> In my Father's house are many rooms; if it were not so, would I have told you that I go to prepare a place for you? And when I go and prepare a place for you, I will come again and will take you to myself.' (Jn 14:2–3)

To convey the image of travel between heaven and earth, John cleverly employs the 'Son of Man' terminology borrowed from Jewish apocalyptic eschatology, with the cloud as the vehicle of celestial transport, an imagery that started with Daniel and is richly documented in the New Testament. An upward journey to heaven is envisaged in Daniel 7:13 ('Behold, with the clouds of heaven there came one like a son of man'), Acts 1:9 ('He was lifted up and a cloud took him out of their sight') and 1 Thessalonians 4:16–17 ('We who are alive ... shall be caught up ... in the clouds to meet the Lord in the air'). On the other hand, in the narratives of the Second Coming (Mark 13, Matthew 24, Luke 21) the movement is from the celestial regions to earth. John's Son of Man, symbolizing Jesus, is a seasoned traveller in both directions. As for the 'Son of Man' image, despite its enriched theological content in John, it still maintains the idiomatic significance attested in the Synoptic Gospels (see Chapter 2, p. 34) that derives from the original Aramaic expression, *bar nasha* or *bar nash*, that is an oblique third-person reference to the speaker: 'Truly, truly I say to you, unless you eat the flesh of the *Son of Man* and drink his blood, you have no life in you; he who eats *my* flesh and drinks *my* blood has eternal life, and *I* will raise him up at the last day' (Jn 6:53–4).

In the religious outlook of the Fourth Gospel, the Son is sent by God the Father, not as the ultimate judge, but as a dispenser of life. He is the Redeemer who came 'not to condemn the world, but that the world might be saved through him' (Jn 3:17). The dreadful harshness of the last judgment is softened in John. Logically, damnation is a failure of the divine plan, as Origen was to maintain in the third century and thereby scandalize the later church (see Chapter 9, p. 222). Eternal life is the ultimate aim and it is to be obtained by means of faith in Christ. His followers are promised the 'bread of life' (Jn 6:47–8) and the spring of vivifying water (Jn 4:13–14). The other source of everlasting life is love. It comes from above, where it unites the Father and the Son in heaven (Jn 3:35; 17:23), and spreads earthwards through the union of the Father and the Son with the believers. The latter are also animated by their reciprocal love towards the Father and the Son (Jn 17:23) and, in an unspecified way, towards one another (Jn 14:21; 15:12). It should be remarked that John is clearly addressing a non-Jewish readership. It is only for them that Jesus' precept to love one another can be called a *new* commandment (Jn 13:34). The Gentile majority of the Johannine church seem to be unaware of the Mosaic Law, 'You shall love your neighbour as yourselves' (Lev. 19:18). Brotherly love is presented by the Jesus of the Synoptic Gospels to his Galilean disciples as the great *old* commandment, not as a new one: 'You have heard that it was said, You shall love your neighbour . . .' (Mt. 5:43; 22:39; Mk 12:31; Lk. 10:27).

The mutual abiding of the Father in the Son, the Son in the Father lifts the Son to mystical heights and results in a kind of apotheosis of Christ. Father and Son share the same knowledge and glory. They are both viewed in some sense as equals – but not always so, as will be shown a little further on (pp. 123–4). Moreover, Christ is described as the true image of God; hence he is entitled to say, 'He who has seen me has seen the Father' (Jn 14:9). Son and Father are actually one and this absolute exaltation of the Son affects in some way all the believers.

> The glory that you have given me I have given them, so that they may be one as we are one. I in them and you in me that they may become completely one . . . Father, I desire that those also whom you have given me, may . . . see my glory which you have given me because you loved me before the foundation of the world. (Jn 17:22–4)

In addition to the redemption of mankind from sin, the purpose of the incarnation of the Son is the ultimate deification of the believers. The seemingly pantheistic picture of the elevation of the disciples of Christ to the celestial domain happens in time and follows the earthly mission of the Son, whereas the Son's union with the Father is eternal and precedes the creation of the universe. This Johannine vision, together with the *Logos* doctrine to be outlined presently (see pp. 127–30), served as a pattern for much of the Christological development in the second and third centuries.

The notion of pre-existence, the dominant feature of the Prologue, is strikingly expressed in one of the so-called 'I am' (*ego eimi*) sayings of John. This type of formula is usually followed by a metaphor: 'I am the bread of life' (Jn 6:35); 'I am the way, the truth and the life' (Jn 14:6). But in a polemical passage it mysteriously stands on its own bereft of predicate. A group of quarrelsome Jews criticized Jesus for asserting that those who listened to his teaching would never taste death. In their judgment only someone under the influence of Satan could claim that, unlike the holy patriarchs and the prophets of the biblical past who had all died, Jesus' followers would escape the grave. Did he pretend to be greater than Abraham? To which Jesus retorted, shocking and confusing them: 'Before Abraham was, I am' (8:51–8). The reason for this startling statement remains unexpressed, but it seems to be linked to an ancient Jewish idea that the name of the Messiah was created by God in eternity; it came into being since before the world was produced, and was later revealed to Abraham. In consequence, Christ mystically existed in the form of his name from before the foundation of the cosmos, long before the birth of the ancestor of the Jewish people.

Subconsciously the evangelist was aware that his enthusiasm was taking him beyond the permitted limits of Judaism, be it native or adopted depending on whether 'John' descended from Hellenized Jewish stock (as I am inclined to think), or was a Gentile proselyte from Ephesus, as Alfred Loisy reckoned (*Le Quatrième Évangile*, 1921). Nevertheless, while insisting on the oneness of Jesus with God, John somehow implied that this did not always strictly amount to equality. In a polemical context he therefore inserted an escape clause. Having allowed his Jesus to declare, 'The Father and I are one' (Jn 10:30), which the hostile listeners found blasphemous, he made him afterwards dilute the saying by metaphorically downgrading the meaning of the term 'God':

> Is it not written in your law, 'I said, you are "gods"?' [Ps 82:6] If those to whom the word of God came were called 'gods' . . . can you say that the one whom the Father has sanctified and sent into the world is blaspheming because I said 'I am God's Son'? (Jn 10:34–6)

It should also be underlined that the Fourth Gospel insinuates throughout that the Son stands below or is second to the Father. The Father always has priority over the Son. It is the Father who sends the

Son, not the Son the Father. In his action, the Son imitates the Father, not vice versa; the message conveyed to his followers by the Son originates with the Father (Jn 5:19; 7:16). In particular, there is at least one passage in which the inferior status of the Son is unquestionably asserted, with Jesus proclaiming: 'The Father is greater than I' (Jn 14:28). This statement is clearly incompatible with and indeed directly contradicts the notion of co-equality. Although a transcendental whirlwind was lifting John up towards the seventh heaven, nonetheless occasionally basic Jewish monotheism reasserted itself. Be this as it may, John's mystical vision, situating the Son from all eternity in the celestial domain, has the last, and as far as the literary arrangement is concerned the first, word in that unique theological gem that is the Prologue to the Fourth Gospel (Jn 1:1–18).

Jesus, the Lamb of God

The Johannine Son of God was not only the revealer of the Father and the 'deifier' of the believers; he was also their saviour and redeemer through his self-offering or sacrifice. To express this idea, John has introduced a metaphor, the 'Lamb of God', unused in the Synoptic Gospels though indirectly paralleled by Paul when he calls Christ 'our Passover', that is, our Passover Lamb (1 Cor. 5:7). In the Fourth Gospel Jesus is publicly identified as 'the Lamb (amnos) of God' by John the Baptist, thus allegorically conveying the idea of redemption: Jesus is 'the Lamb of God who takes away the sin of the world' (Jn 1:29, 36). The term 'Lamb' symbolizing Christ, but with the use of a different Greek word (arneion), figures a dozen times in the Book of Revelation, but never as 'Lamb of God' (amnos Theou).

The allusion recalls the lamb sacrifices offered for the expiation of the sins of Israel in the Temple, and in particular the paschal lamb slaughtered in the afternoon of the eve of Passover (14 Nisan) on behalf of every Jewish family, for the regular residents as well as for the pilgrims who came to celebrate the great spring festival in Jerusalem. According to John's peculiar Passion chronology, in which the sentencing and execution of Jesus take place on the day preceding Passover, the death of the crucified Christ at 3 p.m. coincides with the time of the killing of the Passover lambs in the Temple court. In this way the Baptist's prediction (Jn 1:29) is presented as fulfilled: 'Behold, the Lamb of God, who takes away the sin of the world.' In this way, the atonement symbolized by all the lamb offerings and especially the Passover sacrifice was depicted as accomplished through the historical fact of the death of Jesus on Golgotha. A similar allegory is expressed in the Aramaic Targum on Exodus 1:15. In a dream of Pharaoh, Moses, the first redeemer of the Jews, typified by a lamb, was placed on one of the scales of a balance and all the Egyptians stood in the other scale, but Moses outweighed them, implying that he would triumph over them and deliver his people from slavery.

Another 'Lamb of God' is encountered in the sacrifice of Isaac in Genesis 22. We have already seen in Chapter 4 on Pauline Christianity that Jewish interpretative tradition portrays Isaac, the lamb of Abraham, as gladly consenting to play the role of the sacrificial victim the Patriarch was to offer on Mount Moriah (pp. 101–3). According to the oldest Jewish tradition on the subject (Jub. 17:15), the quasi-immolation of Isaac took place on 15 Nisan, the date of the future feast of Passover. John's inspired use of the 'Lamb of God' imagery cleverly encapsulates and transmits the rich Christian theological concept of universal redemption achieved by the sacrificial death of Jesus.

Excursus on the Holy Spirit

Before turning to the Prologue, a brief consideration must be given to the Holy Spirit in the theological complex of John's Gospel. In general, neither in the Hebrew Bible nor in the New Testament is the Holy Spirit treated as a person. Holy spirit or spirit of holiness is the name given to the power through which God has performed his actions in the world ever since the beginning of the creation when it was hovering like a bird over the primordial waters (Gen. 1:2). In the Old Testament the spirit of holiness cleanses impurity and inspires the prophets. In the Synoptic Gospels John the Baptist announces that Jesus will baptize by means of two purifying elements – the holy spirit and fire – or just with the holy spirit (Mt. 3:11; Mk 1:8; Lk. 3:16), and in the Acts of the Apostles the holy spirit takes possession of all the disciples of Jesus.

By contrast, in the Fourth Gospel the mystically personified Spirit is the successor of Christ and the continuator of his work. The Holy Spirit is the 'other Counsellor' or 'Advocate' (*paraklētos*, Jn 14:16,

26), dispatched by the first one, Jesus (1 Jn 2:1). Its task is to be always with the Johannine community, remind its members of the message delivered by Jesus, and convey to them the whole truth: 'But the Counsellor, the Holy Spirit, whom the Father will send you in my name, he will teach you all things, and bring to your remembrance all that I have said to you' (Jn 14:26).

The Holy Spirit dwells in the believers in the same way as the Father and the Son dwell in them (Jn 14:17); it proceeds from the Father in the same way as does the Son (Jn 15:26) and passes on to the believers the teachings that the Son has received from the Father and entrusted to the Spirit without himself directly communicating them to his disciples (Jn 16:13–15). The constant procession from Father to Son culminates in the Holy Spirit. John's theology of the Holy Spirit contains and foreshadows the idea that the whole revelation was not handed down by Jesus during his life, nor was it immediately and fully understood by his disciples. Here lie the seeds of the idea of doctrinal development that the authoritarian church, suspicious of change, has always found difficult to accommodate.

THE PROLOGUE: QUINTESSENCE OF THE JOHANNINE RELIGIOUS OUTLOOK

The Prologue of John chronicles a new creation. Like Genesis 1:1, it starts with the phrase 'In the beginning', and compresses in 251 carefully chosen words the substance of the Christological doctrine of the Fourth Gospel. The nature of the relationship between the Prologue and the rest of the Gospel is much debated among its interpreters. For some, like the well-known British New Testament expert C. K. Barrett, it is a piece of solid theological writing produced by the evangelist himself. The Prologue puts in a nutshell the history of Jesus recounted in the Gospel and the Gospel story explicates the theology of the Prologue (Barrett, *The Prologue of St. John's Gospel*, 1971, pp. 27–8). For others, the piece is a mystical hymn, composed quite independently of the Gospel by a writer belonging to a Hellenistic Jewish milieu, so R. E. Brown (*The Gospel According to John I–XII*, 1966, pp. 18–23), rather than to a Palestinian Jewish-Christian community, as John Ashton concludes (*Studying John: Approaches to the Fourth*

Gospel, 1998, p. 6), or to Gentile-Christian circles from Syria in the opinion of Rudolf Bultmann (*The Gospel of St. John: A Commentary*, 1971, p. 12).

A detailed analysis of the Prologue suggests that its composition follows, rather than precedes, the main narrative of John. The situation resembles that of the Infancy accounts of Matthew and Luke compared to the main body of those Gospels. In both cases, the introductory sections are aware of the essential themes of the subsequent reports, but the latter do not echo the characteristic ideas of the opening parts. Just as the topic of virginal conception is ignored in the rest of the Jesus story recounted by Matthew and Luke (see G. Vermes, *Jesus: Nativity – Passion – Resurrection*, 2010, pp. 157–62), the typical Hellenistic philosophical idea of the Word (*Logos*) that dominates the opening verses of the Prologue (where it is used four times in verses 1–2 and 14) makes no appearance whatsoever in the rest of the Fourth Gospel. The best explanation of this phenomenon is that the Prologue stands at the end of the process of composition of John and not at the beginning, despite its place at the opening of the finished work. Assuming that it started life as an independent hymn, it was subsequently anchored to the main body of the Gospel with the help of allusions to the historical figure of John the Baptist, who acted as the witness to the Word in the age of Jesus (Jn 1:6–8, 15). A second chronological indicator is a reference to the earlier Jewish lawgiver Moses (Jn 1:17). The hymn was then prefixed to the main body of the Gospel to serve as a condensed introductory synopsis to the somewhat diffuse essential teaching of the evangelist regarding the peregrinations of the eternal Son of God and his relation to God the Father and to his terrestrial followers.

The initial words of the Prologue, 'In the beginning', are unquestionably patterned on the opening of Genesis, the first book of the Hebrew Bible. Both texts take the reader to eternity, before the moment of the creation, before events determined by space and time, prior to the conflict between darkness and light. 'In the beginning God created the heavens and the earth . . . And darkness was over the face of the deep . . . And God said, "Let there be light"', we read in Genesis 1:1–3. In John's Prologue, too, the primeval darkness of the pre-creation phase is illuminated by the eternal and all-powerful divine Word or *Logos* that transforms non-existence into luminous reality.

In the beginning was the Word, and the Word was with God, and the Word was God . . . All things were made through him . . . In him was life, and life was the light of men. The light shines in the darkness, and the darkness has not overcome it . . . The true light . . . was coming into the world. (Jn 1:1–2, 4–5, 9)

However, John introduced an unprecedented novelty into the Genesis imagery when he identified God's supertemporal creative Word with Jesus of Nazareth, whom he presented as Son of God incarnate, born in the fullness of time and living for a short period in a human body to reveal to men God the Father. 'And the Word became flesh and dwelt among us . . . The only Son who is in the bosom of the Father has made him known' (Jn 1:14, 18).

While the dualistic notion of light/darkness perfectly suits the purpose of the evangelist in his proclamation of Jesus as the Redeemer Son of God, the ultimate clue of the message of the Prologue lies elsewhere. Regarding the darkness/light symbolism of John, it is often associated with the Dead Sea Scrolls where phrases such as 'sons of light', 'ways of light' and 'spirits of light', and their opposites, frequently occur, especially in the Community Rule and the War Scroll. But compared with the numerous uses of the concepts of light/darkness in the Qumran manuscripts, 'sons of light' is not a typical Christian idiom. The expression 'sons of light' appears no more than three times in the Prologue, and only once elsewhere in John (Jn 12:36), outside the Prologue, whereas the idiom 'sons of darkness' is nowhere attested in the New Testament.

The key term in the Prologue is the Greek noun *Logos*, which has a rich Hellenistic past but possesses an important Hebrew and Aramaic background too. Moreover, the *Logos* concept is pivotal in the thought of the Jewish philosopher Philo of Alexandria (*c.* 20/10 BC– after AD 39/40) as well as in Hellenistic mysticism known as Hermeticism, contemporaneous with the Fourth Gospel. Hermes or Hermes Trismegistos – Hermes Thrice-Greatest – was the Hellenized reincarnation of the Egyptian deity Thoth, the source of wisdom, who was believed to deify man through knowledge (*gnosis*). The influence of Philo and Hermetism on Hellenistic Christianity is generally acknowledged. In Hermetic literature the *Logos* is identified as the 'Son of God' and in Philo it is also a mediator figure, the instrument of creation in God's hand. In the Platonic philosophical language the *Logos* is the Demiurge, the Craftsman responsible for the creation of the world.

John is familiar with all these ideas. The *Logos* was there before the creation, was with God and was indeed divine. The *Logos* is portrayed as the Son abiding in the bosom of God the Father who revealed himself in the fullness of the ages to the hostile darkness of the world as life and light during the ministry of John the Baptist, who introduced the timeless pre-existing Word into Jewish history. The Jews, Jesus' 'own people' (Jn 1:11), represent darkness, and they are depicted in the whole Fourth Gospel as his mortal enemies who sought to kill him from the start. This is in stark contrast to the Synoptic Gospels where only Jewish leaders oppose Jesus, not the people as a whole.

One may also ask whether Hebraic and Aramaic ideas connected with the creation story of the biblical book of Genesis also lie concealed beneath the powerful Hellenistic garb of the *Logos*. Such a supposition could be meaningful in the hypothesis that 'John' was a Hellenized Jew who, like Paul, also had a Palestinian education. As has been noted, both Genesis and the Fourth Gospel start with the phrase 'in the beginning'. In the Bible creation is launched by means of a divine command: 'And God said, "Let there be light"; and there was light' (Gen. 1:3). Likewise according to the Prologue of John, all things were made by the eternal Word of the Almighty and as a result light shone in the primeval darkness (Jn 1:1–4).

Though the Jewish literary sources which also contain these concepts postdate the Fourth Gospel, in the not unlikely hypothesis that they reflect earlier ideas, a cursory glance at them is justified. Ancient rabbinic interpretative tradition recorded in the Palestinian Targums or Aramaic paraphrases of Genesis present a twofold understanding of *be-reshit* ('in the beginning'). The term is rendered by the ancient exegetes either as 'with Wisdom' (*be-hokhmeta*) or 'with the Word' (*be-Memra)*, both expressions being the fruit of deep expository thinking. 'With wisdom' is the outcome of the reading of Gen. 1:1, 'In the beginning God created the heavens and the earth', in conjunction with Proverbs 3:19, 'The Lord by *wisdom* founded the earth; by understanding he established the heavens.' As for the omnipotent divine Word, or *Memra*, often substituted in the Palestinian Targums for the sacrosanct name of God (YHWH), it no doubt alludes to the

verbs that expressed the divine commands by which the various created realities (light, firmament, etc.) were ordered to come into being.
In the Mishnah (Abot 3:15), Rabbi Akiba, who suffered martyrdom
during the second Jewish rebellion against Rome in AD 135, asserts
the relatedness of Wisdom to *Memra* and Torah (the Law) when he
declares that God bestowed on Israel 'the precious instrument by
which the world was created' and proves it from Proverbs 4:2, 'For I
give you good precepts; do not forsake my Torah.' Since for the rabbis
the Law was in existence before the creation of the world (bPes 54a;
bNed 39b), they imagined that God consulted the Torah when he
decided to create and used it as a blueprint, an architect's drawing, as
the Midrash puts it, for bringing the world into existence (Genesis
Rabbah 1:1).

The conceptual world of ancient Jewish Bible interpretation provides therefore a most helpful intellectual framework for a writer
with a dual traditional Jewish and Hellenic background for the understanding of the creative role of the *Logos*. Suddenly the stark statement
that in the beginning God produced everything with his Word becomes
more easily intelligible. The pointed message of the Prologue consists
in the identification of the divine *Logos* in action since all eternity
with the historical personage of Jesus in whom the Word became
flesh. This preface to the Fourth Gospel, together with the subsequent
teaching about the Holy Spirit, is the principal source of the developing ideas of the Greek church regarding the doctrine of the Holy
Trinity. Without John, the Christian message would have been quite
different and would have lacked some of its true poetic dimensions.
Indeed, the *Logos* idea played a crucial role in the development of
Christology in the early church, in the works of Justin and Origen and
throughout the whole Arian controversy in the fourth century.

THE JOHANNINE RELIGION

To perceive the reality of the Johannine religion, it must be set against
the type of religious life outlined in the teaching of Jesus and in the
letters of St Paul. Both the religion of Jesus and that of Paul are centred on the expectation of the Kingdom of God, awaited directly by
Jesus and his disciples, and in the form of the *Parousia* or Second

Coming of Christ by the Pauline church. Both groups strove towards the ultimate ideals along practical pathways, by means of the adaptation of the Mosaic Law to the peculiar circumstances of the end time, or through emphasis on its spiritual demands without the necessary observance of the whole Torah. Jesus reinterpreted some of the precepts and Paul added to them a few of his own. In sum, Christ is seen as the Redeemer and the Revealer of the way to the Kingdom, but the steps to follow are concrete. Not so in the Johannine religion, notwithstanding the odd-man-out, 1 John 2:3, where knowledge of Jesus is loosely identified with the observance of his commandments.

The whole Johannine corpus, the letters as well as the Gospel, meanders along in a vague, less down-to-earth, and altogether dreamier manner than Jesus or Paul. As far as the relationship with God and Christ, or the Father and the Son, is concerned, in John *faith* is the key word. If my counting is correct, the verb 'to believe' (*pisteuein*) occurs seventy-seven times in his Gospel, to which we can add eight examples from the First Letter of John. Faith in the divine sonship of Jesus, in his mission to the world by the Father and his intention to lift the believers to the heavenly home, is the essential summing-up of the Johannine religion. In metaphorical language religion is the move from darkness to light, from the kingdom of Satan to that of the Father and the Son. Human religious action can also be epitomized in the single idea of love. Members of the Johannine communities must love the Father, the Son and one another. In fact fraternal love is the ultimate criterion of true religiousness: 'If anyone says, I love God, and hates his brother, he is a liar; for he who does not love his brother whom he has seen, cannot love God whom he has not seen' (1 Jn 4:20).

The only specific feature of the Johannine faith, stressed in the letters of John, is the insistence on the reality of the incarnation, namely that Jesus Christ came 'in the flesh' (1 Jn 4:2; 2 Jn 7) in reaction against the Docetists, Cerinthus and other early Gnostic teachers alive in Asia Minor during the decades that followed. Their idea that the birth, life and, in particular, the suffering and death of Jesus were not true but merely imaginary will be a standard theme of the great debate with Gnosticism in the second century.

Unlike the Christianity of the Acts of the Apostles and of Paul, the Johannine literature contains no clear hint at the basic religious rituals of the early church – baptism and the breaking of the bread, the sacred communal meal in imitation of Jesus' Last Supper with his apostles. Allusion to the latter can hardly be expected in John. The Fourth Gospel knows of no Passover supper-like ritual: in John Jesus' last meal with his apostles took place not at the start of 15 Nisan, but twenty-four hours earlier. The only incidental reference by Jesus to baptism is inserted in the dialogue with Nicodemus, where the spiritual rebirth of the believer is said to be due to water and Spirit (Jn 3:5). In the Fourth Gospel water is always presented as the source of life, and not as a means of purification. Neither does the imagery of eating the body and drinking the blood of Christ in John chapter 6 point to a regularly repeated ceremony. This partaking in the body and blood symbolizes spiritual nourishment by faith rather than a ritual weekly custom. While Matthew belatedly attaches a couple of allusions to the church, and Acts and the letters of Paul frequently mention it, the fourth evangelist abstains from hinting at an organized community established by Jesus. The closest we come to it is in John 21, a chapter later appended to the Gospel (see p. 117 above), where Jesus appoints Peter as the shepherd of his flock, a metaphor for the church. The final denouement of the mystery, the transfer of the followers of Jesus to their heavenly mansions, is the object of unhurried hopeful expectation, foreseen in the not too distant future. 1 John 2:18 quietly asserts that the faithful were living in the last hour and almost nonchalantly adds that not only one, but many antichrists have already come. In the Johannine age the eschatological excitement of the earlier years was already cooling down and the new era of the post-apostolic church was dawning.

In conclusion, the most notable contribution of John to the further development of Christianity consists in a clearer proclamation of the divinity of Jesus than anywhere else in the New Testament. One would search in vain for such a statement in the Synoptic Gospels, and Paul is at best equivocal (see pp. 106–11). John, on the other hand, not only makes Jesus assert his oneness with the Father even though on a somewhat inferior level (Jn 10:30; 14:28), but declares that the Word, which was to become incarnate in the person of Jesus, was God. The relevant verses of the Prologue deserve repeating. 'In the beginning was the Word, and the Word was with God, and *the Word was God* . . . And the Word became flesh.'

With these not altogether harmonized statements that Christ was equal yet inferior to the Father, John set into motion the heated doctrinal debates which stretched from the fourth to the sixth centuries. The Christological controversies among Church Fathers and at ecumenical councils (Nicaea in 325, Chalcedon in 451 and Constantinople in 553) all arose from the message first enunciated in the Fourth Gospel, and especially in its Prologue's startling claims that Jesus was the Word and the Word/*Logos* was God.

6

The Didache and Barnabas

PRELIMINARY NOTE

In our examination of the New Testament evidence it is reasonable to presume that all the readers of this book possessed some familiarity with the sources. However, in dealing with the Greek and Latin works representing the doctrinal legacy of early Christianity from roughly AD 100 to 325, the style of presentation will require substantial adjustment as these texts are known less well or not at all by non-specialists. One possible model to follow would be a direct historical-critical investigation of the development of the Jesus image in the early church, similar to the magisterial work of the German Jesuit Aloys Grillmeier, *Christ in Christian Tradition* (2nd edn, 1975). But since this type of book is useful only to specialist theologians, I have decided to broaden the approach and discuss the literature of the early Church Fathers in fuller detail, giving a description of both the authors and the contents of the writings, so that the essential elements of Christology, the patristic teaching dealing with the person of Jesus and the role attributed to him by the church in the celestial realm and on earth, can be put into its proper context. The number of direct citations will be increased to allow the readers to judge on the basis of direct evidence.

For the benefit of those unacquainted with the life and thought of the early church it should also be noted that a complete, if somewhat antiquated, English translation of all the relevant texts is available in *The Ante-Nicene Christian Library: The Writings of the Fathers down to AD 325*, by Alexander Roberts and James Donaldson. Originally published in Edinburgh by T. & T. Clark between 1867 and 1873, it is easily accessible on the Internet in *Christian Classics Ethereal*

Library (www.ccel.org/fathers.html) and in *New Advent* (www. newadvent.org/fathers/index.html). A select updated bibliography is included in this book (pp. 245–56).

To prepare the ground for the study of the so-called post-apostolic Church Fathers in the second century, it will be helpful to start with the presentation of the contrasting theological ideologies contained in two significant writings which originated close to AD 100, before the most recent units of the New Testament appeared. These are the Didache or the Teaching of the Twelve Apostles, probably composed during the last two or three decades of the first century AD, and the Epistle of Barnabas, written before, but presumably not much before, the second Jewish rebellion against Rome in AD 132–5. The Didache is the product of Jewish Christianity and Barnabas is a typical Gentile-Christian writing.

The Didache, though it was patently used in antiquity as a model for later church regulations – it influenced the third-century *Didascalia* and the fourth-century Apostolic Constitutions – was nevertheless classified by the famous church historian Eusebius (*c.* 260–339) as being among the 'spurious', i.e. non-canonical, books distinct from the New Testament (*EH* 3.25, 4). Preserved in an eleventh-century manuscript, known as the Codex Hierosolymitanus, it was rediscovered by the Eastern Orthodox prelate Philotheos Bryennios in 1873, who published it in 1883. The Greek text is further attested in a papyrus fragment of the fourth century (P. Oxyrinchus 1782) and in a Coptic translation (P. Lond. Or. 9271) from the third/fourth century, as well as in Latin, Ethiopic, Syriac and Georgian renderings. The Didache has been acclaimed as one of the most significant literary treasures of primitive Christianity, describing the initiation of new members and the essential rites and organization of the infant church. Testifying to the earliest extra-scriptural understanding of Jesus, it provides a very important source for our quest.

The Epistle of Barnabas, on the other hand, came close to being accepted as part of the New Testament, possibly because of its fictional attribution to Barnabas, the senior colleague of St Paul in Antioch according to the Acts of the Apostles. The epistle was acknowledged as belonging to the canon of sacred Christian literature by the great third-century Alexandrian authorities, Clement and Origen, and as such was included in the oldest Greek Bible, the fourth-century

Codex Sinaiticus. Subsequently however it was firmly downgraded by the church and relegated to the category of the extra-canonical writings, as we learn both from Eusebius (*EH* 3.25, 4) and from St Jerome (*De viris illustribus* 6).

Interestingly both the Didache and Barnabas contain a section dealing with morality, entitled the 'Two Ways'. Didache 1–5 speaks of the ways of life and death, while Barnabas 18–21 prefers to refer to the ways of light and darkness. It has long been suspected, and since the publication in 1951 of the Qumran Community Rule (1QS 3:12–4:26) it has become obvious, that the two Christian manuals of ethics were patterned on a pre-existent Jewish model.

The Didache and Barnabas furnish a valuable insight, independent from the New Testament, into the life and ideas of the early followers of Jesus, the former probably envisaging communities in Palestine or Syria, whereas the home ground of the Epistle of Barnabas is supposed to be Egypt, most likely Alexandria, as its characteristic use of allegorical Old Testament interpretation would suggest. They permit a precious glimpse into two types of communities in the nascent church, and exemplify their way of life as well as their fundamental beliefs. It is hardly necessary to add that both have been written and preserved in Greek.

THE DIDACHE OR THE TEACHING OF THE TWELVE APOSTLES (*c.* AD 50–100?)

The nature of the document

Nothing is formally stated in the text of the Didache about its author or its audience. The work transmits anonymously a primitive form of Christian message attributed to the twelve apostles of Jesus and most of the material implies that the audience or readership was of Jewish rather than of Gentile background. That at some stage it was meant to address non-Jews too is intimated by the secondary title: 'The Teaching of the Lord through the twelve apostles *to the nations*', and also by the reference in 6.3 to abstention from food deriving from sacrifice to pagan gods, a prohibition included also in Paul's First

Letter to the Corinthians (8:1–12). Everything else is perfectly adapted to Jewish communities of Jesus' followers in the Holy Land, where there were also Gentile cities in the coastal region, or to Christians living in neighbouring Syria, say at Antioch, where the church consisted of Jews and Gentile converts according to the Acts of the Apostles (11:19–21).

The Didache contains no identifiable chronological pointer, such as an allusion to the fall of Jerusalem or the destruction of the Temple, and can conceivably be dated any time in the second half of the first century up to AD 100, though many scholars are inclined towards the latter part (AD 70–100) of this timescale. The work possibly precedes the definitive redaction of the Synoptic Gospels as the Didache's quotes from the teaching of Jesus are not strictly identical with the transmitted form of Matthew and Luke, and consequently may reflect a more primitive version of these texts. Also, and very significantly, apart from the passage concerning idol food, nothing echoes the letters of Paul. We have every reason to think that the Didache envisages a rather primitive and rudimentary form of Jewish-Christianity, not unlike, and doctrinally even less developed than, the church described in the first twelve chapters of the Acts of the Apostles.

The community of the Didache

So how can one portray the life of this embryonic Jesus party, whose members the author of the Didache addresses as his 'children'? The terminology recalls the style of speech of that other shepherd of souls, the guardian of the Essene Damascus sect (CD 2:4). As has already been pointed out, the conduct of the Didache community is modelled on a Jewish moral code, the doctrine of the Two Ways, which springs from the Old Testament and is magnificently summed up in another Qumran text, the Community Rule (1QS) dating from c. 100 BC.

In outlining the substance of religious action, the Didache adds the so-called Golden Rule to the quintessential summary of the Mosaic Law – the love of God (Deut. 6:5) and the love of neighbour (Lev. 19:18). It is important to note, however, as far as the religious-cultural background of Didache 1.2 is concerned, that the Golden Rule is given not in the positive form attested in the Gospels of Matthew and Luke – 'Whatever you wish that men would do to you, do so to them'

(Mt. 7:12; Lk. 6:31) – but in the older negative Jewish form – 'Whatever you do not want to happen to you, do not do to another' – as we find it also in the apocryphal book of Tobit (4:15), in Philo (*Hypothetica* 7.6), in the Palestinian Targum (Pseudo Jonathan to Leviticus 19:18) and in the Talmud (bShab. 31a; see Chapter 2, p. 55). These three basic precepts are expounded in the Didache by what seems to be a free quotation from the Gospels in a passage which is considered by some experts as a supplement inserted by a later hand:

> Bless those who curse you, pray for your enemies, and fast for those who persecute you. For why is it so great to love those who love you? Do not the Gentiles do this as well? But you should love those who hate you – then you will have no enemy. Abstain from fleshly passions. If anyone slaps your right cheek, turn the other to him as well, and you will be perfect. If anyone compels you to go one mile, go with him two. If anyone takes your cloak, give him your shirt as well. If anyone seizes what is yours, do not ask for it back, for you will not be able to get it. (Did. 1.3–4)

A comparison of this passage with the wording and the order of the commandments in the corresponding Gospel verses clearly indicates that the compiler of the Didache did not have the traditional form of Matthew and Luke before him.

> Love your enemies and pray for those who persecute you ... For if you love those who love you, what reward have you? Do not the tax collectors do the same? And if you salute only your brethren, what more are you doing than the others? Do not even the Gentiles do the same? If any one strikes you on the right cheek, turn to him the other also ... You must be perfect ... If any one would ... take your coat, let him have your cloak as well; and if anyone forces you to go one mile, go with him two miles. (Mt. 5:44, 46–7/ Lk. 6:28, 32–3, 35; Mt. 5:39, 48; Mt. 5:40–41/ Lk. 6:29–30)

The instruction handed down in the Didache reminds us of the Jerusalem church depicted in the opening section of the Acts of the Apostles. The members of the apostolic community, like those of the Didache, continued to live and pray as Jews, but combined their Judaism with the doctrinal legacy they received from the Gospel of Jesus through his apostles. An important reference is supplied in passing to religious communism: 'Share all things with your brother and do not say that anything is your own' (Did. 4.8). This precept, not unlike the one mentioned in Acts (2:44; 4:32), is missing from the Gospels, but ultimately recalls the Qumran-Essene rule of common ownership of property.

The document comprises also a conditional recommendation to bear the entire yoke of the Lord. It is sometimes considered as a secondary addition. Whether this means the practice of the eschatological ethics of Jesus or adherence to the Mosaic Law is uncertain. Be this as it may, the faithful, who by that time may have included Gentile Christians too, are told that those who cannot attain perfection should at least try to do as much as possible: 'For if you can bear the entire yoke of the Lord, you will be perfect; but if you cannot, do as much as you can' (Did. 6.2). A further hint may amount to an encouragement of non-Jews to observe as far as possible the Jewish dietary rules: 'And concerning food, bear as much as you can', with the proviso that food sacrificed to idols must be avoided (Did. 6. 3).

The ritual of initiation

The candidates wishing to enter the community of the Didache, having completed their preliminary instruction, were declared fit to undergo baptism, the solemn initiation ritual of the Jesus fellowship. The author supplies the earliest detailed regulation for the baptismal ceremony. The Gospel of Matthew (28:19) gives only the formula 'In the name of the Father and the Son and the Holy Spirit' to be recited, with no further particulars. The Didache requires that both the baptizer and the candidate should prepare themselves for the ceremony by fasting, probably implying a single meal in the evening, the baptizand being duty-bound to do so for one or two full days. As a rule, baptism was to be administered by immersion in running water – the Qumran Community Rule stipulates 'seas and rivers' for the sectarian baptism – but if no running water was available, any water, hot or cold, could be used. In the absence of a river or a pool, the baptismal rite could be performed by pouring water three times on the candidate's head.

Whichever way the baptism was performed, the surviving text of the Didache imposes the ritual formula attested in Matthew 28:19 of Father, Son and Holy Spirit (Did 7.1 and 3). Bearing in mind, however, the slow progress of Trinitarian theology in the early church, the historicity of the Didache's wording appears questionable for two reasons. At the earliest stage of the primitive church, according to both the Petrine and Pauline sections of the Acts of the Apostles (chapters 1–12 and 13–28), baptism was administered not by invoking the Father, the Son and the Holy Spirit, but simply in the name of Jesus (Acts 2:38; 19:5). Secondly, and perhaps more significantly, the Didache itself lays down apropos the Eucharistic meal that the participants of this solemnity must be baptized, not in the name of the Trinity, but 'in the name of the Lord' (Did. 9.5), the Lord being always identified as Jesus in this writing. Once more, we are brought face to face with a very early form of Christianity.

Fasting and prayer

The mention of the obligatory fast before baptism leads to further consideration of the rules about abstinence from food, which carry with them highly important historical-sociological consequences. The argument is centred on regular fasting for two days a week. It appears that there was disagreement within the Christian community concerning the fast days. The group instructed by the author did not see eye-to-eye with another faction referred to as the 'hypocrites', who apparently also belonged to the same Jewish-Christian community. These 'hypocrites' fasted on Monday and Thursday, but '*you* [the group of the Didache] should fast on Wednesday and Friday' (Did. 8.1). From the New Testament (Luke 18:12) we learn that twice-weekly fasting was a Pharisee custom, confirmed also in the Mishnah (Taan. 2:9), where it is specified that a two-day public fasting had to take place on Monday and Thursday, and a three-day fast on Monday, Thursday and on the following Monday or on Thursday and the following Monday and Thursday. Extreme Jewish ascetics, such as the Essene-like Egyptian Therapeutai, fasted on three, and even six consecutive days (Philo, *Contemplative Life* 34–5).

Who, then, were these Judaeo-Christian 'hypocrites', who continued a practice generally prevailing among pious Pharisaic Jews, and distinguished themselves from the 'us'-party of the Didache by adopting different weekdays for fasting? As is well known, in the New Testament, in the Gospel of Matthew chapter 23, the term 'hypocrites' is a regular epithet given to the members of the party of the Pharisees, with hypocrisy implying lack of sincerity and ostentatiousness. But such ordinary Pharisees and scribes were not part of the Jewish-Christian church, and could not form a separate group within the congregation. On the other hand, Acts 15:5 alludes to members of the Jesus movement who were *former* Pharisees, and were associated with the church of Jerusalem headed by the arch-conservative James, the brother of Jesus. As we learn from Paul's letter to the Galatians (2:12–13), the arrival of such ex-Pharisees in Antioch compelled all the Jewish members of the mixed Judaeo-Gentile church of that city, Peter and Barnabas included, to revert to the customary Jewish dietary behaviour. In Paul's eyes the discontinuation of the table fellowship with the local Gentile Christians made Peter guilty of hypocrisy (*hypocrisis*), and in connection with Barnabas the verb *sunhypokrinomai* ('to act hypocritically') is used.

It seems therefore reasonable to conjecture that the 'hypocrites' of the Didache were Jewish-Christians who remained attached to Pharisaic customs, such as the fast days on Monday and Thursday rather than on Wednesday and Friday. If so, the 'hypocrites' divided the community by sticking to their former Jewish traditions, while the author of the Didache displayed a more independent and innovative attitude recommending fasting on different days.

The same innovation applied to the formal communal prayer. Unlike the 'hypocrites', the Didache community recited three times daily the Lord's prayer as commanded by Jesus in his Gospel (Did. 8.2–3). The wording in Didache 8.2 is similar, but not quite identical, to the text of Matthew 6:9–13. If one tried to guess the identity of the prayer of the 'hypocrites', the choice would fall between the two main daily prayers of Pharisaic-rabbinic Judaism, the *Shema'* ('Hear O Israel', Deut. 6:4–5) and the *Shemoneh 'Esreh* or Eighteen Benedictions. Of the two, the *Shemoneh 'Esreh* is more likely since it, like its substitute in the Didache, was recited three times, morning, afternoon and evening, whereas the *Shema'* was rehearsed only twice, morning and evening.

The Thanksgiving meal

After baptism, fasting and prayer, the Didache lists the Thanksgiving meal as the fourth cult practice of the members of the

Jewish-Christian church. The communal meals, also called 'breaking of the bread' or Thanksgiving (Eucharist), which were celebrated in church on Sunday, the Lord's day (Did. 14.1), have been discussed earlier in connection with the Acts of the Apostles (2:42, 46; 20:7; Chapter 3, p. 75) and with Paul's description of the church of Corinth (1 Cor. 10:16–17; 11:20–34; Chapter 4, pp. 91–2). Only baptized persons were allowed to partake of it. A similar exclusion of the not fully initiated was also in force in the Qumran-Essene sect, according to the Community Rule. Outsiders were excluded and novices had to undergo two years' training before being fully admitted to the common table.

The communal Eucharist was a real meal and not just a religious ritual. Its purpose was to feed the participants and it went on until they had all had enough to eat. At the same time it was a symbol reminding the members of the spiritual food and drink, and the eternal life that Jesus promised to the church. But the liturgy of the Thanksgiving meal also possessed an eschatological ingredient. The bread broken into many morsels denoted the dispersed members of the church who were due to be reassembled from the ends of the earth, or from the four winds, into the one Kingdom of God (Did. 9.4; 10.5). The terminology used by the Didache in connection with the cup of wine exhibits a formula to my knowledge not attested anywhere else: the congregation asks for God's blessing on 'the vine of David'. The eschatological atmosphere and the colourful Davidic Jewishness find further expression at the end of the meal in a series of exclamations, as will be shown below (p. 145). In connection with the 'breaking of the bread', let it be stressed that neither the parallel accounts of Acts nor the Didache discloses knowledge of any theological symbolism linking the sacred communal meal of the early church with the Last Supper. For Paul, however, the ritual of the Lord's Supper was a reiteration of the sacrificial death of Jesus and implied a mystical participation in his immolated body and blood. The Eucharistic ideas transmitted in the Didache are definitely non-Pauline, and may even be pre-Pauline.

But before this conclusion is accepted, we must find an explanation for the threefold use of 'sacrifice' (*thusia*) apropos the communal meal in Didache 14.2 ('Let no one quarrelling with his neighbour join you until they are reconciled, that your sacrifice may not be defiled. For this is the sacrifice mentioned by the Lord: "In every place and time, bring me a pure sacrifice"').

The short answer is that we are facing here a mistranslation. The term *thusia* appears in the Didache's allusion to a command in the Sermon on the Mount (Mt. 5:23–4), where Jesus demands reconciliation between quarrelling neighbours to prevent their Temple offering from being defiled by their bad temper. Here the Didache erroneously replaces Matthew's 'gift' (*dôron*) by 'sacrifice' (*thusia*). The ultimate culprit is in fact the Septuagint that loosely renders in the proof text of Malachi 1:11, quoted in Didache 14.3, the Hebrew word *minhah* ('offering') as *thusia* ('sacrifice'): 'In every place and time, bring me a pure sacrifice [*thusia*].' But neither Matthew, nor the Hebrew Malachi passage speaks of a *zebah*, a sacrifice where the victim is slaughtered. Consequently any attempt to interpret the Didache's presentation of the Eucharist in the light of the Pauline theology of Jesus being the Passover Lamb is baseless.

The teaching authority

The end section of the Didache (11–15), prior to the last chapter, offers archaic regulations relating to the teaching authority of the church and the duties of the faithful towards their spiritual leaders. Here again we find ourselves in non-Pauline territory with only an incidental mention of bishops and deacons, who served as the backbone of Paul's ecclesiastical organization. Once more echoes of the earliest Palestinian communities of the Acts of the Apostles are heard in the Didache.

The church leaders first introduced were not attached to communities, but were itinerant apostles and prophets, resembling Jesus and his emissaries (Lk. 10:1–20). The main difference lies in the fact that Jesus' envoys travelled two by two, whereas the Didache's missionaries were single individuals evangelizing on their own.

To understand the prophets of the Didache, one must recall the picture of the nascent church sketched in the Acts of the Apostles. Some of these charismatic prophets are said to have travelled from Jerusalem to Antioch (Acts 11:27–8) and are again mentioned in the company of teachers active in the same Syrian city (Acts 13:1; 15:32). One of them, Agabus, later predicts in AD 58 in Caesarea the impending arrest of Paul (Acts 21:10–11). The picture is completed by prophesying women, the four daughters of the deacon or evangelist Philip, active in Caesarea. Christian prophets are found in the church of Corinth, too, and their ministry met with Paul's warm approval (1 Cor. 12, 14).

In the communities of the Didache, as in the churches of Acts and Paul, the teaching activity, especially in the case of the prophets, was surrounded by what was considered the manifestation of the Spirit (Did. 11.7–9). One may therefore conclude that in the congregations of the Didache the charismatic phenomenon still played a prominent part, although the faithful were advised to rely on their own discernment:

> Not everyone who speaks in the Spirit [i.e. in charismatic frenzy] is a prophet, but only one who conducts himself like the Lord . . . Do not listen to anyone who says in the Spirit, Give me money . . . But if he tells you to give to others who are in need, let no one judge him. (Did. 11.8, 12)

In order to prevent abuse, strict rules were laid down in regard to the treatment of the wandering teachers and prophets. Preachers of true doctrine were to be received with open arms and looked after, as long as they did not overstay their welcome. But this statutory welcome was of short duration: one or a maximum of two days. 'If he stays for three days, he is a false prophet' (Did. 11.5).

If a true prophet or teacher decided to settle in a community, his livelihood was secured by the payment of the tithe from 'the wine vat . . . the threshing floor . . . cattle and sheep' as well as from 'your money, clothing and everything you own' (Did. 13.3, 7). Paul, too, exhorted his churches to take care of their pastors (1 Cor. 9:8–12). The Didache also ruled that ministers of the gospel were to be looked after in the same way as Jews catered for the Temple personnel since, significantly, the Christian prophets are granted the dignity of 'chief priests' (Did. 13.3). In the absence of prophets and teachers, the tithe was to be distributed to the poor. If an ordinary fellow believer from another place wished to take up permanent residence in a church community, they were allowed to do so as long as they were able to earn their living. The cheat was viewed as a 'Christ exploiter' (*Christemporos*) and was firmly rejected.

The Didache appears to represent a transitional stage in church development. In addition to charismatic prophets and teachers, it entrusts the running of the communities to bishops and deacons, as was the case in the churches of St Paul, except that in the Didache these officials, meek characters with no interest in money, were democratically elected by the community instead of being appointed by apostles (Did. 15.1).

Eschatological expectation

The eschatological atmosphere finds expression in connection with the Thanksgiving meal in a series of exclamations: 'Hosanna to the God of David!', 'May grace come and may this world pass away!', and the Aramaic cry, *Maranatha* (see also 1 Cor. 16:22), an expression that can mean either 'The Lord has come' (*Maran atha*), or more likely, 'Come, our Lord!' (*Marana tha*). The latter understanding is parallel to the Greek invocation, 'Come, Lord Jesus!' in Revelation 22:20.

Didache 16 further demonstrates that the eschatological spirit, symptomatic of the preaching of Jesus and of the earlier writings of Paul, was still alive: 'Be watchful ... be prepared. For you do not know the hour when our Lord is coming' (Did. 16.1). The false prophets, announced in the eschatological discourse in the Gospels (Mk 13:22; Mt. 24:24) and elsewhere in the late writings of New Testament (1 Jn 4:1; Rev. 16:13; 19:20; 20:10), were ready to pounce on the unsuspecting and the naïve, and the 'seducer of the world', who labelled himself the 'Son of God', was performing false 'signs and wonders' (Did. 16.3–4). But at the end three signals of the truth were expected to herald the return of Jesus in the midst of his celestial cortège: the opening of heaven, the sound of an angelic trumpet and the resurrection of the righteous dead. 'Then the world will see the Lord coming on the clouds of the sky' (Did. 16.8).*

It is often assumed that the text breaks off here and the Didache remains unfinished. However, it can be argued even more strongly

* The (Caucasian) Georgian translation of the Didache develops the theology of the concluding phrase by adding: 'Then the world will see the Lord *Jesus Christ, the Son of Man who is the Son of God*, coming on the clouds of the sky.' These supplements reflect later Christianity, and in any case the Georgian version is of doubtful authenticity.

that the abrupt ending is intentional and produces a compelling and dramatic finale.

The Jesus portrait of the Didache

The Didache paints a detailed and colourful canvas of the life and organization of an early Judaeo-Christian church, arguably the last such picture produced by a Jewish author and almost certainly the only one free of the all-pervading influence of Paul and John in later writings. Now the moment has come to ask the question regarding the representation of Jesus in the pages of the Didache. How is he understood in this early Christian manual?

The vocabulary is immediately revealing. Paul was on the point of calling Jesus God; where does the Didache stand in this respect? The term 'God', once called in a definitely Jewish way the 'God of David' (Did. 10.6), appears ten times in the work. However, Jesus is never identified as God. The divine name 'Father' or 'our Father' also figures ten times, but God is never designated specifically the Father of Jesus. There is no equivocation with the title 'Lord'. It is encountered twenty times, always relating to Jesus, never to the heavenly Father.

Still with the focus on the vocabulary, in the whole sixteen chapters of the Didache, containing roughly 2,000 words, the title 'Christ' is nowhere mentioned on its own, nor is the messiahship of Jesus anywhere stressed. This absence of the messianic, which distinguishes the Didache even from the primitive Christology of the Acts of the Apostles, is in harmony with the unwillingness of the historical Jesus to accept the designation Christ/Messiah (see Chapter 2, p. 50). The combined title 'Jesus Christ' appears only once in the benediction formula, 'For the glory and the power are yours through Jesus Christ for ever' (Did. 9.4), where 'Christ' may have been quasi-automatically appended to 'Jesus' in the course of the transmission of the Didache in antiquity. It must also be underlined that the Didache completely avoids the use of 'Son' or 'Son of God' in relation to Jesus. The idiom 'Son of God', as has been observed, is found only once, where it is the self-designation of the Antichrist, the 'seducer of the world' (Did. 16.4).

The most striking aspect of the Didache's rudimentary Christology is the use of the epithet 'your Servant', which accompanies the name of Jesus four times, three times in the Greek text and once in the Coptic translation. The Greek *pais* can be rendered either as 'servant' or as 'child', and some of the translators of the Didache, no doubt in order to cater for Christian sensibilities, prefer the second translation as it is not far distant from 'Son'. However, on reflection, the choice of 'Jesus, your Servant' imposes itself. As has already been seen in Chapter 3 (p. 84), 'Servant' or 'Servant of God' are among the earliest titles applied to Jesus in the Acts of the Apostles, and since both in Acts (4:25) and in the Didache (9.2) Jesus and David are designated as *pais* in neighbouring passages, the expression must possess the same meaning, whether it refers to Jesus or to David, *pace* the influential commentator on the Didache, the Dominican J.-P. Audet (see *La Didachè: L'Instruction des apôtres*, 1958, p. 428). In other words, if our understanding of *pais* is correct, the Didache uses only the least elevated of all the qualifications attached to the name of Jesus in early Christian literature.

In short, the Jesus of the Didache is essentially the Servant of God, the great eschatological teacher who is expected to reappear soon to gather together and transfer the dispersed members of his church to the Kingdom of God. The ideas of atonement and redemption are nowhere visible in this earliest record for Jewish-Christian life. Nor can one find any hint at the sacrificial character of Jesus' death and its Pauline symbolical re-enactment in the rituals of baptism and the Eucharist. Needless to say, the Johannine idea of the eternal and creative *Logos* is nowhere on the horizon either.

In sum, while handed down by Jewish teachers to Jewish listeners, as in Acts and in the Didache, the image of Jesus remained close to the earliest tradition underlying the Synoptic Gospels. The switch in the perception of Jesus from charismatic prophet to a superhuman being coincided with a geographical and religious change, when the Christian preaching of the Gospel moved from the Galilean-Judaean Jewish culture into the surrounding Gentile Graeco-Roman world. The disappearance of Jewish teachers opened the gate to an unbridled 'Gentilization' and consequent 'de-Judaization', leading then to the 'anti-Judaization' of nascent Christianity.

It is not surprising, therefore, that the Didache displays no sign of animosity against the Jews. In fact, the term 'Jew' nowhere occurs in the whole work, no doubt because the author and most of his original audience still considered themselves part of Jewish society. The mean-ingfulness of this silent solidarity with the descendants of the Patriarchs and David will become manifest as soon as we reach the next stop along our path, the Epistle of Barnabas.

THE EPISTLE OF BARNABAS
(c. AD 120–35)

The contents of the Epistle of Barnabas point to a pseudonymous Greek-speaking Gentile Christian author. The work incontestably belongs to the post-AD 70 period as it mentions the destruction of the Temple of Jerusalem by the enemies of the Jews, the Romans (Barn. 16.4). On the other hand, as no reference is made to the rebuilding of Jerusalem as the pagan city of Aelia Capitolina by Hadrian, or to the suppression of the second Jewish revolt against Rome under the lead-ership of Simeon ben Kosiba or Bar Kokhba, it must antedate AD 132–5. Pseudo-Barnabas's letter falls into two unequal sections. A long anti-Jewish diatribe (chapters 1–17) is followed by a shorter sec-tion of moral instruction (chapters 18–21), which re-uses the existing Jewish tractate on the Two Ways, called here the Way of Light and the Way of Darkness, and is similar to the Didache's section on the Way of Life and Way of Death.

The first and weightier part of the epistle requires detailed consid-eration by those concerned with its Jesus image. It is straightaway obvious that, contrary to the largely expository Didache, Barnabas has the appearance of a confrontation. The epistle presents two quar-relling groups, referred to as 'we–they' or 'us–them', who both consider the Scriptures of the Old Testament as their own property. The 'we/us' party is naturally the Christian community, instructed by Pseudo-Barnabas, the author of the letter, whereas the opposition remains nameless, though its Jewish identity is beyond question. The writer seeks to assure his readers about the correctness of the 'we' party and that those referred to as 'they' are, have always been, and will for ever be wrong. The argumentation reveals a remarkably broad and deep knowledge of the Greek Bible, or possibly the use of a col-lection of proof texts, that is to say, Old Testament extracts considered as prophetic predictions of New Testament personalities and events.

These excerpts are usually designated as testimonies or *Testimonia*, inspired by the many scriptural debates contained in the Acts of the Apostles (see Chapter 3, pp. 77–8; for Barnabas, see P. Prigent, *Les Testimonia dans le christianisme primitif*, 1961). The Dead Sea Scrolls' Messianic Anthology (4Q174) and *Florilegium* or Commentary on the last days (4Q175) demonstrate that such lists or chains (*catenae*) of biblical evidence already existed among Jews in pre-Christian times.

Allegorical exegesis

The overall purpose of the author of the epistle is to provide his readers with 'perfect knowledge' (Barn. 1.5). He tries to underpin their faith with such *gnosis* ('knowledge') when it comes to comprehending the meaning of some of the essential notions of the Old Testament such as covenant, fasting, sacrifice, circumcision, food laws, Sabbath and the Temple. He stresses that the institutions and precepts of the Jewish Scriptures must never be taken literally; they must be understood figuratively in the light of the allegorical Bible exegesis in vogue first in classical and Hellenistic-Jewish, and later in Christian Alexandria.

Indeed, and here we immediately touch on the Jesus concept, those endowed with true *gnosis* know that the old rules given to Moses have been spiritualized and superseded by the new law revealed by Christ (Barn. 2.5). The biblical prophets already proclaimed the worthlessness of the old Temple sacrifices (Barn. 2.4). As a result, 'they' – the Jews – deceive themselves, but 'we' – believers in Jesus – are aware that what God requires now, and has always required, is not a sacrifice amounting to a cultic act of slaughter, but its symbolical equivalent, the broken heart (Barn. 2.10); and that forgiveness of sins, destruction of death and resurrection are obtained, not through the killing of animals, but through the mystical power of the sprinkling of the Lord Jesus Christ's blood (Barn. 5:1–6). Pauline theology, ignored in the Didache, is in the forefront of the thought of Barnabas.

Fasting, too, the author argues, should consist, not in literally abstaining from food in the Jewish fashion, which was adopted also by the Didache, but figuratively, metaphorically or allegorically, in accordance with the saying of the prophet Isaiah (58:6–10), through putting an end to injustice, liberating the oppressed and, more concretely, through sharing one's food with the hungry (Barn. 3.1–5). As for circumcision, a major issue in Gentile Christianity of Pauline colouring, its understanding as the severance of the foreskin is a misconception implanted in the mind of the Jews by the evil angel Satan. In any case, that sort of circumcision has been useless and has never been to the exclusive advantage of the Jews as it has also been practised by idol-worshiping priests, as well as by all the Syrians, Arabs and Egyptians.

The symbolical meaning of the circumcision was revealed to and understood by Abraham when he was ordered to undergo the rite not just by himself, but with 'eighteen and three hundred' male members of his household. The true full meaning is this. In Greek the numerical value of the letters *I* and *H* is 10 and 8, and the letter *T* stands for 300. But the figure 318 also conceals a mystery since the two letters *IH* form the beginning of the name of Jesus (*IESOUS*) and the letter *T* has the shape of the cross. Those who possess *Gnosis* are aware that it was through the cross that the grace of the true circumcision of the heart was dispensed, rendering the corresponding mutilation of the flesh wholly redundant (Barn. 9.3–7).

The same framework of allegorical interpretation applies to prohibited food. Thus the swine symbolizes a man who forgets God when he lives in luxury, but cries out when he is hungry (Barn. 10.3–11). Likewise the Temple is not an edifice made by human hands, but a spiritual sanctuary built for God in the heart of man (Barn. 16.1–10), and the Sabbath does not relate to the last day of the earthly week, but to the Sabbath of the creation. It also typifies the final stage of the present era after six days/6,000 years – for in God's eyes one day equals 1,000 years – and after the Sabbath, the eighth day is for rejoicing as it marks Jesus' resurrection from the dead and his ascension to heaven, and with them the inauguration of the new world without end (Barn. 15.1–9).

In short, Judaism, the religion of the 'they/them' party, has turned into a complete fiasco. Led astray by Satan, the Jews misunderstand and misapply all the commandments revealed by God to their Lawgiver, Moses. What is more, their covenant is a sham. Indeed, it never came into being as it was never ratified. When Moses came down from the mountaintop to present the two tables of the covenant to the people of Israel, he found them engaged in idol worship and in his fury he smashed to smithereens the tables inscribed with God's hand. This is why the agreement between God and the Jews became null and void from the start and was replaced in time by the covenant that 'the beloved Jesus' sealed in the heart of the Christian believers through his blood as their Redeemer (Barn. 4.6–8; 14.1–7). Moses was merely the prototype of Jesus; the victory over the Amalekites, secured by his outstretched hands, and the erection of a tree with a bronze serpent attached to it as an emblem of protection against snake bites in the Sinai desert, symbolized liberation from sin which originated with the serpent in Paradise. Thus Moses simply prefigured the deliverance from the consequences of the disobedience of Adam, which Jesus actually achieved on the cross (Barn. 12.2–7; cf. Justin, *Trypho* 90–91).

Jesus also fulfilled the typology of Isaac, who was placed on the altar by his father, Abraham, as a sacrificial victim to be offered to God (Barn. 7.3). Consequently Barnabas concludes that the covenant is not 'theirs', but 'ours'. The Jews permanently lost it and have no entitlement whatsoever to it. According to the epistle's message in a nutshell, ever since Sinai the Jews practised their religion the wrong way, whereas 'we', Christians, benefit from the Mosaic symbolism.

Are we witnessing here a real rhetorical debate, where Barnabas is engaged in an intellectual contest with a representative of the Jewish community? The answer is uncertain. For while a hostile undercurrent runs through the whole writing, it nevertheless may be theoretical, lacking the sharpness and acerbity of an actual dispute. For instance, it is quite remarkable that, whereas the biblical Israel is named a dozen times in the document, the pejorative term 'the Jews', the name of the actual opposition to Jesus and Christianity in the terminology of some of the Gospels, is never used in Barnabas. A likely explanation is that the epistle does not deal with a genuine controversy provoked by some real life crisis. It is not an answer to a competing Jewish messianic movement, or to rumours about plans to rebuild Jerusalem and the Temple, or even to the willingness of some members of the church to admit that the Jews had some entitlement to the Bible and to the Mosaic covenant. On the whole the Epistle of Barnabas bears all the attributes of an intra-Christian treatise addressed to church members and endeavouring to establish the supremacy of the apostolic teaching over Judaism. The aim of the epistle is not to confute the Jews, but to reassure the faithful that they are the people of God's covenant, and to depict for them the real figure of Jesus.

How does the author of the Epistle of Barnabas proceed in his theological reinterpretation of the Old Testament? He is extremely well versed in the Greek translation of the Jewish Bible, or constantly uses a collection of selected sayings from it, but curiously Barnabas never directly quotes the words of Jesus. He has two rather general hints at the authority given by Jesus to his apostles to preach 'the gospel' (Barn. 5.9; 8.4) and shows knowledge of the Synoptic evangelists' interpretation of Psalms 110:1, according to which Jesus is not the 'son', but the 'lord' of David (Mk 12:35–7; Mt. 22:41–5; Lk. 20:41–4). He further alludes in Barnabas 7.9 to Jesus' enemies admitting that they were responsible for ill-treating and crucifying the 'Son of God' (see Mk 14:61–2; Mt. 26:63–4; Lk. 22:70). Nevertheless, Barnabas's extracts are less explicit than the four Gospel references in the Didache (Did. 8.2; 11.3; 15.3, 4), in one of which the Lord's prayer, with wording similar to Matthew's, is actually claimed to be part of the Gospel (Did. 8.2).

The nearest we come to a Gospel quotation is with Barnabas 4.14: 'Many of us were found called, but few chosen', which is close to Matthew 22:14: 'For many are called, but few are chosen.' Curiously, the Jewish exegetical introductory formula, 'as it is written', normally leading to a quotation of a biblical text from the Old Testament, is prefixed to it. Again, and even more curiously since the main theme of the epistle – the new covenant abolishing the old – is a Pauline topic, the author nowhere makes use of the genuine correspondence of Paul, even though Barnabas's epistle resembles the deutero-Pauline letter to the Hebrews in its insistence on the substitution of the sacrifice of Jesus, the Son of God, for the sacrifice offered by the high priest in the Jerusalem Temple.

The Jesus of Barnabas

Measured against the Didache, in which Jesus is defined as God's 'Servant' (see pp. 146–7), the epistle attests a considerable degree of doctrinal development and reaches Pauline, and once even Johannine heights. The title 'Lord' (Kyrios) is applied both to God and to Jesus.

Jesus is also called 'Master' and 'Ruler' (*despotês*), but since among the Jews none of these epithets was exclusively divine, no valid conclusion can be drawn from their use. The terms 'Son' or 'Son of God', which figure no less than twelve times, are more significant. In the singular, the title 'Son of God' indicates not simply a holy man especially close to God, but a person of a higher order. In the typology of Joshua son of Nun, 'Jesus son of Naue' in Greek, the announced annihilation of the Amalekites at the end of time would be achieved by Jesus Christ, not by the earthly Jesus acting *qua* 'Son of Man' and defeating an historical foe, but as Jesus the 'Son of God' in his eschatological triumph over the final enemy.

In parenthesis, the Epistle of Barnabas and the letter of Ignatius of Antioch *To the Ephesians* (20.2) are the earliest Christian witnesses contrasting the two expressions, 'Son of Man' and 'Son of God' in a Christological context. It should be added in passing that the phrase 'sons of God' in the plural designates the Christian believers who must resist the present lawless age and all the stumbling blocks that Satan, the 'Black One', will place before them in the future (Barn. 4.9).

The superhuman understanding of 'Son of God' is further strengthened by the writer's assertion that 'the Son' was not only above the human category, but he was also pre-existent since eternity and was active already before the creation. It was to him that God's words 'Let us make man according to our image and likeness' were directed at the time of 'the foundation of the world' (Barn. 5.5; 6.12). By postulating a Johannine *Logos*-like Son of God, Barnabas may imply acquaintance with the Prologue of the Fourth Gospel. But he goes even further in implicitly asserting Christ's strictly divine character by explaining that the reason for the incarnation of the eternal Son of God was that without the concealment of his true self under a human body, people would not have been able to look at him and survive (Barn. 5.9–10). The argument is tacitly, but unquestionably, based on Exodus 33:20, where Moses is told by God, 'You cannot see my face, for no one shall see me and live', so Moses was allowed, according to the colourful metaphor of the rabbis, to see God from behind in the 'vision of the buttocks'.

This is clearly Barnabas's paraphrase of the Word becoming flesh as described in John chapter 1. But whereas in the Prologue the aim of the Word in becoming human was to reveal God the Father to mankind, Barnabas combines the Johannine vision of the *Logos* revealing the face of the Father with Paul's redemption theology. The ultimate purpose of the descent of 'the Lord of the entire world' among men was to allow himself to suffer 'for our sake . . . in order to destroy death and to show that there is resurrection of the dead' (Barn. 5.5–6). Contrary to the Judaeo-Christian Didache, Barnabas is permeated by Pauline thought, and combining it with a dose of John's mystical vision, he constructs for his readers a Saviour image in which Jesus is God in all but in name. We are not to wait for too long to cross this major hurdle along the meandering path of Christology.

A comparative glance at the Jesus portraits of the Didache and Barnabas discloses the main difference between the two documents. The late first century (*c.* 70–100) Didache, with its exclusively Jewish-Christian outlook less advanced than John or even Paul, offered Jesus and the Christian message to a non-Jewish audience or readership. In it, Jesus remains the Servant (*pais*) of God and is never referred to as 'the Son of God', nor does the Didache call God the Father of Jesus.

By contrast, Barnabas, most likely written under Pauline/Johannine influence for Gentile Christians in the third decade of the second century AD (*c.* 120–35), recognizes in Jesus the eschatological Son of God, who existed before his appearance on earth. While he is not expressly portrayed as God, his human body is seen as a deliberate and benevolent disguise of his underlying divine character. The parting of the ways between the Jewish and the non-Jewish followers of Jesus is obvious already at this early stage of doctrinal development, and since the Didache is the first and last expression of Judaeo-Christianity after the New Testament, doctrinal evolution will from now on continue exclusively on the Gentile-Christian line.

7

The Apostolic Fathers

1 and 2 Clement, Ignatius, Polycarp, Hermas and Diognetus

After the survey of the Didache and the Epistle of Barnabas, two odd-ities in early Christian literature, the next task of the inquiry is to consider the primitive church and its Jesus image in the rest of the early patristic sources, that is to say in the works of authors who flourished between the end of the first century and the middle of the second century AD. In their own way, they all supply fascinating insights into the organization of the young Christian communities as well as into the understanding of Jesus during those initial years of the history of the church.

CHRISTIANITY AND THE ROMAN EMPIRE

Almost from the beginning the Christians were in violent conflict with the ruling power of the Roman government, and the ensuing struggle became a determining factor in the evolution of the nascent church. The execution of Peter and Paul in Rome, probably in the mid-60s of the first century AD, is alluded to in the so-called Epistle of Clement to the Corinthians, or 1 Clement, and two of the authors to be discussed in this chapter, Ignatius and Polycarp, died themselves as martyrs of the faith. Hence the attitude of the Roman state to Christians from Nero to Constantine will be the subject of a preliminary survey.

Rome, whether republican or imperial, was liberally inclined to-wards other religions, provided their practice did not lead to rebellion or encourage what the Romans considered immorality. Judaism enjoyed favourable treatment both in Palestine and in the countries of the Diaspora owing to privileges granted by Julius Caesar and Augustus, but Jews had first-hand experience of the harshness of the empire towards rebels following the first uprising (AD 66–70/3) put down by Vespasian and Titus, as well as after the failure of the Bar Kokhba war (AD 132–5) during the reign of Hadrian (Martin Goodman, *Rome and Jerusalem*, 2007, pp. 445–511). Foreign cults were tolerated as long as their worshippers were prepared to bow also to the Roman gods and in particular to the deified emperor. Lip service sufficed, but complete refusal of worship was interpreted as atheism, an act offending the state and Caesar, and had dire consequences. The Jews managed to circumnavigate the dangers thanks to their recognized ancient immunities, but the new unpopular Christian *superstitio* found itself in more treacherous waters, especially as it was remembered that its founder, *Christus*, after whom his followers were named, was crucified as an anti-Roman revolutionary by Pontius Pilate, governor of Judaea, during the reign of Tiberius.

Rome's first act of hostility towards the Christians came about as a pure accident. After the great fire of the city in AD 64, rumour spread that Nero himself, intent on rebuilding the capital, secretly engineered the conflagration. To escape suspicion, the emperor looked for somebody to blame, and the unpopular group of outsiders, the Christians, were selected to serve as suitable scapegoats. The suspects were rounded up and convicted, not so much as arsonists, but for the crime of *misanthropy*, 'the hatred of the human race' ('*odium humani generis*'). Tacitus, who records the story, remarks that the people of Rome did not truly believe in the guilt of the Christians. 'There arose a sentiment of pity, due to the impression that they were being sacrificed not for the welfare of the state, but to the ferocity of a single man' (*Annals* 15.44, 5).

Having found his culprits, Nero proceeded to have fun. Covered with wild beasts' skins, the condemned Christians were thrown before dogs to be savaged by them. Others were fastened on crosses and after the fall of darkness they were set alight to serve as lamps by night (Tacitus, *Annals* 15.44, 2–4). As has already been noted, 1 Clement, written some thirty years later, indicates that early Christian tradition counted the apostles Peter and Paul among Nero's most important victims (1 Clem. 5.4–7).

A much more illuminating picture of the official attitude of Rome may be garnered from the consultation addressed by the governor of Bithynia, Pliny the Younger, to the emperor Trajan in AD 110/11 about the treatment of Christians, and from the corresponding imperial rescript sent by Trajan to Pliny (Pliny, *Letters* 10. 96–7; see Fergus Millar, *The Emperor in the Roman World*, 1977, pp. 557–8). Clearly, by that time the worship of the Roman gods and of the emperor was considered as an absolute requirement for the residents of the empire, except for the Jews who were exempted, and a negative attitude amounted to disloyalty to the state. On this basis, Pliny had no hesitation in sentencing to death people who replied yes to the thrice-repeated question: Are you a Christian? A positive answer, which implied refusal to worship, was judged to be obstinacy that deserved capital punishment. However, if the Christians happened to be Roman citizens, they were not executed in the province but were dispatched to the capital. As a fair-minded judge, Pliny asked the emperor for guidance with regard to specific particulars as charges of being Christians were levelled against an increasingly large number of men and women of every age and social class.

Was he right, Pliny inquired, to declare not guilty people whose names figured on an anonymously produced indictment (*libellus sine auctore*) or those who denied that they were Christians, and publicly prayed to the Roman deities, offered wine and incense to Trajan's statue, and cursed the name of Christ – something, Pliny added, true Christians would never do? But his main doubt concerned the handling of people who, having admitted to having been Christians in the past claimed that they had ceased to be members of the sect, and proved it by worshipping the Roman gods and Caesar as well as by cursing Christ. After all, Pliny commented, in every other respect their conduct was innocuous. All they did was to foregather on a certain day (on Sunday) before dawn to sing hymns to Christ as god, swear that they would not commit any crime and reassemble later on the same day for a common meal. The veracity of their account was confirmed by the testimony obtained under torture from two slave women whom they called deaconesses. Apart from unwillingness to participate in Roman worship, being a Christian meant in Pliny's opinion no more than practising a harmless superstition. In short, should people without discernable criminal behaviour be prosecuted for having been formerly Christians? In other words, did the very name 'Christian' carry criminality attached to it?

Compared to the length and detail of the consultation, Trajan's response was concise, careful and stuck to general principles. He had no quick answer or an all-purpose formula to offer, but he gave three guidelines on how to handle Christians. First of all, officials were not to take the initiative to ferret them out. Secondly, they must not act on anonymous accusations. According to the progressive-minded Trajan, such charges without identified accusers 'are terrible examples and not at all in keeping with our age' (*'Nam et pessimi exempli nec nostri saeculi est'*). Thirdly, the due process of the law should be applied to persons brought before the court. If at the end they were found guilty, they had to be punished, but if they offered prayers to the gods of Rome, they were to be pardoned on account of their repentance, irrespective of their past behaviour. Trajan discretely remained silent on the subject of imperial worship.

For more than a century, Christians were dealt with along the lines laid down by Trajan and further refined by Hadrian. In a rescript sent in AD 121/2 to Minucius Fundanus, proconsul of Asia, in fact answering the inquiry of his predecessor, Q. Licinius Silvanus Granianus, Hadrian insisted on the necessity of formal court proceedings against Christians and not mere popular denunciations by 'petitions or shouts'. The accusers had to prove that the Christians had acted against the laws. And Hadrian menacingly added: 'By Hercules, if anyone takes this course in order to make a mischievous accusation, take cognizance of his wickedness and consider how to punish him' (quoted from Justin, 1 *Apology* 68). Rome was puzzled by the behaviour of the Christians; nevertheless the emperors insisted on the strict application of the law.

Trajan and Hadrian supplied the legal framework of the conflict between Christianity and the Roman Empire until the initiative for promoting the persecution of the church was directly taken by the emperor Decius in AD 249/50. As an innovation, Decius and later Diocletian and Maximian personally presided over trials of Christians.

In this historical context attention can now be focused on the literary sources reflecting the development of Christianity from the end of the first to the middle of the second century AD. All the works are in

Greek and they include the First and the Second Epistles of Clement of Rome, the seven authentic Letters of Ignatius of Antioch, the Letter and the Martyrdom of Polycarp of Smyrna, *The Shepherd* of Hermas and the Epistle to Diognetus.

THE EPISTLE OF CLEMENT TO THE CORINTHIANS (*c.* AD 95/96)

The title, 'First Epistle of Clement', is a misnomer as there is no real Second Epistle. The so-called Second Epistle, as will be shown, is not an epistle at all but a sermon, nor was it written by the same Clement as the present document.

The First Epistle is a lengthy exhortation addressed by the church of Rome to the church of Corinth, in which the Romans urge the Corinthians to calm down the troubles caused by the deposition of the governing bishops and deacons of their congregation by a local clique of ecclesiastical 'young lions'. The aim of the epistle was the re-establishment of harmony and peace. Communal harmony or *homonoia* is a key word in this document, as well as in the letters of Ignatius of Antioch. The church of Rome sought to engineer a return to the status quo in Corinth through the reinstatement of the unjustly deposed worthy leaders, originally installed in their office by the legitimate successors of officials who were themselves appointed by the martyred apostles Peter and Paul (1 Clem. 5.4–5; 44.1–2). The Corinthian system was clearly different from that of the Didache, where bishops and deacons were *elected* by the congregation.

The epistle voices the views of the Roman community as such; no individual is identified in it as the author. The only persons mentioned by name are the three otherwise unheard of bearers of the message: Claudius Ephebus, Valerius Bito and Fortunatus. The attribution to someone named Clement is secondary and extraneous; the letter itself is in fact anonymous. According to the *Ecclesiastical History* of Eusebius (*EH* 3.4, 15), the Clement to whom the authorship is assigned was the third bishop of Rome, Peter being the first, but Tertullian describes him as Peter's immediate successor. On the other hand, Hermas, who wrote *The Shepherd* before the middle of the second century AD, mentions a Clement whose job was to keep the Roman Christian community in touch with other churches: 'Clement will send [the little book he had received from Hermas] to the foreign cities, *for that is his commission*' (Visions, 8.2). Since the writer of the letter nowhere speaks with the authority of a major church leader, as would have been the case if he had been Pope Clement, the second or third bishop of Rome, his identification with Clement, secretary of the Roman church in charge of foreign relations, may be considered as a reasonable hypothesis. The work is usually dated to AD 95/96, the end of the reign of the emperor Domitian, which would make it, apart possibly from the Didache, the oldest Christian writing outside the New Testament.

The structure of the church

Interesting details emerge from the letter regarding the organization of the churches in the dying years of the first century. It is needless to remind readers that no teaching about the church can be traced back to Jesus, and that the Synoptic Gospels are silent on the matter with the exception of the few glosses added to Matthew (see Chapter 2, p. 59). Contrary to the Pauline world, in which the communities during the apostle's life time had monarchic bishops, such as Timothy in Ephesus and Titus in Crete, the Corinthian church of the First Epistle of Clement, like that in the Didache, was governed by a plurality of bishops and deacons (1 Clem. 42, 44). Both classes were also referred to in a confused way as presbyters or elders (1 Clem. 44.4; 47.6; 54.2; 57.1 and possibly 1.3). Concerning the nature of the office of these church leaders, some respected interpreters (for example, Altaner and Henry Chadwick) express the opinion that it mostly consisted in the 'offering of the sacrificial gifts', that is to say, the eucharistic meal (1 Clem. 44.4). However, this interpretation appears somewhat forced; when the text asserts that it is sinful to 'depose those who offer in a blameless and holy way the gifts of the episcopal office' (*dôra tês episkopês*), it is too restrictive to apply this statement to the sacred communal repast alone, as it is likely to include also all the educational and pastoral duties of the bishops.

Another important area of information contained in 1 Clement relates to the role played by Holy Scripture in the life of the churches.

Clement, like Barnabas, was extremely well versed in the Bible including the Apocrypha (the Wisdom of Solomon is quoted and Judith is mentioned), and he even praised his Corinthian readers for their familiarity with the Bible (1 Clem. 53.1). It is worth noting, for example, that he refers to the typology of Isaac as foreshadowing the sacrifice of Jesus. It also figures implicitly in Paul (see Chapter 4, pp. 101–2) and explicitly in Barnabas 7.3, but Clement, thanks to his awareness of an ancient Jewish exegetical tradition, stresses the voluntary nature of Isaac's role, namely that he 'gladly allowed himself to be brought forward as a sacrifice, confident in the knowledge of what was about to happen' (1 Clem. 31.3), viz. that God would stop Abraham from accomplishing the deed. Clement was also acquainted with the Synoptic Gospels, but quoted them less often than the Old Testament. He cited from the words of Jesus (e.g. 1 Clem. 46.7–8) and also explicitly mentioned 'the epistle of the blessed apostle Paul' in which the latter complained about earlier divisions in the church of Corinth (alluding to 1 Cor. 1:12). This shows that the canonization of the Gospels and the Pauline epistles was already advancing, but the New Testament was not yet considered as authoritative a guide in matters of Christian belief as the Septuagint Bible of the Hellenized Jews, produced (according to the legend) by seventy translators.

Clement never displays anti-Jewish sentiments resembling those of Barnabas, nor does he regularly subject the Old Testament to allegorical exegesis. His straight citation of Moses' prayer, asking God to forgive the idolatrous Jews for their worshipping the golden calf while he was bringing down for them the tables of the covenant from Sinai, would have made Barnabas feel apoplectic (1 Clem. 53.2–5 compared to Barnabas in Chapter 6, pp. 150–51). For Barnabas the breaking of those stone tables meant the abolition of the divine covenant with the Jewish people before it had ever gained force.

The Jesus of the First Epistle of Clement

Regarding Christology or the theological image of Jesus in vogue in the early church, Clement marked a step forward compared to the Didache, where Jesus was simply 'the Servant' (*pais*) of God. This same lowly title of 'Servant' or 'beloved Servant' appears three times in Clement too, but its use is exceptional as it is confined to chapter

59. It is possible therefore that the prayer in which the phrase figures was lifted by the author from an earlier source with a less developed Christology. In general, Jesus is designated in the Clementine terminology as 'Son of God' (1 Clem. 36.4; 59.2–4), but he is also called 'the benefactor of our souls', and 'the High Priest', as he was in the Epistle to the Hebrews (1 Clem. 36.1; 61.3; 64.1).

1 Clement's Christological vocabulary resembles the Pauline and deutero-Pauline phraseology. Jesus is definitely distinguished from God and is inferior to him. God as 'Master' speaks about his 'Son' of not quite the same status (1 Clem. 36.4) and, as in Paul's benediction formulas, it is always God who is blessed 'through Jesus Christ' (1 Clem. 20.11; 50.7; 59.2–3; 61.3; 64.1), and never Jesus on his own. The style of the prayer, 'As God, the Lord Jesus Christ and the Holy Spirit all live' (1 Clem. 58.2), does not necessarily testify to a conscious trinitarian theology. It may simply represent without any deeper reflection the tripartite baptismal formula of Matthew's Gospel (28:19). The doctrine of the Holy Trinity was not yet in the forefront of speculation at the turn of the first century.

The main doctrinal message of the Epistle of Clement relates to the redemptive character of the 'blood' of Christ (1 Clem. 7.3; 21.6; 49.6), another central topic of Pauline theology. A colourful typological formulation of this idea is given in the story of the prostitute Rahab from the Old Testament book of Joshua. For her friendly behaviour towards the Israelite spies, Rahab was promised that her home in Jericho would be protected from the conquering Jewish army provided that she displayed a crimson cord in her window (Josh. 2:18). This cord now figuratively predicted that it was 'through the blood of the Lord that redemption would come to all who believe and hope in God' (1 Clem. 12.7).

In summary, the main contribution of the Epistle of Clement to the understanding of the changing faces of Christianity in the post-apostolic age refers to the early, still ill-defined, hierarchical structure of the church. In the portrayal of Jesus, Clement goes beyond the Didache, but does not quite reach the level of the Epistle of Barnabas. On the whole, it continues roughly the Pauline theological speculation with Jesus being considered as Son of God without any further specification.

THE SECOND EPISTLE OF CLEMENT
(c. AD 140)

The so-called Second Epistle of Clement has nothing epistolary in it; it is in fact the earliest Christian homily outside the sermons of Peter, Stephen and Paul in the Acts of the Apostles in the New Testament. Though attributed to Clement by church tradition, it is clearly the work of an author other than that of 1 Clement, and is thought to originate from shortly before the middle of the second century. The sermon it contains enriches the image of post-apostolic Christianity on several important points. It is a moral exhortation to the faithful with particular emphasis on charity, almsgiving being given the pride of place among the virtues: 'Giving to charity is as good as a repentance from sin. Fasting is better than prayer, but giving to charity is better than both' (2 Clem. 16.4).

The preacher addresses a Gentile-Christian audience, people who were formerly idolaters, 'worshipping stones and pieces of wood, and gold and silver and copper' (2 Clem. 1.6). Gentile Christianity adopted the language of the Jews in their caricature of pagan religion. The church organization in question was similar to that of Corinth as depicted in 1 Clement. It was run by several presbyters with no mention of a single bishop. Opinion regarding the homily's place of origin fluctuates between the churches of Corinth, Rome and Alexandria. The only major innovation regarding the idea of the Christian community is the distinction between the mystical true church devised by God since all eternity, the first church, the spiritual church, the church that was 'created before the sun and the moon . . . the church of life', the church which is 'the body of Christ', and that other failed house of God directed by the unfaithful that can be qualified 'a cave of thieves' (2 Clem. 14.1–2).

The Bible in 2 Clement

Perhaps the most significant contribution of 2 Clement to our study of the historical evolution of Christianity concerns the author's attitude to the Bible and to Jesus. The homilist regularly quotes from the Prophets, especially from Isaiah, but oddly ignores the Mosaic Law altogether. In connection with the New Testament, two points stand out. 2 Clement appears to be the first Christian writer to apply the term 'Scripture' to a quotation from the Gospel: 'And also another Scripture (*graphê*) says, "I did not come to call the righteous, but sinners"' (2 Clem. 2.4 citing Mt. 9:13; Mk 2:17), thereby assigning biblical status to the words of Jesus and granting them the same dignity and authority as the Old Testament. The same idea is implicit in the phrase: 'The Bible and the Apostles indicate . . .' (2 Clem. 14.2), where 'Bible' refers to the Septuagint and 'the Apostles' to the New Testament.

The text of the Gospels quoted by 2 Clement is not quite the same as our own traditional text. Some of the words attributed in it to Jesus do not figure either in the Synoptic Gospels or in John. For example, a loosely reproduced version of Matthew 10:16 is followed up by a dialogue unknown to the canonical evangelist, but appropriate in days of persecution experienced by Christians in the Roman Empire in the second century:

> For the Lord said, 'You will be like sheep in the midst of wolves.' But Peter replied to him, 'What if the wolves rip apart the sheep?' Jesus replied to Peter, 'After they are dead, the sheep should fear the wolves no longer. And you also, do not fear those who kill you and then can do nothing more to you; but fear the one who, after you die, has the power to cast your body and soul into the hell of fire.' (2 Clem. 5.2–4)

At a later stage, Jesus' advice for eschatological vigilance is formulated thus: 'When the Lord himself was asked by someone when his kingdom would come, he said, "When the two are one, and the outside like the inside, and the male with the female is neither male nor female"' (2 Clem. 12:1–2). This saying, as far as its substance if not its purpose is concerned, is in fact inspired by the Gospel of Thomas, a composition which was hovering close to the edge of the New Testament.

> Jesus saw some babes nursing. He said to his disciples, 'These nursing babes are like those who enter the kingdom.' They said to him, 'Then shall we enter the kingdom as babes?' Jesus said to them, 'When you make the two into one, and when you make the inner like the outer and the outer like the inner, and the upper like the lower, and when you make the male and the female into a single one, so that the male will

not be male nor the female be female, when you make eyes in place of an eye, a hand in place of a hand, a foot in place of a foot, an image in place of an image, then you will enter' [the kingdom]. (Thom. 22)

Nevertheless, the questions asked in the two works are not the same. 2 Clement is concerned with determining the moment of the eschatological D-day, the time of God's final manifestation, whereas Thomas seeks to describe in an excessively verbose style the babe-like qualities that Christians will have to display if they wish to enter the Kingdom of heaven.

The Jesus of 2 Clement

The most important contribution of 2 Clement to the evolution of Christian thought is its implicit high Christology, on a par, as will be seen, with that of Ignatius of Antioch. It bursts into the open in the very first sentence of the work: 'Brothers, we must think about Jesus Christ as we think about God' (2 Clem. 1.1). The formula is reminiscent of the phrase that Pliny the Younger quoted in his letter to the emperor Trajan. In it he described the Christians as people accustomed to 'to sing hymns to Christ as God' ('*carmen dicere Christo quasi deo*') (see above, p. 157). It would seem, therefore, that the trend towards the formal deification of Jesus was gaining momentum among the Greek Christians of Asia Minor and Syria early in the second century AD. However, no trinitarian allusion can be found anywhere in 2 Clement. The work contains a single doxology, which appears at the end and its object is God alone without explicit reference to the Son and the Spirit. 'To the only invisible God, the Father of truth, who sent us the saviour and founder of incorruptibility, through whom he also revealed us the truth and the heavenly life – to him be the glory for ever. Amen' (20.5).

THE LETTERS OF IGNATIUS OF ANTIOCH (*c.* AD 110)

The letters written by Ignatius of Antioch constitute a particularly rich mine for the investigation of early Christian theological thought.

He was the immediate successor of Peter as bishop of Antioch according to Origen (Homily 6 on Luke), or, if Eusebius's testimony is preferred (*EH* 3.22, 36), he was the third leader of the Syrian church following Peter and a certain Evodius. For undisclosed reasons, no doubt on account of his refusal to worship the Roman gods and the emperor, he was condemned to death by the state authorities in Syria. During the reign of Trajan (AD 98–117), most likely around AD 110, he was sent to Rome to be thrown to the wild beasts in the arena for the entertainment of the spectators. Ignatius gladly welcomed his fate, and was almost maniacally keen to die. He even prayed that the animals, God's chosen instruments, should promptly become his executioners and his tomb (*Romans* 4.2; 5.2). In the same spirit, Ignatius begged his Roman co-religionists not to take steps to save him and thereby delay his much longed-for encounter with God.

Under the guard of a unit of ten soldiers, referred to as 'ten leopards', Ignatius travelled overland from Antioch, through Asia Minor to Smyrna, and having been granted relative freedom, he was able to meet the local bishop Polycarp and to receive delegations from the neighbouring churches of Ephesus, Magnesia and Tralles. From Smyrna he wrote four letters, to the Ephesians, Magnesians, Trallians and to the Roman Christians. The next port of call was Troas on the Aegean coast, from where he busily dispatched three more letters to the Philadelphians, Smyrneans and to Bishop Polycarp of Smyrna. Ignatius' life ended – no doubt as he hoped it would – in a Roman amphitheatre. Polycarp in his letter to the Philippians (9.1) merely alludes to the fact of Ignatius' martyrdom, but does not give any further detail. The seven epistles of Ignatius just mentioned were already listed by Eusebius and they are the only ones held to be authentic by modern scholars. The original texts were in Greek, but owing to Ignatius' influence and popularity there exist also Latin, Syriac, Coptic and Armenian translations. The six further spurious letters, five of them attributed to Ignatius and one addressed to him, are thought to be fourth-century forgeries.

The church organization

Apart from a general exhortation to piety, the main theme running through the letters refers to church discipline. Ignatius insisted on the duty of all the Christians to subject themselves to their bishop, to a single usually named bishop in each single church, and to the colleagues of the bishop, the presbyters and deacons. The hierarchy was quintessential in Ignatius' ecclesial system. For him, the bishop symbolized the Lord and shared the mind of Jesus (*Ephesians* 3.2; 6.1) and the presbyters were like the council of God (*Trallians* 3.1). The hierarchical structure of the church is presented as essential and the role of the clergy, in particular of the monarchic bishop, is depicted as extending over the whole life of the community. For example, unlike the vagueness of the author of the Didache or even of Clement, Ignatius places the eucharistic meal under the control of the bishop or his delegate (*Smyrneans* 8.2), and even matrimony between Christian spouses required episcopal approval to ensure that it was entered into for the sake of the Lord and not for lust (*Polycarp* 5.2). The idea of the church, totally absent from the teaching of Jesus, had now become a dominating principle eighty years after the cross.

Judaizers and Docetists

Christianity as a body of belief and practice was treated by Ignatius not as a theory, but as an established tangible reality. The believers formed a real community whose members first bore the name 'Christians' in Ignatius' Antioch, according to the Acts of the Apostles. They were the initiates of a new cult society, as was already 'Paul, the holy one' (*Ephesians* 12.2). The church was an organization to which one had to belong not just nominally but in truth; the believers had to embody Christianity and live according to its rules (*Magnesians* 4, 10.1; *Romans* 3.1).

Since neither Graeco-Roman paganism, nor the oriental mysteries such as Mithraism, etc., appeared on the Christian apologists' horizon until later in the second century – in 2 Clement, the Epistle to Diognetus, the Martyrdom of Polycarp, Justin's First Apology and his Dialogue with Trypho – Ignatius contrasted Christianity with two other systems of false teaching or heresy. He defended his religion against 'Judaism', understood in a special sense, and against Docetism. Both had already been encountered in the Acts of the Apostles as well as in the Pauline and Johannine writings.

The Judaism of Ignatius is not the religion practised by the Jews of his time, but the Christian heresy of the Judaizers, people who insisted on the compulsory observance of the Mosaic Law and Jewish customs by all the members of the church, whether they were of Jewish or of Gentile stock. For Ignatius, it was wholly improper to embrace this sort of Judaism and simultaneously proclaim faith in Jesus Christ (*Magnesians* 10.3). No Christian should lend his ears to someone who was expounding such a doctrine. It was permissible to listen to a circumcised person (a church member of Jewish origin) preaching Christianity, but they had to turn away from someone putting forward a Judaizing message even if it was done by an uncircumcised Gentile Christian (*Philadelphians* 6.1). This would suggest that the trend initiated to Paul's deep annoyance some sixty or seventy years earlier by the emissaries of James the brother of Jesus was still flourishing in Ignatius' days.

The use of the proof texts from the Jewish Bible in relation to the Gospels was one of the subjects of debate between ordinary Gentile Christians and the Judaizing branch in the church. Ignatius regularly referred to Scripture, more often to the Gospels than to the Jewish Bible, but was less scripturally minded than Barnabas or 1 Clement. Not surprisingly, his method of arguing without relying on the Old Testament did not deeply impress his Judaizing opponents. They refused to believe in the Gospel if its teaching did not find support 'in the ancient records' of the Jews. Ignatius' habit was to counter their objection and prove his contention with the vague general remark, 'it is written', but without quoting chapter and verse. However, his antagonists were not satisfied and wanted him to be more explicit. No doubt exasperated, and possibly short of actual evidence, he came up with a generic answer: contemplated in the context of the cross, the death and the resurrection of Jesus, 'the ancient records' were redundant (*Philadelphians* 8.2).

While the threat of 'Judaizing' was normal and foreseeable in the churches of Syria and Asia Minor, which had a Jewish background and Jewish surroundings, the other type of heresy, 'Docetism', had its home ground in the Gentile, Hellenic environment. Already echoed, as has been noted, in the letters of John (see Chapter 5, p. 131), Docetism objected, curiously for the modern mind, not to the divinity of Christ, but to the concrete fleshly reality of the 'Incarnation'. Jesus

Christ may have been the Son of God, but he could not truly be a Son of Man. With their Greek philosophical logic, these first Christian thinkers rejected the possibility of the existence of a spiritual God revealing himself in a material body.

These Docetists, whom Ignatius treats as 'atheists' or 'unbelievers', were especially hostile to the idea of the suffering and death of the Son of God, the basic tenets of the Pauline and Johannine religion and of Christianity in general (*Trallians* 10.1). For the bishop of Antioch, the easiest way to discard their stance was the firm reassertion of the factuality and strict historicity of every detail of the story of Jesus. Christ was a genuine Son of Man. 'You should be fully convinced of the birth and suffering and resurrection that occurred in the time of the governor Pontius Pilate. These things were truly and certainly done by Jesus Christ' (*Magnesians* 11; see *Smyrneans* 1.1–2).

The most detailed treatment of the life of the Son of God is given in the Letter to the Smyrneans, where the reality of Jesus' suffering is emphatically stated: 'He truly suffered ... not as some unbelievers say ... only in appearance' (*Smyrneans* 2.1). He was not a 'bodiless spirit', but ate and drank and could be touched even after his resurrection (*Smyrneans* 3.1–3). In the last resort, Ignatius opted for ridiculing his opponents: If the events of Jesus' life had been accomplished only in appearance, Ignatius' chains, too, would be worn only in appearance (*Smyrneans* 4.2). In practice, the Docetic teaching was in his eyes nothing less than blasphemy (*Smyrneans* 5.2). Moreover, those who adhered to it excluded themselves from the Christian community when they refused to participate in the eucharistic meal on account of their rejection of the idea that it signified Jesus Christ's suffering for human sins in the flesh (*Smyrneans* 7.1). We witness here the emergence of the Gnostic troubles that were to plunge the church into a long-lasting crisis during the second and third centuries.

The Jesus image of Ignatius

Towering above all the other witnesses of post-apostolic Christianity, the letters of Ignatius constitute a particularly rich reservoir of Christological doctrine in the early church. Parallel to the phrase, 'and the Word (*Logos*) was God', from the Prologue of John (Jn 1:1), and no doubt antedating 2 Clement's solitary example (see p. 165), the letters of the bishop of Antioch were the first to declare the divinity of Jesus not just once but more than a dozen times, in plain words as well as in images. He spoke of Jesus as 'our God', 'our God Jesus Christ', 'the God that is Jesus Christ', 'the only Son' who is 'our God'. Also when he referred to the 'suffering of my God', he could only have had Jesus in mind (*Romans* 6.3). The divine character of Jesus is revealed in his existence since all eternity, in being 'with the Father from before the ages' (*Magnesians* 6.1). Echoing the Johannine imagery, Jesus Christ was for Ignatius the manifestation of God, 'his Word that came forth from silence' (*Magnesians* 8.2).

Emphasis on the divinity of Jesus went hand in hand with his earthly reality, with the fact that in him 'God became manifest in a human way (*anthrôpinôs*)' (*Ephesians* 19.3). This anti-Docetic insistence induced Ignatius to implant Jesus into the historical concreteness of the Jewish and Graeco-Roman world. At the start of the second century AD, he produced what seems to be a rudimentary formula of Christian profession of faith, similar to the earliest forms of the Old Roman Creed dating from the mid-second century AD. The terminology used in it serves to underline Jesus' true humanity. The most developed version is included in the Letter to the Smyrneans 1.1–2:

You are fully convinced about our Lord, that he was truly from the family of David according to the flesh, Son of God according to the will and power of God, truly born from a virgin, and baptized by John that all righteousness might be fulfilled by him. In the time of Pontius Pilate and the tetrarch Herod, he was truly nailed for us in the flesh – we ourselves come from the fruit of his divinely blessed suffering – so that through his resurrection he might eternally lift up the standard for his holy and faithful ones, whether among Jews or Gentiles, in the one body of his church.

There are two more embryonic credal sketches:

Our God Jesus Christ was conceived by Mary according to the plan of God; he was from the seed of David, but also from the Holy Spirit. He was born and baptized. (*Ephesians* 18.2)

Jesus Christ . . . is from the race of David according to the flesh, and is both Son of Man and Son of God. (*Ephesians* 20.2)

It is worth observing that the historical anchors in the political domain are Pontius Pilate, the Roman prefect of Judaea, and Herod Antipas, the tetrarch of Galilee. Ignatius never links Jesus to the Jewish people as such. He is silent on Annas and Caiaphas, the high priests responsible for the handing over of Jesus to the Romans, and he sees Jesus' chief ancestor not in Abraham, as in the Gospel genealogies, but in David, following Paul's formula in Romans 1:3, 'his Son who descended from David according to the flesh'. Jesus' birth of a virgin is also expressly asserted. However, it may be wondered whether with the combination of 'conceived by Mary ... from the seed of David, but also from the Holy Spirit', Ignatius left the door ajar, as did the Sinaitic Syriac version of Matthew 1:16 ('Joseph begot Jesus'), for an active role of Joseph, son of David, in the paternity of Jesus (see G. Vermes, *Jesus: Nativity – Passion – Resurrection*, 2010, p. 34). But these issues concerning Mary's dignity as God-bearer, hotly debated in the church in the fourth and fifth centuries, are beyond the scope and the time-scale of the present inquiry.

To end the survey of the Christological contents of the letters, mention should be made of two trinitarian phrases which do not seem to serve any particular purpose. In the first, Ignatius prays that the Magnesians may prosper in everything they do 'in flesh and spirit, in faith and love, *in the Son and the Father and in the Spirit*' (13.1). In the second, the Ephesians are depicted as 'stones of the *Father*'s temple ... being carried up to the heights by the crane of *Jesus Christ*, which is the cross, using as a cable the *Holy Spirit*' (*Ephesians* 9.1). No theological reflection is attached to this imagery.

In an *obiter dictum* of a different kind, Ignatius notes that he and his contemporaries lived in 'the end times' (*Ephesians* 11.1). The subject is not developed, indicating that eschatological expectation was not a central issue for Ignatius.

Ignatius of Antioch testifies to a number of highly significant changes in Christian religious practice and belief, the most important of them being the plain assertion of the divinity of Jesus. However, nothing suggests that these changes were actually thought through and that the implications of the various doctrinal claims were perceived and elaborated in depth. It took another two hundred years for the church to work out a systematic definition of what was to be understood by Christ's divinity and his relationship to God the Father, and reconcile the new concept with the monotheism inherited from Judaism. The first major steps towards these aims will be discovered in the work of the later second-century apologists, philosophers and theologians, starting with Justin Martyr (*c.* AD 100–*c.* 165), whose thought will be investigated in the next chapter.

ST POLYCARP (*c.* AD 69/70–155/6)

Polycarp, bishop of Smyrna, is said to have been a disciple of John the Elder (see Chapter 5, pp. 117–18) and the teacher of another Smyrnean, the great theologian St Irenaeus. His surviving letter, written in answer to the request of the church of Philippi for copies of the correspondence of Ignatius which he had in his possession, and the glorified account of Polycarp's own martyrdom, yield only a small amount of fresh evidence for our inquiry into the development of Christianity in the first half of the second century. According to the Martyrdom, the elderly Polycarp was put to death after having served Christ for eighty-six years. Denounced both by pagans and by Jews, he was sentenced as an atheist for refusing to swear by Caesar's goddess of Fortune.

It is surmised by many scholars that originally Polycarp wrote two letters, the first soon after the death of Ignatius in *c.* AD 110 (*Philippians* 9.1), and another dispatched by him some thirty years later, and that the two ended up by being conflated to constitute the surviving document. Polycarp used the Gospels, but unlike most other writers of this period only seldom either the Jewish Bible or the Apocrypha. He condemned the heretics who refused to confess that Jesus Christ had come 'in the flesh', that is to say the Docetist Gnostics, whose leader (possibly Marcion, see Chapter 8, pp. 194–5) bore the title 'the firstborn of Satan' (*Philippians* 7.1). Nothing very original appears in the domain of Christology; we find only commonly used phrases going back to the New Testament like 'Saviour', 'eternal Priest' and 'Son of God'. By contrast, in The Martyrdom of Polycarp we encounter three times the still current phrase *pais*, 'Servant' (*Martyrdom* 14.1, 3; 20.2), a primitive Christological designation, first witnessed in the Acts of the Apostles, but regularly used in the Didache, and also occasionally in 1 Clement.

The Shepherd OF HERMAS
(c. AD 110–c. 140)

According to the Muratorian Fragment, the earliest list of the books of the New Testament from the end of the second century, Hermas was the brother of Pope Pius, bishop of Rome from AD 140 to 154. His work, consisting of five Visions, twelve Mandates or Commandments and ten Parables, enjoyed considerable popularity in the second and third centuries and was considered Scripture by no lesser ecclesiastical authorities than Irenaeus and Tertullian. Origen, too, held it to be canonical although seldom read in a liturgical service. By contrast, the Muratorian Fragment, while denying its canonical status, considers it as permitted reading in the church.

The apocryphal apocalypse entitled *The Shepherd* is a work without great depth but with wide popular appeal. The Shepherd was the name borne by the angel of repentance who conveyed to Hermas moral teachings centred on penance. The interesting characteristic of Hermas's teaching about penitence is that after baptism it can take place only once. Sinning Christians were granted only a single second chance to return to God. Relapse after a second forgiveness carried with it permanent rejection from the church and eternal damnation.

Like most early ecclesiastical writers apart from Ignatius, Hermas is vague about the hierarchical structure of the church and speaks in the plural of presbyters and bishops with no firm emphasis on monarchic episcopacy. We already know that the author of the Mandates makes use of the moral doctrine of the Two Ways (Mand. 2.4–6; 6.2; 8.1–2). In this borrowing from Jewish ethics, Hermas imitates the Didache and Barnabas. He has some rather curious theological statements when he speaks of the incarnation of the Holy Spirit, apparently associating it with the *Logos*:

> God made the Holy Spirit dwell in the flesh that it desired, even though it pre-existed and created all things ... Since it [the flesh] lived in a good and pure way, co-operating with the Spirit and working with it in everything, behaving in a strong and manly way, God chose it to be a partner with the Holy Spirit. (Parable 5.6)

Later, in Parable 9.1, Hermas declares that the 'Spirit is the Son of

God'. This confusion between the Spirit and the Word made no lasting impact on Christian thought in the following centuries and the idea of the incarnation of the Holy Spirit found little echo in the writings of the later Church Fathers.

THE EPISTLE TO DIOGNETUS (c. AD 150–200)

This epistle contains an apologia for the Christian faith addressed by an anonymous writer to Diognetus, a pagan official about whom we have no further information. The author contrasts the Christian worship of God with Judaism and the religion of the pagans, extols the outstanding Christian virtues, and argues the divine origin of Christianity revealed to men through the Son of God.

Anti-Jewish and anti-pagan polemics

The writer of the epistle is obviously a Greek Christian who is opposed both to pagans and to Jews. A simplistic rejection of Graeco-Roman religion, defined as the worshipping of lifeless stone, copper, silver and gold statues of gods, is followed by an equally firm condemnation of Judaism. Without realizing that they are doing so, the pagans in practice behave ridiculously towards their idols. They worship stone and clay figures but, knowing that they are worthless, they do not guard them – whereas they lock up the silver and gold statues of the deities for fear that they might be stolen. Can these 'gods' not look after themselves? The Jews, in turn, practise monotheism, but do so in an improper way. They bring to God offerings as though he needed gifts, and their concern for food, Sabbath, circumcision, fasting and new moons is totally indefensible. To think that God forbids something good to be done on the Sabbath or encourages the Jews to boast of the mutilation of their bodies is plain superstitious nonsense. The anti-Judaism of the Epistle of Barnabas comes to mind.

By contrast, the Christians of Gentile origin are not inferior to, indeed they are as good as, their pagan compatriots. They live in the same cities, speak the same language and adopt the same lifestyle. The Jews attack them as foreigners and the Greeks persecute them.

The world hates the Christians, but the Christians love those who hate them, and their number increases daily even though they are continuously under duress (*Diognetus* 5–6).

The Jesus image of the letter

The author of the Epistle to Diognetus has something more special to say when he sets out to praise the excellence of the Christian religion and the manner in which it was revealed by God. The messenger was not an angel or an ordinary human mediator, but the Demiurge, the heavenly Craftsman, through whom the world was created. This term, borrowed from Philo of Alexandria and from Platonism, will become part of the Christian theological jargon.

> He sent the Craftsman and maker of all things himself, by whom he created the heavens, by whom he enclosed the sea within its own boundaries, whose mysteries all the elements of creation guard faithfully, from whom the sun was appointed to guard the course that it runs during the day, whom the moon obeys when he commands it to shine at night, whom the stars obey by following the course of the moon ... this is the one he sent to them ... With gentleness and meekness, as a king sending his own son, he sent him as a human to humans, he sent him as a king; he sent him as God. (*Diognetus* 7.2–4)

The writer cleverly ensures that the purely philosophical imagery acquires Christian colouring by identifying the 'Craftsman' with the 'Servant/*pais*' (*Diognetus* 8.9; 9.1) and indeed with 'the Son of God' ('*ho huios tou theou*'; *Diognetus* 9.4). Without ever directly naming Jesus, the author of the letter gives here a splendid elaboration of the *Logos* doctrine of the Johannine Prologue, using the technical term 'Demiurge' which will play a prominent role in the Arian controversy at the time of the Council of Nicaea. Although apart from the concept of the Demiurge the Epistle to Diognetus does not provide anything wholly new, it furnishes an excellent synopsis of the development of Christology in a strictly Graeco-Roman setting by the middle of the second century.

To sum up the teaching of the Apostolic Fathers, the following observations will be helpful.

Their concept of the church still fluctuated, but was definitely developing. Ignatius of Antioch was, in particular, the champion of the monarchic episcopacy with each church being under the total control of a single bishop, who was seen as the terrestrial representative of Jesus and the indisputable head of his assistants, the priests and deacons and the whole congregation of believers. This church progressively acquired a growing consciousness of being God's community, capable of confronting the Judaizers, i.e. Christians wishing the continuation of life under the Mosaic Law, the Jews, the Gnostic heretics who rejected the bodily reality of Jesus, and the pagans, for whom Christianity was a ridiculous superstition. They even faced up to the persecuting Roman state, strengthened by the conviction of their divine election.

Most important to note are the elements of the Christological image of the Apostolic Fathers. While 'Servant' (*pais*), that primitive title of Jesus formulated in Judaeo-Christianity, together with the other main evangelical and Pauline epithets like 'Son of God', 'High Priest' and 'Saviour', was still current in 1 Clement, the Martyrdom of Polycarp and the Epistle to Diognetus, a close reading of the sources reveals progressive steps in the domain of Christology. The most significant of these are connected with the upgrading of Jesus from 'charismatic Prophet', 'Messiah' and undefined 'Son of God' to the full status of divinity, chiefly under the impact of Ignatius of Antioch, but echoed also by 2 Clement.

Some of the traditional terms, such as 'Son of God', were further enriched. In Jesus God manifested himself in a human form; the Son was with the Father before the ages, but was still inferior to God, and the incarnate Christ was real and not just apparent as the Docetists claimed (1 Clement, Ignatius, Polycarp). The true humanity of the Redeemer is directly linked to the blood of Christ, the Saviour (1 Clement), and is also emphasized in rudimentary historical Creeds (Ignatius).

Finally, the Epistle to Diognetus is the forerunner of later theological speculation founded on the Johannine Prologue in depicting the revelation of Christianity by the Word/*Logos* as the work of the divine 'Craftsman' (Demiurge), who was also God's chosen instrument in the creation of the world.

8

Apologists and Theologians of the Second Century

Justin, Melito and Irenaeus

Christian religious thinking advanced by leaps and bounds in the second half of the second century and its progress may be illustrated by considering the works of the three leading Church Fathers of that period. The first of them, Justin Martyr, was an innovator in providing theological speculation with philosophical foundation, but he played a pioneering part in biblically based controversy too. The second, Melito of Sardis, left to posterity a moving homily with a powerful doctrinal basis, but one that is also spiced with virulent anti-Judaism. The third, Irenaeus, was the first major biblical theologian who was also celebrated as a leading apologist of orthodox Christianity against Gnosticism and Judaism. All three of them made a substantial contribution to the shaping of Christology, moving the image of Jesus further and further from his origins.

JUSTIN MARTYR

With Justin the reflective, philosophical-theological presentation of the Christian religion, and in particular that of the person and mission of Jesus, entered a new phase. His three surviving major works, two *Apologies* and his famous *Dialogue with the Jew Trypho*, present a much more rationally oriented picture of Christianity than either the New Testament or the authors of the post-apostolic age surveyed in the previous chapters. The *Apologies*, the first addressed to the Roman authorities (the emperor and the senate) and the second to the Roman people, offered a defence of Christianity against the charge of atheism, and the *Dialogue with Trypho* faced up to Jewish criticism of the new faith in the form of a discourse with a learned rabbi, who is portrayed as fully conversant with the style and method of classical rhetorical debate.

Justin was born *c.* AD 100 in the city of Samaria, renamed in AD 72 by the emperor Vespasian Flavia Neapolis (Nablus), not far from the ancient biblical city of Shechem. He described himself as an 'uncircumcised man' of Greek pagan stock. He was the 'son of Priscus and grandson of Bacchius', and claimed Samaritan nationality (1 *Apol.* 1; *Trypho* 28.2; 120.6). As a young man he decided to become a professional philosopher whose main aim was to investigate whether there were several gods or only one, and whether the deity was detached and aloof or whether he cared for his creatures (*Trypho* 1.4).

Justin started his training with the study of Stoicism, but soon abandoned this course of inquiry when he realized that his teacher knew nothing about God, nor was interested in religious ideas. He was equally unlucky with his next master, an Aristotelian, whose apparent chief concern was the collection of tuition fees from his pupils. Justin then tried to enter the Pythagorean school to study philosophy, but his admission was made conditional on first acquiring broader culture and familiarizing himself with music, astronomy and geometry. Refusing to delay his search for God through the study of subjects outside his concern, Justin attached himself to a leading Platonist, who taught the intellectually hungry disciple about immaterial things and the contemplation of ideas. With the unbridled enthusiasm of youth, 'he expected forthwith to look upon God ... the end of Plato's philosophy' (*Trypho* 2.6), but was again disappointed. There was no fast track to the divine. Meanwhile he discovered that Plato lifted from the Jewish lawgiver Moses some of his ideas, those of the creation and the association of the *Logos* (Word) with the cross. He also realized that the Greek poets' concept of *erebos* (darkness of the underworld) also came from Moses (1 *Apol.* 59–60).

An unnamed elderly Christian, whom Justin accidentally met in a park in Ephesus, advised him that if he wanted to learn about God, instead of the Greek philosophers who were ignorant of the subject, he had to turn to wiser men of considerably greater antiquity, namely the biblical prophets. Inspired by the Holy Spirit, these sages revealed God the creator and Father of all things, and his Son, Christ. Captivated by the words of the old man, Justin promptly embraced

Christianity, which his classically trained mind recognized and proclaimed as the sole profitable and true philosophy (*Trypho* 3–8).

He put on the uniform of the profession, the pallium, the cloak by
which he was easily recognized by Trypho as a philosopher (*Trypho*,
1.2), and opened a school in Rome. His most famous pupil was the
Assyrian Tatian, author of the renowned *Diatessaron*, or 'Harmony of
the Four Gospels'. According to this same Tatian, Justin was denounced
as a Christian by his philosophical opponent, the Cynic Crescens, and
was tried by the prefect of Rome, Junius Quadratus (*Address to the
Greeks*, 19). Having refused to sacrifice to the Roman gods, he was
declared an atheist, was scourged and finally decapitated in AD 165.

Justin's writings

Justin's extant works are two *Apologies of the Christian Faith*, the
first addressed as a petition, a 'booklet' (Greek *biblidion*, Latin *libellus*), to the emperor Antoninus Pius (AD 138–61), to his son Verissimus
the Philosopher, and to Lucius the Philosopher (on the genre of *libelli*,
see Fergus Millar, *The Emperor in the Roman World*, 1977, pp. 243–
4, 562–3). The second *Apology* was destined for the Roman senate
under Marcus Aurelius (161–80) and Lucius Verus (161–9). Justin's
third writing, the *Dialogue with the Jew Trypho*, is purported to
reflect – according to Eusebius (*EH* 4.18, 6) – a two-day disputation
in Ephesus with a group led by the educated Jew Trypho, normally
residing in Greece and sometimes identified, probably mistakenly, as
the Tannaitic Rabbi Tarfon of the Mishnah. This encounter took place,
we learn from incidental remarks of Justin (1 *Apol.* 31; *Trypho* 1.3;
9.3; 16.2; 108.3), some time after the rebellion of Bar Kokhba (AD
132–5), in the course of which, Justin informs us, Christians were
threatened by Jews with cruel punishment 'unless they would deny
Jesus and utter blasphemy' (1 *Apol.* 31). The three compositions of
Justin contain a substantial amount of reliable information regarding
the church's understanding of itself and Jesus in the mid-second century world.

In his *Apologies* Justin cleverly argued that the fate of the Christians, condemned to death for refusing to worship the gods and
Caesar, is the latter-day repetition of the injustice inflicted on Socrates
who, owing to the machinations of demons, was also executed as an

atheist (1 *Apol.* 5). The argumentation used in the two *Apologies* substantially differs from that we find in the *Dialogue*. The one addressed to pagans is essentially philosophical and the biblical element merely consists of using scriptural personalities as authorities more ancient than the Greek philosophers. The second type of argument is meant for Jews, unless the debatable view is adopted that the *Dialogue with Trypho* is merely a literary device, and that the apparently anti-Jewish apology is actually intended for internal Christian consumption. The Dialogue displays, in addition to some philosophical reasoning, Justin's mastery of biblical polemic against Jews. For this reason it will be examined separately following the *First and Second Apologies*.

The *Apologies*

The starting point of Justin's philosophical theology is his Judaeo-Christian understanding, via Philo and the Prologue of John, of the Platonic notion of the *Logos* (the divine Word or creative power). He intended to portray Jesus Christ as this *Logos* for Graeco-Roman intellectuals. The pagan philosophers, Justin argued, did not possess the whole doctrine of the *Logos*, available only in Christ; they had only partial understanding and as a result, owing to the machinations of the devils, they tended to contradict themselves (2 *Apol.* 8, 10).

Justin's doctrine: the Logos

Using Plato to envelop Christianity with a favourable aura, Justin injected two novelties into his teaching. The first was the assertion, coherent with his general Christian theological outlook, that Plato and the other Greek philosophers were not wholly original, but borrowed from Moses and the biblical prophets their understanding of the *Logos*. Secondly, he thought that, owing to his incomplete perception of the message of the Jewish Scripture, Plato was confused and spoke of three Gods. The first God put the second, the *Logos*, crosswise in the universe (this is a distorted representation of the brazen serpent attached by Moses to a cross in the wilderness), and the third God was the Spirit, who was said to be floating upon the waters (1 *Apol.* 60).

The *Logos* is the crucial topic in Justin's thought. It is presented as the first power after the Father and followed next by the Spirit

(1 *Apol.* 13). The *Logos* is not of the same standing as the Father and his function is comparable to that of the god Hermes, who is the divine Word interpreting the supreme Zeus (1 *Apol.* 21). However, the 'Christian' *Logos* has a distinguishing feature in that it became a man and was born of a virgin (1 *Apol.* 31, 63). The information derives from the Jewish Scriptures. The human birth of the *Logos* happened in conformity with the prophecy of Isaiah 7:14 ('Behold a virgin shall conceive and bear a son'), and the event came about 'by power' and not 'by intercourse', in a way similar to Zeus' lust for women (1 *Apol.* 33; for the Isaiah prediction see *Trypho* 43.3; 67.1). Begotten of God the Father before the creation of the world, and in time becoming a human being for the destruction of the demons, the *Logos*-Christ was distinguished by his mighty works, which were not the fruit of magic but marked the fulfilment of divine prophecies. The eternal *Logos* was realized in the virginally born Jesus Christ of the Christian Creed, who came to heal the sick and raise the dead. He was hated and crucified, he died, rose again and ascended to heaven as Son of God (1 *Apol.* 13, 30, 31, 60).

Justin advanced a threefold proof to demonstrate that 'a man crucified under Pontius Pilate, procurator of Judaea in the time of Tiberius Caesar' was 'the Son of God' and 'the Saviour'. The first evidence is that the humiliating defeat inflicted on the Jews by the Romans and the devastation of their land were divine punishment for their rejection of Jesus. The second is the success of the mission of the apostles among the Gentiles; Justin notes that by the middle of the second century the pagan converts largely outnumbered the Jewish Christians in the church. Thirdly, belief in Jesus' sonship of God was vindicated by the astounding power of the Christian charismatics: they could expel demons no other exorcists were able to overcome (1 *Apol.* 13, 53, 60; 2 *Apol.* 6).

Baptism and Eucharist

In regard to Christian religious life, the *Apologies* of Justin have only a few details to reveal. Baptism is depicted as an ablution for the remission of sins, and the sacred communal meal is identified as the nourishment of the faithful by the flesh and blood of Christ. Neither sacrament is outlined with strictly Pauline colouring: baptism is not said to be a symbol of the burial and resurrection of Christ nor the Eucharist the memorial of the Last Supper. On the other hand, Justin remarks in passing that the words of the Eucharist have been appropriated and plagiarized by the worshippers of Mithras: 'For the apostles, in the memoirs . . . which are called Gospels, have delivered to us what was enjoined upon them . . . which the wicked devils have imitated in the mysteries of Mithras' (1 *Apol*. 66). Justin further notes that the Eucharistic assembly was held on Sunday, a day appropriately chosen for religious celebration because it was on the first day of the week that God began the work of the creation and Jesus Christ rose from the dead (1 *Apol*. 67).

The Dialogue with the Jew Trypho

Although it has all the appearances of an urbane scholarly debate between a Christian philosopher and a Jewish teacher, the *Dialogue with Trypho* is nevertheless interspersed with occasional politely worded scathing comments. Justin accuses the Jews of murdering Christ and the prophets, and standing up to God by refusing to recognize Jesus (*Trypho* 16.4). In turn, Trypho qualifies as 'foolish' the Christian doctrine envisaging the incarnation of God (*Trypho*, 48.1). On the whole, the work reveals a powerful intellectual clash between Christianity and Judaism, built on the common ground of the Greek Old Testament (see Tessa Rajak, 'Talking at Trypho' in *The Jewish Dialogue with Greece and Rome*, 2001). Indeed, although Justin knows the New Testament, and in 1 *Apology* 66 specifically alludes to the apostles' memoirs called Gospels, in his polemic with Trypho he relies only on quotations from the Septuagint translation of the Hebrew Bible. Nevertheless, he is less violently anti-Jewish than the author of the Epistle of Barnabas. As will be remembered, for Barnabas the Sinai covenant with Israel was never enacted; in consequence, it lacked validity and did not entitle the Jews to call themselves God's chosen people (see Chapter 6, pp. 150–51). Justin never goes that far and his milder anti-Judaism resembles that of 1 Clement (see p. 161).

The two main themes of the *Dialogue* focus on the relationship between Judaism and Christianity and the demonstration from biblical prophecy that Jesus was the Son of God, ultimately endowed with divinity in some mysterious way. According to Justin, Jewish hostility towards Christianity sprang from a double rejection. First the Jews repudiated and killed Jesus and his forerunners, 'the Just One and his prophets before him'. Secondly, they did the same also to the believers in Christ and cursed them in their synagogues, blaming them for spreading their 'godless heresy' in all the lands. In Justin's opinion, the Jews justly suffered for their crimes. Even circumcision, which they proudly consider as the emblem of their election has in fact become a distinguishing mark, setting them apart for divine punishment as the recent events – the two failed rebellions against Rome – had demonstrated (*Trypho* 16–17).

Trypho, on the other hand, stressed in his counter-argument that the Jews obtained God's mercy through obedience to the Law, that is to say, by means of the observance of the Mosaic precepts relating to circumcision, the Sabbath, the feasts and the new moons, practices to which Justin and his co-religionists firmly objected. How could, Trypho wondered, the Christians consider themselves pious when, on the whole, their lifestyle did not differ from that of the pagans? They conducted themselves without any God-given rules of behaviour, and their specific hope simply rested on a crucified man, whom they believed to be the Christ. Even if such a man had ever existed, he would not have been aware of his messianic status or possessed the appropriate spiritual power without being anointed and proclaimed Messiah by the returning prophet Elijah. But Trypho was convinced that Elijah had not yet returned. Consequently he thought the Christians must have invented a Messiah for themselves and it is for the sake of this imaginary Christ that they are 'foolhardily perishing' (*Trypho* 8.3).

In his answer Justin turned on Judaism. He advanced that the Mosaic Law, imposed on the Jews because of the hardness of their hearts, was useless as it had been abrogated once and for all in favour of the law given by Christ (*Trypho* 11.2). It goes without saying that every new law and covenant cancels all the previous arrangements. For example, the new offering ordained by Jesus Christ, 'the Eucharist of the bread and the cup', is well pleasing to God, while the offerings presented by the Jewish priests in the past were utterly rejected according to the testimony of the spokesmen of Judaism, the prophets of the Bible (*Trypho* 117.1). It is quite amusing to note that in this disputation Justin comes up with a surprising objection against circumcision as a means of justification: as a ritual applicable only to males, it was against sex equality! His principle, *mutatis mutandis*, has a contemporary ring and should well embarrass present-day opponents of women's ordination in the traditional Christian churches.

> The inability of the female sex to receive fleshly circumcision proves that this circumcision has been given for a sign, and not for a work of righteousness. For God has given likewise to women the ability to observe all things which are righteous and virtuous. (*Trypho* 23.5)

The Messiahship and divinity of Jesus

The main disagreement between Justin and Trypho springs from the principal teachings of Christianity: the messianic status and the accepted, but not yet clearly defined, divinity of Jesus. For Trypho and his Jewish colleagues the claim that a man who died on the cross can be the divine Christ was both unproven and nonsensical:

> When you say that this Christ existed as God before the ages, then that he submitted to be born and become man, yet that he is not man of man [being miraculously conceived], this assertion appears to me to be not merely paradoxical, but also foolish. (*Trypho* 48.1)

Trypho further challenged Justin to show that the Bible, and in particular the prophets, envisaged the existence of another God besides the Creator of all things (*Trypho* 55.1). The Christian reply was that Scripture indeed speaks of 'another God', but that it envisages him as being of not quite the same standing as the Creator of the universe. The Bible depicts this 'other God' as an 'Angel and Lord', that is to say, Angel/Messenger 'because he announces to men whatsoever the Maker of all things – above whom there is no other God – wishes to announce to them' (*Trypho* 56.4; 58.3). In *Trypho* 59.1 Justin goes even further and designates the same envoy as 'Angel, and God, and Lord, and man', who appeared in human form when visiting Abraham and Isaac, and who according to the Book of Exodus also conversed with Moses in the burning bush in the form of a flame of fire.

Justin keeps on hammering home the same message that this Angel, who is God, revealed himself to Moses (*Trypho* 60.1). He further insists that, following the testimony of the Bible, before the created beings of the world God begot a rational Power called by the Holy Spirit 'now the Glory of the Lord, now the Son, again Wisdom, again an Angel, then God, and then Lord and *Logos*'. The *Logos*/Word of Wisdom is the God engendered by the Father of all; he is the Word, the Wisdom, the Power and the Glory of the Begetter (*Trypho* 61.2). The Jewish riposte was that these terms did not constitute real plurality and that when God said, 'Let *us* make man' (Genesis 1:26), he used an ordinary human speech form. As people often do, he addressed himself, or he spoke to the elements of which man was formed. Trypho's negative reply was countered by a scriptural citation which for Justin indisputably indicated that God conversed, not with himself, but with another rational being. For in Genesis 3:22, God says, 'Behold Adam has become as *one of us*.' This means that several persons, minimum two, are envisaged, namely that God was communicating with 'an Offspring that was generated by him, who was with him before all the creatures'. This Offspring was his eternal Word, the *Logos* (*Trypho* 62.4), whose pre-existence is thereby postulated.

In Justin's account, Trypho gives the impression that he has been shaken by all these scriptural arguments. However, he comes up with what he considers as a trump card, the words of Isaiah 42:8: 'I am the Lord God; that is my name; my glory I give to no other, nor my praises.' In other words, there is no second God. Justin's rejoinder is that the broader context of Isaiah 42:5–13 implies that there is one person, the Servant of the Lord, with whom God shares his glory, and this person is his Christ (*Trypho* 65.1–3).

Trypho then sets out to demolish the Christian claim that the various divine names like Angel, Glory, etc. really correspond to separate entities. For him and for Judaism they merely represent diverse forms or modalities under which the one and only God is perceived.

> The power sent from the Father of all which appeared to Moses, or to Abraham, or to Jacob, is called an Angel because he came to men (for by him the commands of the Father have been proclaimed to men). It is called Glory, because he appears in a vision sometimes that cannot be borne. It is called a man, and a human being, because he appears arrayed in such forms as the Father pleases. They call him the Word, because it carries tidings from the Father to men, but maintain that this power is indivisible and inseparable from the Father. (*Trypho* 128.1)

Justin, in his turn, firmly maintains that the various manifestations of God in biblical history correspond to an actual distinction between

God the Father and Christ, who according to the writings of the prophets was 'God, the Son of the only, unbegotten, ineffable God' (*Trypho* 126.1). Trypho and his fellow Jews are surely mistaken if they imagine that the eternal, unbegotten God himself descended from his heavenly abode to wander from one location to another to meet men.

> For the ineffable Father and Lord of all neither has come to any place, nor walks, nor sleeps, nor rises up, but remains in his own place, wherever that is, quick to behold and quick to hear, having neither eyes nor ears, but being of indescribable might; and he sees all things, and knows all things, and none of us escapes his observation; and he is not moved or confined to a spot in the whole world, for he existed before the world was made. (*Trypho* 127.1)

For Justin and for the Christians, Jesus, the Son of God, is the subject of all these manifestations. None of the patriarchs, nor Moses, or any other human being was able to behold the ineffable Lord of the universe; they saw him manifested in his eternal Son, who is God, or in the Angel/Messenger, who performed God's will, or in the appearance of fire which talked to Moses from the bush on Sinai, or in the human being born of the Virgin (*Trypho* 127.3). These various expressions of Power were generated by God's will, and did not result from severance or division as though the essence of the Father could be partitioned. Nevertheless, the Offspring begotten by the Father was numerically distinct from the Begetter (*Trypho* 128.4). Here we witness perhaps for the first time a philosophical-theological attempt to distinguish between what later theologians called 'persons' within the one mysterious substance of the Godhead.

Virginal conception

The miracle of the virginal birth of Jesus is an essential and heavily emphasized constituent of the *Logos*-Christology of Justin and simultaneously an easy target for Trypho's attack. Justin puts forward as an undeniable fact that in the entire history of the race of Abraham, Jesus was the only person who was conceived by a virgin without sexual intercourse (*Trypho* 43.7; 66.3; 67.1–2). Trypho launches a two-pronged rebuttal. First Isaiah, the source of the doctrine, did not speak of a virgin but of a young woman (*neanis*), as we find it in the second-century AD Greek versions of the Old Testament of Aquila, Symmachus and Theodotion. Secondly, the prediction related not to Jesus, but to a biblical king, contemporary of the prophet, who was born in the eighth century BC.

> The whole prophecy refers to Hezekiah, and it is proved that it was fulfilled in him, according to the terms of this prophecy. Moreover, in the fables of those who are called Greeks, it is written that Perseus was begotten of Danae, who was a virgin; he who was called among them Zeus having descended on her in the form of a golden shower. And you ought to feel ashamed when you make assertions similar to theirs, and rather should say that this Jesus was born man of men. And if you prove from the Scriptures that he is the Christ, and that on account of having led a perfect life according to the law, he deserved the honour of being elected to be Christ, it is well; but do not venture to tell monstrous phenomena, lest you be convicted of talking foolishly like the Greeks. (*Trypho* 67.1–2)

It is hard to understand why Trypho omitted to mention the philological crux, namely that the word for 'virgin' (*betulah*) does not figure in the original text of Isaiah. In fact, the prophet announces that a 'young woman' (*'almah*) will give birth to a son. Justin, ignorant of Hebrew, preferred to stick to the Septuagint's reading of *parthenos* ('virgin'), the term that figures in Matthew 1:23 too: 'Behold, a *parthenos* shall conceive.' Indeed, Justin explicitly accused Trypho and the Jews of falsifying their old Greek Bible, which the Hellenized church also considered as her own property.

> You in these matters venture to pervert the expositions which your elders that were with Ptolemy king of Egypt gave forth, since you assert that the Scripture is not so as they have expounded it, but says, 'Behold, the young woman shall conceive,' as if great events were to be inferred if a woman should beget from sexual intercourse: which indeed all young women, with the exception of the barren, do. (*Trypho* 84.3)

Since, as stated, the three second-century AD Greek translators of Isaiah – Aquila, Theodotion and the Jewish-Christian Ebionite Symmachus – correctly rendered the Hebrew *'almah* with the Greek *neanis* ('young woman'), Trypho was not on his own and from the linguistic point of view his case was fully justified. But Justin shuns philology and prefers to focus on Trypho's debatable though probably historically correct interpretation of the passage as referring to the birth of King Hezekiah. Trypho's earlier hint at the Greek legend relative to the mythical begetting of Perseus by Zeus of Danae was meant to ridicule what amounted in his mind to crass credulity on the part of Christians.

A modern observer of the debate would admit that in this round Trypho definitely won on points. However, Justin was determined to conduct the rhetorical exchanges on his own ground, the Greek of the Septuagint. We have to wait until Origen in the third century to find a Christian controversialist capable of appreciating the Jewish philological point of view. For Justin, the ultimate move of Trypho and his co-religionists should be conversion to Christianity without delay as the Second Advent of Christ may not be far away: 'So short a time is left for you in which to become proselytes. If Christ's coming shall have anticipated you, in vain you will repent, in vain you will weep; for he will not hear you' (*Trypho* 28.2).

It is worth remarking that, contrary to most of the authors examined previously who showed some, or like Ignatius and 1 Clement, a considerable amount of concern for church organization and the role of the bishops and presbyters, Justin only occasionally discusses questions of worship (baptism, Eucharist), and displays no particular interest in the ecclesiastical aspect of Christianity. Rhetorical debate is his home ground, and his field of expertise is the Greek Bible.

Some of Justin's ideas sounded out of true, indeed plainly unorthodox, a century or two later. While he would have been outraged if someone had accused him of polytheism, he undoubtedly gave the impression that the Father, the *Logos* and the Spirit were in some undetermined way different entities. Also, his trinitarian concept cannot escape the charge of implying inequality between God the Father and God the Son.

> We reasonably worship him, having learned that he is the Son of the true God himself, and we are holding him in the *second place*, and the prophetic Spirit in the third ... They proclaim our madness to consist in this, that we give to a crucified man a place second to the unchangeable and eternal God, the Creator of all. (1 *Apol.* 13)

This is clearly a subordinationist statement that asserts the superiority of God, the transcendent Father, over the less transcendent *Logos/* Son. Another peculiar teaching of Justin derives the divine Sonship of Christ from his wisdom rather than from his being God's specially begotten Offspring (1 *Apol.* 22; *Trypho* 61.1) and his third oddity relates to the self-generation of the *Logos* in a virgin (1 *Apol.* 33). Such 'unorthodox' statements are, however, unsurprising, indeed normal in ante-Nicene Christology.

Eusebius of Caesarea justifiably qualified Justin's literary work – the three surviving writings and the five further titles now lost – 'the products of a cultured mind' (*EH* 4.18). He opened a new chapter in the history of Christian thought.

MELITO OF SARDIS (DIED BEFORE AD 190)

Melito, bishop of Sardis in the Roman province of Asia (north-western Asiatic Turkey), was described by Eusebius as a 'eunuch who lived entirely in the Holy Spirit' and as a 'great luminary' of the church (*EH* 5.24, 5). Whether by eunuch he meant castrated or celibate is open to debate. Melito visited the Holy Land with a view to establishing the list of the canonical books of the Old Testament. According to Eusebius (*EH* 4.26), his list does not contain the book of Esther, which incidentally is also missing from the biblical remains of the Dead Sea Scrolls found at Qumran.

The extensive literary work of Melito, listed by Eusebius, survived only in fragments and quotations until 1940, when his Easter homily preserved in a Chester Beatty-Michigan papyrus was first published (see C. Bonner (ed.), *The Homily on the Passion*, 1940), followed twenty years later by the edition of the same text from papyrus XIII of the Bodmer collection, edited by M. Testuz.

Having presented the defence of Christianity to the emperor Marcus Aurelius in a now lost appeal in *c.* 172, Melito can justifiably be classified among the apologists. Nevertheless, his surviving Passover sermon is essentially a theological treatise – unless its powerful anti-Jewish stance would classify it as an apologetical writing. The Jews whom he blames are the Jews of the past, in particular the hostile Jews of the age of Jesus envisaged in an abstract sense, and not the real Jews of the second century, such as those Polycarp accused of joining the pagans in proffering charges against the Christians before the Roman authorities (see p. 172).

Melito was a champion of the 'Quatrodeciman' Easter, the celebration of the Christian feast on the evening of the fourteenth day of Nisan, coinciding with the start of the Jewish Passover. He is listed among the Asian bishops – who were also supported by Irenaeus from Gaul (see below) – when they defended their liturgical tradition against Victor, the authoritarian bishop of Rome, who was ready to excommunicate all the dissenters from his tradition in which Easter was to be celebrated on the Sunday following the Jewish feast day (Eusebius, *EH* 5.23–4). It is not surprising that Melito was anxious to deliver a major Easter sermon filled to the brim with theological implications.

Continuous doctrinal musings underlie Melito's homily, which is based on the typological significance of the events of the Mosaic Passover. In the reality of the suffering, death, burial and resurrection of Christ the prefiguration of the Old Testament stories were seen fulfilled. The antecedents of the Egyptian Passover are traced back as far as the events of the Garden of Eden. The act of disobedience of Adam and Eve enslaved their posterity to wickedness and sensual pleasure, to the 'tyrannical transgression', which later received the designation of 'original sin' (Homily 49–50), and the mark of which, imprinted on the soul, brought death to every human being (Homily 54).

Atonement for Adam's trepass was preplanned by Christ in biblical history. It was prefigured by the trials inflicted on the patriarchs, the prophets and the whole people of Israel. In turn, the mystery of the suffering of Christ was typically anticipated in the death of Abel, the binding of Isaac, the sale of Joseph, the exposure of Moses in the Nile, and the troubles of David and the prophets (Homily 57–9). Finally Christ closed the circle when he descended from heaven. Having become a man capable of suffering, he killed death (Homily 66) and plunged the devil into mourning (Homily 68).

The fulfilled predictions inspire in Melito a breathtaking poetic awe. The worshipper realizes that in truth it was Christ who was murdered in Abel, bound on the altar in Isaac, exiled in Jacob, sold in Joseph, exposed in Moses, hunted down in David and dishonoured in the prophets. After acquiring the real body of a man in a virgin, he was executed in Jerusalem. He was put to death for healing the lame, cleansing the leper, giving light to the blind and reviving the dead; but he was also crucified, buried and resurrected to lift up mankind from the grave to heaven (Homily 69–72).

The death of Jesus

The Jews killed Jesus Christ because it was necessary for him to suffer and die. But they deceived themselves. Instead of praying, 'O Lord, if your Son is to suffer . . . let him suffer but not through our intermediary; let him suffer by the hands of foreigners, let him be judged by the uncircumcised men' (Homily 74–6), the Jewish people enjoyed destroying him and in doing so, they destroyed themselves.

> You sang songs, he was judged;
> you issued the command, he was crucified;
> you danced, he was buried;
> you lay down on a soft couch,
> he in a grave and a coffin. (Homily 80)

As a result the Jews lost their entitlement to be called Israel: 'You did not see God' (Melito alludes to the ancient popular etymology according to which 'Israel' means 'the man who sees God'). They did not recognize the Firstborn of the Father, begotten before the morning star, one who guided mankind from Adam to Noah, from Noah to Abraham and the other patriarchs. God saved the Jews in Egypt, gave them manna from heaven and water from the rock and revealed the Law to them on Horeb. He gave them the Promised Land, the prophets and the kings. At the end, God descended to earth to heal the sick and raise the dead, only to be killed by the Jews (Homily 83–6).

Israel set their faces against the Lord, whom even the nations worshipped, and over whom Pilate washed his hands, and they changed the joyous feast into one of acerbity, turning into reality the type of the bitter herbs they were to eat at the Passover meal.

> Bitter is for you Caiaphas whom you trusted . . .
> Bitter is for you the vinegar you produced.
> Bitter are for you the thorns you plucked.

Bitter are for you the hands you bloodied,
You killed your Lord in the midst of Jerusalem.
(Homily 92–3)

The drama reaches its climax when the full horror of the murder committed in the heart of the Holy City is realized. For the one who was hanging on the tree was he who 'hung the world' and 'fixed the heavens'. So if the people did not tremble, the earth quaked instead and Israel reaped their just deserts.

> You dashed down the Lord,
> you were dashed to the ground
> and you lie dead. (Homily 99–100)

Christ, on the other hand, proclaims:

> Come all families of men …
> For I am your forgiveness,
> I am the Passover of salvation …
> I am your resurrection. (Homily 103)

Melito's Christology

Profound theological reflections are hidden within the poetic majesty of Melito's rhetoric. His Passover homily encapsulates a complete Christian synthesis of salvation together with a penetrating view of second-century Christology, starting with the primeval story of Paradise and ending with the glorification of the Son and the Father mutually supporting each other.

> He is the Christ …
> He bears the Father and is borne by the Father,
> to whom be the glory and the power for ever. Amen.
> (Homily 105)

In a remarkably succinct summary, the worshippers are presented with the eternal and temporal history of the Son/*Logos*. He is pictured as existent and active from before the start of the creation and responsible for the making of the heavens, the earth and humanity. He was foretold by the Law and the prophets, and the Christian faith is the fulfilment of these predictions: the Lord became incarnate through a virgin, was crucified, buried, resurrected and raised to celestial heights to be enthroned next to the Father as the judge and saviour of all from the beginning to the end of the age (Homily 104).

Melito's emphasis on the real body taken by the eternal Son in the womb of the virgin is the standard Christian weapon against Docetism and Gnosticism. According to a citation by Abbot Anastasius Sinaita in the seventh/eighth century (Migne, *Patrologia Graeca* 89, col. 229), from one of Melito's lost works, 'The Incarnation of Christ', he directly confronted the Gnostic Marcion's denial of the genuineness of the bodily birth of Jesus. For Melito the flesh of Christ was not a 'phantasm', as Marcion called it, but real and true.

The repeated assertion of prophetic announcements being fulfilled in the earthly life of Christ forms an apologetical arsenal against all the unbelievers, be they Gentiles or Jews. Moreover, Israel's guilt of deicide and consequent loss of election are relentlessly hammered home throughout the whole sermon: '*God has been murdered* ... by the right hand of Israel' (Homily 96).

These words denouncing the Jews as God-killers are emotionally much more powerful than the equally vicious assaults against Judaism of the Epistle of Barnabas. Finally, no Church Father before the fourth century was able to squeeze into a single sentence as much high Christology as Melito when he declared:

> For as a Son born, and as a lamb led,
> and as a sheep slain, and as a man buried,
> he rose from the dead as God,
> being by nature God and man.
> (Homily 8)

IRENAEUS OF LYONS (c. AD 130–200)

Irenaeus was born in Asia Minor, probably in Smyrna, where in his early youth he was taught by the martyr Bishop Polycarp. At some later stage he migrated to Gaul, where he was ordained a presbyter. He acted as an emissary of his church to Pope Eleutherius in Rome, and also intervened on behalf of the bishops of the Roman province of Asia with Pope Victor in the Quatrodeciman controversy, speaking up against the excommunication of entire churches just because they observed the unbroken tradition of their predecessors (*EH* 5.24). Some time after AD 177 Irenaeus succeeded the martyred Pothinus as bishop of Lugdunum (Lyons).

Gnosticism

In addition to being the first major biblical theologian of the church, Irenaeus was also a powerful champion of orthodoxy. While in earlier times Christianity needed to vindicate itself primarily against the persecuting arm of the Roman Empire (Ignatius, Polycarp, Justin), and secondarily against Judaism (Pseudo-Barnabas, Justin and Melito) as well as against Docetism (1 John, Ignatius, Justin), by the time of Irenaeus the chief threat to orthodox Christian belief arose from a more sophisticated Gnosticism propagated by the Egyptian Valentinus and the Asiatic Marcion, both active in Rome from the middle of the second century.

The teaching of these heretics is mainly known from the refutation offered by their orthodox opponents – Irenaeus in the first place, and Tertullian a little later (see Chapter 9, pp. 203–4) – although in the Coptic Gospel of Truth, known since the mid-twentieth century thanks to the Nag Hammadi discoveries in Egypt, we now probably possess a genuine Gnostic work, bearing the same title as the writing attributed by tradition to Valentinus, one of the outstanding masters of Gnosticism. The essence of this doctrine lies in dualism, with a supreme spiritual Deity facing an inferior Creator or Demiurge responsible for the making of the material world, the opposite of the world of spiritual realities. Morsels or sparks of the spiritual entered human beings and their redemption consisted in the deliverance of the spiritual from the prison of matter through knowledge or *gnosis*, thus allowing the return of the wayward sparks to the supreme immaterial God. The divine Christ descended from on high as the bearer of this *gnosis*. Without assuming real fleshly nature through incarnation and without subsequently suffering or dying, he put on a human appearance and dwelt in the unreal body of Jesus.

One of the pillars of Gnosticism, Marcion, son of the bishop of Sinope from Pontus in Asia Minor, was first excommunicated by his father and later by the Roman church. He turned his back on the Judaism of the Old Testament and its angry God, and opted for the wholly different loving deity revealed by Jesus. He redefined the New Testament, accepting only the Gospel of Luke (after cutting off the first two chapters dealing with the birth story of Jesus) and ten out of the fourteen letters of Paul, excising the Pastorals (1 and 2 Timothy and Titus), and the Epistle to the Hebrews. His doctrine was conveyed in a now lost book entitled 'Antitheses', in which the Jewish God of the Law was contrasted with the God of love of the Gospel.

Irenaeus was the leading challenger of Valentinus and Marcion in his five-volume treatise, popularly known as *Against Heresies* but in fact entitled *Unmasking and Refutation of the False Gnosis*. In combating Gnostic dualism, he followed in the footsteps of Justin, whose relevant statement he quotes: 'I would not have believed the Lord himself, if he had preached a God other than the Creator' (*Heresies* 4.6, 2). He also prepared the way for the further anti-Gnostic warfare fought by Tertullian and Clement of Alexandria in the following generation.

The theology of Irenaeus

Apart from championing the traditional belief in a single God-Father, who through his Son and Spirit was the maker of the whole created world, and laying stress on the genuine incarnation of Jesus, both God and man, Irenaeus merely reaffirmed the Christology of the second-century church and crowned this restatement with a masterly vision of the *oikonomia*, the economy or order of the redemptive work of Christ. He reformulated the vision of Justin and Melito, and ultimately that of Paul, concerning the foreshadowing of salvation in the typological figures of the Old Testament and their realization in the destiny of Christ, the incarnate Word/*Logos* and Son of God. In such a context, he defined redemption history as a recapitulation (*anakephalaiôsis*), a full circle from the first man to Christ, from the first to the last Adam.

> It was incumbent on the Mediator between God and man ... to bring both to friendship and concord, and present man to God, while he revealed God to man ... What he appeared, he also was: God

recapitulated in himself the ancient formation of man, that he might kill sin, deprive death of its power and vivify man. (*Heresies* 3.18, 7)

And again:

> [Christ, the eternal *Logos*] took up man into himself, the invisible becoming visible ... the impassible becoming capable of suffering, and the Word being made man, thus *recapitulating* all things in himself. (*Heresies* 3.16, 6)

For his overemphasis of the reality of the divine and human, the *Logos* and the flesh, in Jesus, Irenaeus would have become suspect a couple of hundred years later of harbouring a heretical idea, namely that in the incarnate Christ two persons, a divine and a human, were active. But in the late second century we are not yet ready for the fight against the teaching propounded by Nestorius amid the controversy that would enliven the age of the Council of Ephesus in 431.

It may be added here in parenthesis that the recapitulation of the role of Adam in Jesus is paralleled in Irenaeus' understanding of redemption history by the recapitulation by the Virgin Mary of the part played by the 'Virgin' Eve. To clarify this imagery, it must be remembered that during her days in Paradise Eve was supposed to be a virgin, and thus the two 'virgins' inversely supplemented one another: 'The knot of Eve's disobedience was loosed by the obedience of Mary. For what the virgin Eve had bound fast through unbelief, this the virgin Mary did set free through faith' (*Heresies* 3.22, 4).

In his anti-Marcionite battle Irenaeus felt obliged to stress the significance and importance of the Jewish Bible. By constantly quoting it and treating it as the possession of the church, he sought to prove that both Testaments depended on one and the same God.

> If Christ had descended from another Father, he would never have made use of the first and greatest commandment of the law; but he would undoubtedly have endeavoured by all means to bring down a greater one than this from the perfect Father, so as not to make use of that which had been given by the God of the law. (*Heresies* 4.12, 2)

The anti-Gnostic enthusiasm contributed to Irenaeus' special concern for the Eucharist, which *qua* renewal of the sacrifice of the body and blood of Jesus had as its prerequisite the reality of the incarnation, the pet hatred of Marcion and his fellows. All the Gnostics rejected the idea of the salvation of the flesh and with it the notion of Christ redeeming man through the offering of his bodily substance. As a result, believers in Gnosticism could not benefit from the Eucharist, the communion of the flesh and blood of the Saviour (*Heresies* 5.2, 3). The real divine and human duality of Christ is asserted by Irenaeus to be the precondition of the efficacy of the Eucharist.

> For as the bread, which is produced from the earth, when it receives the invocation of God, is no longer common bread, but the Eucharist, consisting of two realities, earthly and heavenly; so also our bodies, when they receive the Eucharist, are no longer corruptible, but have the hope of the resurrection to eternity. (*Heresies* 4.18, 5)

Finally, Irenaeus played an important role in the development of the Christian idea of the church. His involvement in ecclesiastical politics, speaking on behalf of the church of Lyons as well as the churches of the Province of Asia has already been noted. But he also made celebrated statements in regard to the establishment of truth in the doctrinal domain. He stressed the importance of bishops, whose uninterrupted succession from the apostles to his days was the palpable guarantee of the Christian truth. However, since it would be tedious to try to establish the historical chain of every single bishop, it is enough to concentrate on the most famous seat, that is, 'the very great, the very ancient, universally known church, founded and organized at Rome by the two most glorious apostles, Peter and Paul' (*Heresies* 3.3, 2).

The meaning of the somewhat obscure lines that follow is hotly disputed among those who maintain or reject the supremacy of the bishop of Rome in the church, a matter that is outside the interest of this book. In any case, in the next chapter of his work Irenaeus chooses as his guide in the establishment of the orthodox faith not just Rome, but all the ancient churches with apostolic connection.

> Suppose there arise a dispute relative to some important question among us, should we not have recourse to the most ancient churches with which the apostles held constant intercourse, and learn from them what is certain and clear in regard to the present question? For how should it be if the apostles themselves had not left us writings? Would

it not be necessary to follow the course of the tradition, which they handed down to those to whom they did commit the churches? (*Heresies* 3.4, 1)

A last noteworthy yet logical sequel of Irenaeus' anti-Gnostic slant is a lack of animosity against the Jews. His stance is far distant from that of Barnabas and Melito. With dreamy optimism, he tells his readers that the Jews are the best prepared candidates for the acceptance of Christianity. It should be easy to persuade them to embrace the faith because its proof lies in their own Scriptures.

> [They] were in the habit of hearing Moses and the prophets, did also readily receive the First-begotten of the dead, and the Prince of the life of God ... They who were of the circumcision were previously instructed not to commit adultery, nor fornication, nor theft, nor fraud; and that whatsoever things are done to our neighbours' prejudice were evil and detested by God. Wherefore also they did readily agree to abstain from these things, because they had been thus instructed. (*Heresies* 4.24, 1)

In contrast to the Jews, the Gentiles constitute a rocky ground. They must be prevailed upon to

> depart from the superstition of idols, and to worship one God, the Creator of heaven and earth ... and that his Son was his Word, by whom he founded all things; and that he, in the last times, was made a man among men; that he reformed the human race, but destroyed and conquered the enemy of man ... [and that adultery and the like] were wicked, prejudicial, and useless, and destructive to those who engaged in them. (*Heresies* 4.24, 1–2)

Consequently, Irenaeus imagined that the apostles and the Christian missionaries had a harder task to face in the pagan world than those who preached the Gospel to the Jews.

To sum up, Justin, Melito and Irenaeus are three powerful supports of the progressively rising edifice of Christology. Their works combine philosophical insight with scriptural argument and theological speculation.

With Justin, Christian theology was born, a theology linked to

Greek philosophy and totally different from Jesus' non-speculative mode of thinking. A professional Platonic philosopher, though not an outstanding thinker by Greek standards, Justin was well equipped to offer a rational defence of his beleaguered faith against the political and religious opposition vis-à-vis imperial Rome and self-confident Judaism. He transmitted the traditional chief tenets of Christianity – Jesus being Son of God and God, as we have already seen in the work of Ignatius of Antioch – but the circumstances and the presentation are novel. While originally and up to the Didache people of Jewish origin formed a majority in the church, Justin expressly states that in his days the proportions were reversed. In fact, he uses this change as a proof of divine favour for Christianity, replacing the heavenly privilege previously granted to the Jews.

His main contribution to the future development of Christian thought relates to the philosophical grounding of the *Logos* doctrine and the crystallization of the system of fulfilment interpretation of biblical prophecy in the person and history of Jesus of Nazareth.

In turn, Melito marshalled a powerfully moving poetic synthesis for demonstrating, in a world imbued with Gnosticism, the reality of the incarnate and redeeming Son of God through the typological exegesis of the Old Testament. With this he managed to pinpoint the major themes of the later Christological debates in the church: the simultaneous divinity and humanity of Christ, the problem of his two natures, divine and human, and his eternity and temporality.

As for Irenaeus, he excelled in both the fight against Gnosticism and in the overall evaluation of Christology as affecting all the various aspects of the theological thinking of the church. The stress he laid on the validity of the Old Testament and the redemptive 'economy' in biblical history and his idea of inverse 'recapitulation' of the roles of Adam and Eve as against Jesus and Mary made lasting marks on theological thinking. As for his insistence on the importance of the Roman tradition for the establishment of orthodox doctrine, it was to play a significant role in later ecclesiastical debate.

Justin, Melito and Irenaeus have prepared the ground for the last bounces of mental effort that transformed the charismatic religion of Jesus into the majestic philosophical theology of the Greek church.

9

Three Pillars of Wisdom

Tertullian, Clement of Alexandria and Origen

In the course of the third century, self-defence against the persecuting Roman state and the fight against Gnosticism continued to form the main motivation of Christian literary activity. The towering figure of Tertullian, a professional lawyer, played one of the leading roles in the drama. Clement and Origen, successive heads of Alexandria's famous *Didaskaleion* or Christian Catechetical School, were the two other prominent personalities who left an indelible mark on the development of Christianity up to the middle of the third century. They were thoroughly steeped in classical culture, and Origen was in addition the most prominent biblical scholar of the Greek-speaking church.

Compared to the previous period, one can note two interesting differences. The authors discussed in the last three chapters came from various corners of the Roman Empire – the writer of the Didache originated in Palestine or Syria, Clement was a Roman, Barnabas an Egyptian, Justin was born in Samaria before moving to Rome, and Ignatius, Polycarp, Melito and Irenaeus all hailed from Asia Minor. By contrast, each of the three Church Fathers of the present chapter was active in North Africa, with Carthage, the home of Tertullian, and Alexandria, the city of Clement and Origen, being the outstanding cultural centres. As a second difference, unlike most of their second-century predecessors, the greatest Christian standard-bearers of the third century were not of episcopal rank. Tertullian was a layman, and so too was Clement. As for Origen, the validity of the priestly ordination conferred on him in Palestine was called into question by his local ecclesiastical superior, Demetrius, bishop of Alexandria. Despite their brilliance, or perhaps because of it, all three were treated as heretics either in their lifetime or after their death. Clement of

Alexandria was honoured as a martyr for centuries until another Clement, Pope Clement VIII (1592–1605), decided to delete his name from the martyrs' register on account of his purportedly unorthodox ideas. Origen, the son of a martyr, was himself grievously tortured during the persecution of Decius in 250, but as he was not killed at once – he died four years later – he was not recognized as a hero of the faith, and was posthumously repeatedly denounced as a heretic. Tertullian, in turn, after a devout orthodox beginning, embraced the Montanist error in 207. From then on, the stern ascetic, who counted himself among the 'spiritual men', the *pneumatici*, of his age, ceased to be *persona grata* in what he disdainfully referred to as 'the church of many bishops' (*On Modesty*, 21).

TERTULLIAN (*c*. 160–*c*. 222)

Quintus Septimius Florens Tertullianus was born in Carthage, the son of a Roman army officer. Eusebius describes him in his youth as 'one of the most brilliant men in Rome', where he trained as a lawyer (*EH* 2.2). He returned to Carthage in 195 and, as writer and apologist, devoted himself entirely to the service of the church. His literary output was spectacular and most of it has survived. A dozen years after his homecoming, he was attracted to Montanism, which was inspired by and imitated the ascetic-charismatic lifestyle of the early Jewish Christianity of the apostles.

The movement was launched in the middle of the second century in Phrygia (Asia Minor) by the eponymous founder, Montanus, with the help of two female associates, Prisca and Maximilla. Montanus was an ecstatic visionary who claimed to have received direct revelations from the Holy Spirit. He was convinced that his Phrygian hometown, Pepuza, would soon witness the descent from heaven of the New Jerusalem as predicted in the Book of Revelation. According to Eusebius, both Montanus and Maximilla ended their lives by hanging themselves in an ecstatic frenzy (*EH* 5.16, 13), but their newborn charismatic Christianity survived and continued in Asia Minor until the sixth century – and thanks to Tertullian's renown, it flourished in North Africa, too.

Tertullian was a brilliant defender of Christianity against both the

Roman state and Marcionite Gnosticism. In his Montanist phase he used the powerful dialectical weapons of an experienced controversialist against what he considered the errors of the Catholic church.

Apology of Christianity

Tertullian was a spokesman of Christian pride, and firmly stood up against the 'rulers of the Roman Empire' (*Apology* 1.1) who were engaged in persecuting the faithful, and did his best to demonstrate their unfairness and even illogicality towards the Christian predicament. Roman justice, he argued, permitted every accused person to plead not guilty either personally or by hiring an advocate. Christians alone were deprived of the right to claim innocence against the charge of criminal behaviour. *Nomen Christianum*, the mere admission of belonging to the Christian community, irrespective of personal conduct, carried with it the death penalty. Also, people accused of ordinary crimes such as theft or murder, who denied their guilt, were subjected to torture in order to force them to *confess* their culpability, whereas the same torment was inflicted on Christians to compel them to *deny* that they were members of the church. So Tertullian eloquently complained of the injustice of the judges:

> Kill us, torture us, condemn us, grind us to dust. Your injustice is the proof of our innocence ... Lately, in condemning a Christian woman to be delivered to a procurer for prostitution [*ad lenonem*] rather than to a lion [*ad leonem*], you admitted that a taint on purity is considered among us more terrible than death ... The more often we are mown down by you, the more we grow in number. *The blood of the Christians is a seed.* Many of your writers exhort to the courageous bearing of pain and death ... yet their words do not find as many disciples as the Christians do, who teach not by words, but by deeds. (*Apology* 50.12–14)

In his eulogy of Christianity, Tertullian went so far as to assert that any tormented human soul,

> when it comes to itself ... waking from sleep or recovering from sickness, and attains something of its natural soundness, speaks of God ... 'God is great and good' ... are the words on every lip ... Such

persons look not towards the Capitol, but towards heaven where they know that the throne of the living God is.

Tertullian crowned these praises with the memorable outcry declaring 'anima naturaliter Christiana', namely that every man's soul is Christian by nature (Apology 17.5–6).

Refutation of heresy

Speaking on behalf of the church, Tertullian adopted a stance of absolute superiority towards Gnosticism. Since, following the lead of Irenaeus, he professed that the truth of Christianity depended on conformity with the teaching of the apostles as handed down within the community of the faithful (see Chapter 8, p. 197), he maintained that only doctrines traceable to the immediate disciples of Jesus could be accepted as valid. Consequently the heretics like Marcion or Valentinus had no leg to stand on because their teachings did not extend far enough into the past. Antiquity reaching back to the first century was an absolute requirement for orthodoxy; any novelty dating from the second century was ipso facto disqualified. The rule of faith or *regula fidei* was contemporaneous with 'the beginning of the Gospel' and antedated the emergence of any of the 'modern' heresies (*Against Praxeas* 2). Conformity with this rule was the guarantee of the Christian truth. In setting out the elements of the *regula fidei*, Tertullian in fact compiled a detailed Christian Creed.

> We . . . believe that there is one only God, but . . . this one and only God has also a Son, his Word, who proceeded from himself, by whom all things were made, and without whom nothing was made. We believe that he was sent by the Father into the Virgin, and was born of her – being both man and God, the Son of Man and the Son of God – and was called by the name of Jesus Christ. We believe that he suffered, died, and was buried, according to the Scriptures, and, after he had been raised again by the Father and taken back to heaven, he is sitting at the right hand of the Father, and will come to judge the living and the dead. He also sent from heaven from the Father, according to his promise, the Holy Spirit, the Paraclete, the sanctifier of the faith of those who believe in the Father, and in the Son, and in the Holy Spirit. (*Against Praxeas* 2)

Invoking against the heretics the principle of *praescriptio*, through which Roman law declared the opponent's claim invalid and consequently unfit to be further debated in court, Tertullian used all his dialectical and rhetorical skill to eviscerate the Gnostic argument against the genuineness of the corporal birth of the *Logos* through the Virgin. In order to lay extra stress on the reality of the humanity of Jesus as opposed to a fictional idealization, Tertullian insisted that he looked ugly: 'His body possessed no human beauty, not to speak of heavenly glory. Had the prophets given us no information concerning his wretched appearance, his sufferings and humiliation would reveal it all' (*On the Flesh of Christ* 9).

In the course of his fight with the Gnostics, Tertullian produced an important and clear formulation of the doctrine of the incarnation of Christ – that he was both man and God – and became the pioneering theologian of the various concepts which became essential in the later Christological debate. In several respects he was miles ahead of his time, and according to the fourth-century Church Father Hilary of Poitiers (Commentary on Matthew 5:1) it was only his Montanist faux pas that neutralized his influence on subsequent Christological thinking, which his brilliant ideas fully deserved.

The Christ of Tertullian

The 'rule of faith' was Tertullian's chief theological banner. 'To know nothing against this rule is to know everything', he asserted (*Prescription against Heretics* 14.5). He focused his attention on the central mystery of Christianity, the concepts of Son of God and Son of Man and their relation to one another, and in particular on the eternal generation of the divine Son by the Father.

> We have been taught that the 'Discourse' [the Greek *Logos* rendered in Latin by Tertullian as *Sermo*] proceeds from God, and in that procession he is begotten, so that he is the Son of God, and is called God because of his unity of substance with God. (*Apology* 21.11)

But this same Word/Discourse, a ray of God, descended in conformity with ancient prophecy into a certain virgin and being made flesh within her, he became at his birth God and man united (*Apology* 21.14).

Fighting against Marcion's Docetism, Tertullian got himself entangled in the terminological complexities of the virginal conception. For the Gnostics, the flesh of Christ was mere appearance: no spiritual God and vile matter could possibly mix. The rule of faith, the church's Credo, reproduced earlier in the quotation from *Against Praxeas*, demanded by contrast belief in the real birth of Christ of a virgin, and Tertullian with all the previous tradition of the church, attested also by Justin and Irenaeus, was a strong defender of the application of Isaiah 7:14 ('a virgin shall conceive') to the miraculous generation of Jesus at the exclusion of the agency of a human father.

His anti-Gnostic stance allowed him to accept that the divinely engineered pregnancy of Mary had as its consequence a real foetus developing in her womb, but landed him in deep waters with the idea of her continued virginity through the birth. The delivery of a real infant could not leave Mary's hymen intact. In Tertullian's view the assertion that the mother of Jesus was still a virgin after childbirth favoured the heresy of the Gnostics. In other words, he professed Mary's virginity before the birth of Christ, but denied it afterwards.

Marcion, who rejected the genuine bodily birth of Jesus, found support for his philosophical stance in Jesus' question, 'Who is my mother and who are my brothers?' (Mt. 12:48), which he took for Jesus' denial of having real earthly relatives. In his effort to pre-empt the Gnostic argument, Tertullian was ready to sacrifice not only the doctrine of Mary's virginal childbearing but also that of her continued virginal status after the Nativity. He implied that after giving birth to her virginally conceived firstborn son, she and Joseph normally procreated the brothers and sisters of Jesus (*On the Flesh of Christ* 7, 23). For Tertullian, these siblings, James, Joses, Judas and Simon, did not represent Jesus' stepfamily but were his real 'blood relations'. The disciples he substituted for them by saying, 'Whoever does the will of God is my brother' (Mk 3:35), were not truer, but worthier brothers (*Against Marcion* 4.19, 11–13).

Tertullian's main doctrinal treatise about Christ with trinitarian implications is contained in his controversy with Praxeas, a heretic native of Asia Minor who, like Marcion and Valentinus, was active in Rome. We are told in *Against Praxeas* that the eternal nativity of the Word (*Logos/Sermo*) took place before the start of the biblical creation of the world when God proclaimed, 'Let there be light.'

According to the words of the Old Testament Book of Proverbs, 'When he prepared the heaven, I [the Wisdom] was present with him' (Prov. 8:27), the *Logos*-Wisdom must be understood as instrumental in the making of everything (*Against Praxeas* 7). Tertullian clearly acknowledges duality in Christ, the man of flesh and blood, conceived and brought forth by the Virgin, and the spiritual Emmanuel or 'God-with-us', the incarnate divine Word (*Against Praxeas* 27.4–6).

> We see plainly the twofold state, not confounded but conjoined, in the one person Jesus, God and man ... The property of each nature is so wholly preserved that the Spirit [the divine quality] did, on the one hand, all things in Jesus suitable to the Spirit, such as miracles, mighty deeds and wonders; and the flesh, on the other hand, exhibited all the conditions that belong to it. It was hungry when tempted by the devil, thirsty when Jesus was with the Samaritan woman, it wept over Lazarus, suffered unto death and at the end actually died. (*Against Praxeas* 27.11)

Such a duality was stated again and again by Tertullian's forerunners, but he was the first to attempt rationally to correlate the two notions. To achieve this, he used or invented Latin neologisms that were to become crucial in the formulation of the doctrine of incarnation and trinitarian theology: person, substance, union, distinction and, ultimately, Trinity.

The theological argument turns on the relationship between God the Father and the Son or *Logos* of God. The Holy Spirit remains opaque in the background although the threesome character of the divinity is constantly stressed. 'I must everywhere hold one only substance in three coherent and inseparable persons' (*Against Praxeas* 12.7). What Father and Son have in common, the source of their unity, is what Tertullian calls 'substance'; the element that divides and distinguishes them is designated as 'person'. There are 'three persons, the Father, the Son and the Holy Spirit; they are three, not in condition, but in degree, not in substance, but in form, not in power, but in aspect, yet of one substance, of one condition, of one power, for God is one' (*Against Praxeas* 2.4). The link between them produces 'three coherent persons, who are distinct one from another' (*Against Praxeas* 25). Hence there is multiplicity in the one God who speaks in the plural in the Bible. Having his Son/Word next to him, and the Spirit linked to the Word, God uses phrases such as 'Let us make' and 'In our image', and declares that Adam has 'become as one of us' (*Against Praxeas* 12.4).

In sum, Christ as Son of God is depicted as completely divine and in his capacity as Son of Man completely human. Father, Son and Holy Spirit possess the same substance or essence, yet constitute three distinct persons in the mysterious unity of the Trinity. In a general and schematic way, Tertullian prefigures on his own the Councils of Nicaea (325) with the definition of the divinity of Christ, Ephesus (431) which asserted that the personality of the incarnate Son of God shared the one and only divine substance with the Father, and Chalcedon (451) that maintained that the Word made flesh possessed two natures, one divine and the other human.

Leaving aside the secondary issue of the perpetual virginity of Mary, it was only in one respect that Tertullian fell short of later orthodoxy. His vision of the Holy Trinity did not include co-equality. For him, and in this he was in agreement with all the ante-Nicene Church Fathers, there existed a difference of degree between the persons of the divine Triad. In one of his polemical writings Tertullian firmly opposed the co-eternity of the Son and endeavoured to demonstrate it in a fashion prefiguring Arius of the age of Nicaea.

> There was a time when neither sin, nor the Son co-existed with the Deity. Sin made God into a judge, and the Son made him into a Father . . . Just as he became Father through the Son and judge through sin, so God also became Lord by means of the creatures he had made in order to serve him. (*Against Hermogenes* 3)

Elsewhere, in conformity with earlier tradition, which echoed the New Testament, Tertullian presented Christ as inferior to God the Father. 'Whatever was the substance of the Word that I designate as a person, I claim for it the name of Son; and while I recognize the Son, I maintain that he is second to the Father' (*Against Praxeas* 7.9).

A little later, Tertullian added further clarification by defining the reason why and how the Father is differentiated from the Son: the Son is only a portion of the Father.

> It is not by division that they differ from one another, but by distinction. The Father is not the same as the Son because they are different in

the mode of their being. The Father is the entire substance, but the Son is a derivation and portion of the whole as he himself acknowledges: 'My Father is greater than I' (Jn 14:28). (*Against Praxeas* 9)

The Eucharist and Tertullian's ethics

Tertullian's comments about the eucharistic worship deserve to be noted. Debating with Marcion, he laid repeated emphasis on the reality of the body of Jesus that was denied by his opponent, and used the figure of bread to ridicule the Gnostic reasoning. If the body of Jesus was a phantom, how could it be symbolized by the real bread of the Eucharist? Besides, why was not the reality (the bread) rather than the phantom fixed to the cross?

> Having taken the bread and given it to his disciples, [Jesus] made it his own body, by saying, 'This is my body', that is, the figure of my body. However, there could have been no figure unless there was first a veritable body. An empty thing or phantom cannot be featured. If, however, as Marcion might say, [Jesus] pretended that the bread was his body, because he lacked true bodily substance, it follows that he must have given bread for us [and not his body]. But then it would suit very well Marcion's theory of a phantom body if bread had been crucified! But why call his body bread, and not rather a melon, which Marcion must have had in lieu of a heart! (*Against Marcion* 4.40)

The cheap concluding sarcasm apart, Tertullian's passage on the Eucharist makes a point of some interest. He expounds the phrase, 'This is my body', as signifying 'This is *the figure* of my body', a formula which appears to imply that for him the bread was a symbolical or allegorical substitute for the body of Jesus and not its mystical reality as later Catholic orthodoxy postulated.

In regard to moral conduct, Tertullian was an ethical rigorist throughout his whole Christian life. He probably felt the need to expiate for his lustful pagan youth in his student days in Rome. Even during his Catholic period he allowed only one penance after baptism, as did Hermas before him (Chapter 7, p. 173). He was also a severe critic of female fashion and beautification and instructed his wife either to remain a widow after his death or, if she really had to, marry only a Christian man. After he had become a Montanist, he outlawed second marriage altogether and qualified it as fornication. Not unlike Muslims, he wanted every woman to be veiled if they ventured outside the home. He held martyrdom obligatory and consequently forbade flight from persecution.

Finally, a glance at Tertullian's moral tractate, 'On Patience' (*De Patientia*) will permit us to end on a slightly humorous note. He opened the tractate by confessing that he considered himself the least qualified person to discourse on this particular virtue. His words were bound to 'blush' if confronted with his usual behaviour: 'I fully confess unto the Lord God that it has been rash enough, if not even impudent, for me to have dared compose a treatise on patience, for which I am totally unfit' (1.1). He remarked, in particular, that the desire for revenge was the greatest enemy of patience. 'If you avenge yourself too little, you will be mad; if too much, you will have to bear the burden. What have I to do with vengeance, the measure of which, through impatience of pain, I am unable to control?' (10).

So the short-tempered controversialist forced himself to compose a work of sixteen chapters in order to instruct himself how to become long-suffering and tolerant. In *The Guinness Book of Records*, *De Patientia* should be listed as the first 'Teach Yourself' book, anticipating the contemporary popular series by eighteen hundred years.

While Justin and Irenaeus were motivated by philosophical considerations in their elaboration of Christology and were equally concerned with the relationship between Father and Son and the redemptive role of Christ, Tertullian followed a different path and disliked philosophy. His saying, 'What has Athens to do with Jerusalem?' (*Prescription against Heretics* 7.9) has become proverbial. Being first and foremost a legally minded critic of Gnosticism, his main target was to demonstrate the authenticity of the human nature assumed in time by the eternally begotten *Sermo/Logos/*Word of the supreme Deity. The razor-sharp intellect of the lawyer combined with an outstanding mastery of language constitute a salient landmark along the path of the doctrinal evolution of Christianity, a landmark that strikes historians of ideas no longer disturbed by Tertullian's heretical 'aberrations' as admirable in the extreme.

CLEMENT OF ALEXANDRIA
(c. 150–c. 215)

Clement was born in the middle of the second century into a pagan family probably in Athens. His thorough education in Greek literature and philosophy is manifest: his writings are decorated with a multitude of quotations from close to four hundred classical writers and poets. After visiting Italy, Syria and Palestine, he settled in Alexandria, attracted there by Pantaenus, the head and probably founder of the *Didaskaleion*, the famous Catechetical School. Around 190, Clement succeeded his master and taught pupils grammar, rhetoric, Scripture, philosophy and religion. Of his many writings only a homily on Mark 10:17–31 ('Whether a rich man can be saved?') and an extensive tripartite work – 'The Exhortation to the Gentiles', 'The Pedagogue' and 'Miscellanies' or *Stromateis* – have survived in full. Clement liked to address himself to the cultured segment of the Christian society of Alexandria at dinner parties with a few glasses of wine (*Strom.* 7.16) in the form of 'urbane high-table conversations', to use the late Henry Chadwick's quiet Oxonian witticism (*The Early Church*, 1967, p. 99).

The persecution of the church by Septimius Severus compelled Clement around 202/203 to relinquish his position and flee from Egypt to Asia Minor, where he died about twelve years later without returning again to Egypt. Origen became his successor as head of the *Didaskaleion* in Alexandria.

Clement's overall aim was to reassure his insecure intellectual listeners and readers that neither Greek philosophy nor heretical Gnosticism constituted a real threat to the Christian faith. Pagan philosophers possessed and conveyed only morsels of the truth, and in any case, he maintained (echoing Justin), they had dishonestly appropriated the wisdom of the Hebrews without ever acknowledging their sources.

> Scripture calls the Greeks thieves of the philosophy of the Barbarians . . . They have imitated and copied the miracles recorded in our books [i.e. the Old Testament]; but we shall prove, besides, that they have investigated our teachings and falsified the most important of them – our writings being, as we have shown, older than theirs – concerning faith

and wisdom, Gnosis and science, hope and love, as well as repentance, continence and the fear of God. (*Strom.* 2.1, 1)

Elsewhere, in his characteristically sophisticated and literate style, Clement confirms this view by citing the sarcastic *bon mot* attributed to his contemporary, the Pythagorean philosopher Numenius from the city of Apamea in Syria, 'What is Plato, but Moses writing in Attic Greek?' (*Strom.* 1.22, 4).

Clement, a devoted Platonist, was convinced that the great Greek sage, no doubt with the help of the biblical prophets, had discovered the basic religious truths, the unity, transcendence and ultimate causality of God, the idea of the Trinity, life after death and the resurrection. He also held that the idea of God was implanted in man's soul in the form of a spark kindled by the divine *Logos* (*Strom.* 1.10, 4) and believed in the prophetic statement of Socrates about the coming just man who shall be 'scourged, shall be stretched on the rack, shall be bound, have his eyes put out; and at last, having suffered all evils, shall be crucified' (*Strom.* 5.14).

Clement's Christian Gnosis

Clement's main personal contribution to church doctrine lay in his representation of Christianity as the true Knowledge (*Gnosis*), which made the various forms of heretical Gnosticism look as mere dwarfs. His perception of the Gnosis springing from the *Logos*/Son of God was the same, though expressed in different words, as Justin's idea that Christianity was the only true philosophy (see Chapter 8, pp. 178–9). Even if not wholly original, his doctrine offered a powerful antidote against the fashionable theories of Valentinus and Marcion that were constantly circulating within the Alexandrian 'chattering classes'. He was not particularly interested in, indeed he shunned, the uncultured 'so-called orthodox', the doers of 'good works without knowing what they are doing' (*Strom.* 1.45, 6).

In Clement's view, the principal argument against the Gnostic heresy was that Christian faith, far from being childish stuff for illiterates, was the only genuine knowledge, the sole medium that could lead to the whole truth. Faith and Gnosis were reciprocal, or as he put it, 'Gnosis is characterized by faith; and faith is characterized by knowledge in a kind of divine mutual correspondence' (*Strom.* 2.4, 16, 2). In consequence, only a Christian, for whom believing was like breathing, could become a true Gnostic worthy of this name and capable of giving a reasoned exposition of what is known by faith.

> As without the four elements it is not possible to live, so no knowledge can be attained without faith. Faith is the support of truth. (*Strom.* 2.6, 31, 3)

> We, are those who are believers in what is not believed, and who are Gnostics for what is unknown; that is, Gnostics for what is unknown and disbelieved by all, but believed and known by a few; and Gnostics, not by words, by the appearance of works, but Gnostics in true contemplation. (*Strom.* 5.1, 5)

Clement's image of Jesus

As far as Christological speculation is concerned, Clement was not an innovator, though he certainly could produce a well-tailored definition: 'The Son is said to be the Father's face, being the revealer, through clothing himself with flesh, of the Father's character to the five senses' (*Strom.* 5.6). Needless to say, ultimately faith is rooted in Christ, the *Logos*, the sole source of real Gnosis, wisdom and truth.

> But we, who have heard from the Lord by the Scriptures that self-determining choice and refusal have been given to men, must rely on the infallible criterion of faith. Thus we shall show that the spirit is willing, since we have chosen life, and believed God through his voice. And he who has believed the *Logos* knows the matter to be true, for the *Logos* is truth, but he who has disbelieved what the *Logos* speaks, has disbelieved God. (*Strom.* 2.4, 1)

This brief sketch of Clement's input into the evolving thought of Christianity might aptly end with his description, typically diffuse, of the reciprocity of God the Father and his Son. It well illustrates Henry Chadwick's remark: 'At times it seems that Clement is almost anxious that nothing should be too clear' (*Early Christian Thought*, 1966, p. 31).

> The Gnostic has been summarily described. We must now return to the careful study of faith; for there are some that draw the distinction that

faith relates to the Son, and our knowledge to the Father. But they forget that, if one has to believe truly in the Son, that he is the Son, and that he came ... one must also know who is the Son of God. So knowledge is not without faith, nor faith without knowledge, as the Father is not without the Son; for as Father, he is the Father of the Son. And the Son is the true teacher regarding the Father. And to believe in the Son, we must know the Father, to whom the Son is related. Again, to know the Father, we must believe in the Son, for it is the Son of God who teaches; for from faith one goes to knowledge; by the Son the Father is revealed. The knowledge of the Son and the Father in conformity with the Gnostic rule – that which is truly Gnostic – is the understanding and discernment of the truth by the truth. (*Strom.* 5.1, 1–4)

Some peculiarities in Clement's teaching need to be signalled. Like Justin before him, he characterized the *Logos* as the cause not only of the creation, but also of his own incarnation. Eternally begotten by the Father, he begets himself in the fullness of time: 'Now the Word proceeds. He is the author of the creation; then he generates himself, when the Word becomes flesh in order that he may be seen (*Strom.* 5.3, 5). Clement's religion, like that of Justin, is an intellectual exercise far distant from the unconditional search of the Kingdom of God that characterized two hundred years earlier the message of Jesus.

ORIGEN (c. 185–254)

Origen, philosopher, theologian and biblical expert all in one, was the most versatile, exciting and influential Church Father in the early centuries of Greek Christianity. His life story was recorded by Eusebius (*EH* 6.1–8, 15–39). Origen was an extremely productive writer; St Jerome credits him with two thousand books (*Ad Rufinum* 2.22). Sadly, no more than a fraction of his original output has survived, sometimes only in Latin translation, the Greek original having disappeared. He is arguably the most outstanding witness of the development of Christological ideas in the pre-Nicene church.

In his teens, having lost his father, Leonides, victim in 202 of the persecution of the Christians by Septimius Severus, Origen was anxious to emulate him and, not unlike Ignatius of Antioch (see Chapter 7,

p. 166), he was fanatically keen to become a martyr himself. To stop the young man from doing something foolish, his mother hid his clothes and thus ensured that he stayed indoors. In a mad enthusiasm, at the age of eighteen he castrated himself, taking literally the hyperbolic counsel of Jesus that his followers should make themselves eunuchs. His practical reason may have been a desire for spiritual freedom in dealing with young female pupils and at the same time to evade 'any suspicion of vile imputations on the part of unbelievers' (*EH* 6.8).

His extreme devotion was translated into continuous fasting and, unlike Clement, he abstained from wine too. Origen slept very little and went everywhere barefoot. By the age of seventeen, this brilliant but eccentric pupil of Clement had already taken charge of the lower section of the Catechetical School in Alexandria. He used his salary and the money received from a rich patroness to provide a living for his widowed mother and six younger brothers. With the flight of Clement from Egypt in 202/3, the eighteen-year-old Origen became the headmaster of the school, which carried with it the supervision of the advanced pupils to whom he taught the Bible in addition to philosophy and literature. His ordination to the presbyterate in Caesarea by the Palestinian hierarchy met with the firm disapproval of Demetrius, the bishop of Alexandria, who considered Origen unfit for the priesthood on account of his castration. As a result, he was demoted from the directorship of the Alexandrian school, but he set up a similar institution in Caesarea, where he spent the rest of his life. He was severely tortured during Decius' persecution and died four years later in 254.

His literary productivity was considerably facilitated by his wealthy Alexandrian patron, Ambrose, who showed deep gratitude to Origen for converting him from Valentinian Gnosticism. We learn from Eusebius that at his own expense Ambrose provided Origen with a whole gang of assistants: 'shorthand-writers more than seven in number ... relieving each other regularly, and at least as many copyists, as well as girls trained in calligraphy' (*EH* 6.23, 2).

Origen, the biblical scholar

As a biblical expert, Origen was an innovator and approached the venerable Septuagint first and foremost as a textual critic. The scriptural knowledge of the Church Fathers who preceded him, such as Justin or Irenaeus, was limited to the old Greek translation of the Hebrew Bible. Origen also familiarized himself with the more recent Greek versions of the Old Testament by Aquila, Theodotion and Symmachus. Even more remarkably, he kept an eye open for new manuscript discoveries, such as a Greek Psalms scroll found during the reign of Antonius Caracalla (212–17) in a jar in the Jericho region, possibly in one of the Dead Sea Scrolls caves in the neighbourhood of Qumran. But, distinguishing himself from his predecessors, Origen also learned Hebrew and consequently was capable of debating on a par with Jews, both parties relying on the original text of the Bible.

His meticulous manuscript inquiry produced the famous Hexapla, an Old Testament presented in six columns. The first contained the Hebrew text written with Hebrew letters and the second the same text in Greek transliteration. They were followed by the critically annotated Septuagint and three and sometimes more different Greek versions. The Hexapla, large sections of which have been preserved in patristic quotations, is still an essential source in biblical research nearly eighteen centuries after Origen's time (published in two huge tomes by Frederick Fields in Oxford in 1875).

The Jesus image of Origen in *Against Celsus*

It is well nigh impossible to present a succinct assessment of Origen's impact on the unfolding of ideas concerning Christ and Christianity, so rich and varied is his literary legacy. A good insight into the Jewish and pagan polemics against Jesus and his followers may be gained from *Against Celsus*, Origen's rebuttal in eight books of a work composed around AD 180 by the Egyptian Platonist philosopher Celsus under the title *The True Doctrine*. Origen was commissioned by his patron, 'the God-loving' Ambrose, to produce a refutation and wrote it probably between 246 and 248, by which time Celsus was no longer alive.

Celsus began his diatribe by presenting first the anti-Christian arguments of an anonymous Jewish teacher of his time, and followed them up by his own criticism of the life and doctrine of Jesus, formulated from a Platonic point of view. Celsus valued only the philosophical arguments and made disparaging remarks about the quarrels and the disagreements between Jews and Christians. In his judgment, these were much ado about nothing, or to use his Greek figure of speech, a fight 'about the shadow of an ass', since in fact both parties agreed that a saviour had been promised by God, and the sole difference between them concerned whether this saviour had actually arrived or was still to come (*Against Celsus* 3.1).

Celsus attributes to his Jewish informer an unpleasant, indeed devastating caricature of Jesus and his early followers, a caricature that reappeared in the Talmud and formed the basis of the hostile early medieval Jewish biography the *Toledot Yeshu* or Life of Jesus (see P. Schäfer, *Jesus in the Talmud*, 2007). Dissecting and maliciously distorting the nativity narrative of Matthew, the Jewish critic contends that Jesus had invented the story of his royal and virginal birth. Far from being of the lineage of King David, he was in fact the adulterine son of a soldier named Panthera and a poor village woman, who was divorced by her carpenter husband for marital misbehaviour. In Origen's view, this was a calumny invented to explain away the miraculous conception of Christ by the Holy Spirit. Nevertheless, he added, it tangentially confirmed the Christian claim that Joseph was not the father of Jesus (*Against Celsus* 1.32).

Origen's handling of the virginal conception of Jesus constitutes a new chapter in Christian apologetics. His predecessors, Justin and Irenaeus, insisted on the total reliability of the Septuagint text of Isaiah 7:14, 'the virgin (*parthenos*) shall conceive and bear a son', reproduced in Matthew 1:23, and accused the Jews of falsifying their own (Greek) Bible by changing 'virgin' (*parthenos*) to 'young woman' (*neanis*). But Origen, the textual scholar, knew that to stand up to Jews, he had to demonstrate his knowledge of the Hebrew Isaiah where, as has been pointed out in connection with Justin (see p. 187), the term employed was *'almah* (another word for 'young woman') and not *betulah* ('virgin' in Hebrew). In the process, he came up with a surprising claim and asserted that the Hebrew of Deuteronomy 22:23–4 proved that *'almah* actually meant virgin:

> If a *young woman*, who is a *virgin*, is betrothed to a man, and a man finds her in the town and lies with her ... you shall stone them to death, the *young woman* because she did not cry for help in the town and the man because he violated his neighbour's wife. (*Against Celsus* 1.34)

The trouble with this explanation is that no known text of the Hebrew Deuteronomy supports Origen's thesis. The word used there is not *'almah* as in Isaiah, but *na'arah* (a further term meaning 'young woman' or 'girl'). So, short of assuming that Origen was deliberately bluffing in the presumption that none of his readers would be able to check the Hebrew text, his statement must be attributed to an uncharacteristic lapse of memory. All the same, even if he was in fact mistaken, he made plain that in scholarly debate the Hebrew text of the Old Testament had to be used, especially when disputing with Jews. In short, instead of displaying a pre-Nicene point of view in which the Greek Septuagint was invested with divine authority, Origen testified to a post-Renaissance attitude and chose to argue from the original Hebrew text of the Bible.

Yet a few pages later Origen fell back on a primitive third-century type of biology when he endeavoured to demonstrate the possibility of virginal conception in the natural world. He asserted that in the animal kingdom some females could have young without intercourse with a male. This is the way naturalists of that age imagined vultures reproduced themselves (*Against Celsus* 1.37; see also Tertullian, *Against the Valentinians* 10). Also, after pouring ridicule on the Greek myths of divine impregnation both in the heroic age, Danae conceiving of Zeus, and in more recent times, Plato's mother being impregnated by Apollo (*Against Celsus* 1.37), Origen contemptuously discarded Celsus' sarcastic argument that since the Olympian gods always lusted after high-ranking and beautiful females, none of them would have fallen for Mary, who was poor and of humble descent, and was not even pretty (*Against Celsus* 1.39).

The Christian doctrine about the divinity of Jesus provoked further mockeries from Celsus' Jewish ally. For him, the miracles of the Gospels did not indicate Jesus' heavenly origin, but were to be ascribed to sorcery. Jesus learned magic during the years he spent in Egypt and used these tricks to persuade his gullible followers that he was God (*Against Celsus* 1.28).

Elsewhere we are told that the Jesus of the Gospel deduced his divine pedigree from the fact that he saw a bird flying towards him when he was bathing with John the Baptist in the river Jordan and heard a heavenly voice calling him Son of God. However, the Jew remarked, this event is without corroboration as there were no other witnesses (*Against Celsus* 1.41). In his refutation of Celsus, Origen interpreted the descent of the dove as the fulfilment of the verse of Isaiah 48:16, 'And now the Lord sent me and his spirit' and treated it as the heavenly proof of the divine election of Jesus (*Against Celsus* 1.46).

Celsus' Jew attributes the recruitment of the circle of the apostles to Jesus attracting to himself 'ten or eleven infamous men, the wickedest tax-collectors and sailors'. He wandered about with them begging in a disgraceful and importunate manner. How could such a lot, devoid even of primary education, persuade multitudes to believe in them (*Against Celsus* 1.62)? Origen sarcastically retorted that Celsus could not count even as far as twelve, and also while as a rule sceptical about the New Testament, he was willing to accept its message as true when it suited him, namely when the evangelist spoke of the apostles' lack of learning (*Against Celsus* 1.68).

Celsus did not tell in detail the rest of the Gospel story, but he made reference to the betrayal of Jesus and his crucifixion, events which were incompatible, in his view, with someone who declared himself God. A genuine God, he maintained, would not have needed to escape to Egypt (*Against Celsus* 1.66). He would not have allowed his associates to betray him, nor would he have tolerated the disgrace of being arrested and crucified by his enemies (*Against Celsus* 2.9, 31). On the contrary, a true God would have destroyed his accusers and his judge, or simply would have walked away from the cross and disappeared (*Against Celsus* 2.35, 68). As for the Christian retort that these happenings had to occur because Jesus had predicted his betrayal, suffering and death, Celsus replied that those prophecies were invented by the apostles (2.13), for if they had been authentic, Judas, and Peter, would not have dared inform on Jesus or deny him (*Against Celsus* 2.19).

For Celsus the resurrection was not worthy of belief. It was based on the testimony of a hysterical woman (Mary Magdalene) and of a man who was deluded by Jesus' magic (Peter). In fact, they were both victims of hallucination (*Against Celsus* 2.55, 70). Here Origen opted for an easy way of escape and reminded his readers that according to the Gospels more than two people had visions of Jesus. Moreover, since some of the apparitions of Jesus occurred in daytime they could not be hallucinations. Hallucination, according to the science of

Origen's age, was a nocturnal phenomenon that affected people with an unbalanced mind or those suffering from delirium.

Furthermore, according to Celsus, the choice of witnesses renders the resurrection story even more unbelievable. Instead of celebrating his pretended triumph over death before the world at large, and especially instead of putting to shame and humiliating his enemies, Jesus chose to appear as a phantom exclusively to the members of his confraternity. The testimony of outsiders would have been more convincing (*Against Celsus* 2.59–60, 70; 3.22). This objection remains unanswered.

In his final criticism Celsus suggests that, although they confess the opposite, Christians adhere to a polytheistic religion. In addition to the one God in heaven, 'they worship to an extravagant degree this man who appeared recently, yet they think it is not inconsistent with monotheism' (*Against Celsus* 8.12). Here Origen maintains that Christians worship only the supreme God, but that according to their faith there are two 'existences' (*hypostaseis*), the Father and the Son, in the substance of this one God.

The Jesus image of Origen

Compared to the style of the Christological discussions offered by earlier Church Fathers, *Against Celsus* now and then gives an astonishingly modern impression. The same cannot, however, be said of Origen's famous manual of theology, *The First Principles* (*Peri Archôn*), composed in Alexandria in the 220s. It typifies a hundred years in advance the great abstruse theological debates of the fourth century.

The Preface of *The First Principles* exhibits a patent anti-Gnostic slant: God is the Creator of the material world; he inspired both the Old and the New Testaments; the *Logos*/Son was pre-existent and his incarnation was real. Using the credal language, Origen asserts that Christ was truly born, truly suffered and died and rose from the grave.

> There is one God who created and arranged all things, who made exist all things when nothing existed ... This righteous and good God, Father of our Lord Jesus Christ, gave the Law, the Prophets and the Gospels, he who is the God of the apostles and of the Old as well as the

New Testament. Then again, Christ Jesus, he who came to earth, was begotten of the Father before every created thing. After he had minis-tered to the Father in the foundation of all things ... in these last times ... was made man ... although he was God ... he remained what he was, God. He took himself a body like our body ... was born of a virgin and the Holy Spirit ... Suffered in truth and not merely in appearance, and truly died our common death. Moreover he truly rose from the dead, stayed with his disciples and was taken up to heaven. (*Principles* Preface 4)

Mixing the Bible with Platonic philosophy, Origen postulated a cre-ation from all eternity because the omnipotent and infinitely good God could not exist without objects on which he could exercise his goodness (*Principles* 1.2, 10). So before making the universe as it is known to man, God brought into existence a world of perfect spirits. Some of these spirits, including the pre-existent human souls, turned away from him, and as a punishment they were exiled into matter (*Principles* 2.8–9). The next eternal happening was the creation of the world by God through his Son/*Logos*. This *Logos*/Word, God's rela-tion to the lower orders, was also entrusted with the revelation of all the divine mysteries. In time, bodily incarnation endowed the *Logos* with human nature in addition to his divine nature (*Principles* 1.2, 1). To formulate this doctrine, Origen invented the concept of *The-anthrôpos* or 'God-man' (Homily on Ezekiel 3.3). He may have also devised Mary's title of *Theotokos* or 'God-bearer', which was to become the slogan at the time of the Council of Ephesus in 431 in the fight against Nestorius, for whom Mary was the mother not of God, but only of the man Jesus.

Like his forerunners, contemporaries and successors, Origen strug-gled with the complexities of the trinitarian theology. He held that only the Father, the source of the divine, was fully entitled to be called '*the* God' (*ho Theos*). The Son, the recipient of divinity from the Father, deserved to be known only as 'God' (*Theos*) with no definite article (Commentary on John 2.1–2, 12–18). In Origen's view Father and Son were both almighty, but the Son was the outcome of the limitless power of the Father (*Principles* 1. 2, 10). Both were great, but the Father was greater as he gave a share of his greatness to the only-begotten Son, the firstborn of all the creation (*Against Celsus* 6.69).

In short, Origen, like all his precursors, ended up with a subordinationist understanding of the relation between the Father and the Son. The Father came first; the Son was the 'second God' (*deuteros Theos*); he took the lower place of honour after the Master of the universe (*Against Celsus* 5.39; 6.61; 7.57), but Father and Son were one in power though they differed in their *hypostasis* or Person (*Against Celsus* 8.12).

> The Father is the primary goodness; as the Son is born of it, he who is called the image of the Father in everything, one can surely say that he is also the image of his goodness. (*Principles* 1. 2, 13)

> It is obvious that we, who maintain that even the sensible world is made by the Creator of all things, hold that the Son is not mightier than the Father, but subordinate. And we say this because we believe him who said, 'The Father who sent me is greater than I' (Jn 14:28). (*Against Celsus* 8.15)

As for the Holy Spirit, Origen declared that it was associated with the Father and the Son in honour and dignity, but could not make up his mind whether it was begotten and could be called Son of God (*Principles* Preface 4).

But while in some way insinuating quasi-equality between the divine persons – the 'image' (Son/*Logos*) of God is of the same dimension as God (*Against Celsus* 6.69) – Origen could not help grading them: the Father was the source of the Son and the Spirit. The Father operated, the Son administered, and the Holy Spirit was the divine postman who delivered the gifts (*Principles* 1.3, 7). Like the *Logos* of Philo of Alexandria (*Heir of Divine Things* 206), Christ the Son was, as it were, 'midway between uncreated nature and that of all created things' (*Against Celsus* 3.34). We are still in the dogmatic nebulosity of the pre-Nicene era. Arius, the catalyst crystallizing what he considered orthodoxy, was still to come.

One cannot fairly summarize Origen's contribution to Christian thought without alluding to his peculiar but admirable doctrine of universal restoration (*apokatastasis pantôn*), an expression he borrowed from the Acts of the Apostles 3:21. It is clearly set out in *The First Principles*:

> The end of the world and the consummation will be given to us, when everyone will have been subjected to the punishment of his sins. At that

time, which only God knows, everyone will have paid his debt. We think that God's goodness will recall all his creation after subjecting and overcoming his enemies. (*Principles* 1.6, 1)

This theory of restoration is built on the double foundation of the goodness of God and the final verse of the eschatological synthesis of St Paul in 1 Corinthians, 'When all things are subjected to him, the Son himself will also be subjected to the one who put all things in subjection under him, so that God may be all in all' (1 Cor. 15:28).

Origen's idea seems to be that at the very end salvation will be extended to all, even the wicked and the damned, even to the devils and Satan. Without universal salvation God would not be 'all in all'. Origen saw in hell fire a purifying instrument, and as a logical thinker, he could not reconcile the idea of eternal punishment, the unquenchable flames of Gehenna, with the infinite goodness of a loving Deity.

The power and the originality of the teaching of Origen were bound posthumously to inspire conflicting attitudes towards the great Alexandrian. His admirers worshipped him and his critics subjected his name to vituperation. Attacks on Origenism, on ideas some of which he actually held and others erroneously attributed to him, continued for centuries. The chief points of controversy concerned the doctrine of the pre-existence of souls, Origen's purported rejection of the literal sense of the Bible in favour of allegorical exegesis and his denial of the eternity of hell. Origenism was condemned at the Council of Alexandria in 400 and again by another Council in Constantinople in 543, at which the emperor Justinian inspired an edict denouncing Origen's errors. The same Council and the one held in 649 at the Lateran pilloried Origen together with the arch-heretics Arius, Nestorius and Eutyches. The greatest mind and the most creative thinker of early Christianity was anathematized by the church of second-rate followers.

10

Nicaea

Eusebius of Caesarea, Arius and Constantine

The Christological debate witnessed no significant innovation in the second half of the third century, so one may directly advance from Origen (d. 254) to the period immediately preceding the first major watershed in the history of Christian theology, the Council of Nicaea in 325. A seismic doctrinal upheaval shook the church of Egypt in 318. The disturbance was triggered by a public disagreement between Alexander, bishop of Alexandria, and one of his presbyters by the name of Arius. They clashed on the subject of the nature of Christ and his relation to God the Father. The discord spread like wildfire and upset the Greek-speaking church, to the utmost annoyance of the peace-seeking Constantine, the first Roman emperor who, instead of being an enemy of Christianity, decided to act as its patron.

After his victory over his rival Maxentius at the battle at the Milvian Bridge in 312, Constantine put an end to the persecution of the church. Bearing in mind the potential impact of the large body of Christians on the realization of his ultimate aim, civic peace in the empire, he took an immediate interest in ecclesiastical matters and was determined to intervene and settle the conflict in Egypt. Perhaps the easiest way to explain and illustrate the situation is through a sketch of the state of play prior to the outbreak of the war of words in Alexandria and a summary presentation of the Christological ideas generally prevailing in the church at the start of the fourth century.

THE CHRISTOLOGY OF EUSEBIUS OF CAESAREA

The doctrinal stance adopted by the famous historian, theologian and ecclesiastical politician Eusebius, bishop of Caesarea (*c.* 260–339), offers a characteristic example. He was in fact the last influential mouthpiece of the pre-Nicene point of view concerning the relationship between God the Father and God the Son, occupying the middle ground between the vague common opinion reformulated with radical clarity by the presbyter Arius and the revolutionary conservative view created by Alexander, bishop of Alexandria, and his young secretary (and later successor), St Athanasius. They both attended the Council of Nicaea, but Athanasius, still being only a deacon and not a presbyter or bishop, was not allowed to take an active part in the synod debates. This did not stop him from exercising considerable influence in the corridors.

Eusebius was a devout follower and champion of Origen even if he did not altogether embrace his understanding of the Father–Son conundrum. Like all the earlier Church Fathers, he was unwilling to place Father and Son on an equal footing in the divine hierarchy. Relying on New Testament terminology borrowed from Paul and John, Eusebius agreed to grant the titles 'Lord' and 'God' to the Son or *Logos*/Word as long as it was recognized that the Son was ranked after and stood below the Father. He used the metaphor of the triple gate of a church for a visual illustration of the Son's and the Holy Spirit's secondary status in comparison with the Father.

> The whole cathedral is adorned with one huge gateway, consisting of the praise of our sovereign Lord, the one only God. On both sides of the Father's supreme power are supplied the secondary beams of the light of Christ, and the Holy Ghost. (*EH* 10.4, 65)

In his view, the pre-eminence of the Father was beyond question. Eusebius persistently avoided before, during and after the council the key word ('consubstantial') introduced in Nicaea that implied co-equality between Father and Son. For him, the chief characteristic of the Father was that he was unbegotten and supreme. The Son, on the other hand, was the minister of the Father. The primitive Christological title *pais* (Servant), attested since the Acts of the Apostles, resurfaced again in Eusebius (*Demonstratio Evangelica* 5.11, 9). Guided by Origen, Eusebius held the Son to be a 'second God', subject to the dominating Lord, God the Father. The *Logos*/Son was the 'Craftsman' (the Greek Demiurge), the tool of the creation in the hand of the Father (see Chapter 7, p. 175), or the 'helmsman' directing the boat in faithful obedience to his Father's instructions (*Demonstratio Evangelica* 4.5, 13).

Eusebius distanced himself from Origen (and anticipated Arius) when he assigned the Son's coming into being to a single act of the Father's will rather than to an eternal, continuous and necessary begetting, inherent to the nature of the Father. In his mind, the birth of the Son was a unique event, not a perpetually lasting process. It followed therefore that the Son was not co-eternal with the Father. In turn, the Holy Spirit was left hovering in the shadowy background of eternity.

Ever since the New Testament era and throughout the next two centuries, equivocation about the divinity of Christ was standard, yet one point was certain. The Son was not recognized as having *quite* the same dignity and standing as God the Father, and the same judgment applied *a fortiori* to the Holy Spirit. Eusebius, like the whole pre-Nicene church, held a subordinationist view, asserting a degree difference within the same sacred class in regard to the persons of the Trinity.

Since philosophy had been introduced into the Christian religious discourse with Justin, Irenaeus, Clement of Alexandria and Origen, the evolving belief in the divinity of Jesus had to contend with various kinds of objection. For Jews like Trypho and pagans like Celsus, the opponents of Justin and Origen, a 'God Jesus', distinct from the Supreme God, was hardly compatible with the idea of monotheism – indeed, it directly contradicted it. As for the Docetists, Gnostics and Platonic philosophers of the type of Marcion and Valentinus, an incarnate God, a divine being who was also a man, implied an unacceptable, not to say unthinkable mingling of the supreme Spirit with the inferior and degrading matter. Christian apologists could easily overcome this second objection with the help of the biblical doctrine that a single Creator God was responsible for both the spiritual and the material worlds, and that in consequence the fundamentally good matter did not constitute an obstacle to the incarnation or humanization of the Deity.

However, the threat of ditheism, let alone tritheism – faith in two or three divine beings – did not go away. Since the reality of Jesus as a born, crucified, dead, buried and bodily resurrected Son of God was an indispensable part of the Christian religion, the theory that Christ was nothing but a different manifestation of the one and only Supreme God did not provide an acceptable alternative or a solution to the dilemma. Justin's Trypho argued along these lines and various early Christian heretics toyed with the same idea. The champions of 'Monarchianism' – monarchy signifying a single ruler – maintained that the divinity of Jesus was nothing real, but a shadow cast over his human personality by divine power. The heresy called 'Sabellianism', named after the third-century Roman, or possibly Libyan, theologian Sabellius, professed that the Father, Son and Holy Spirit simply represented three different aspects of the one and the same God. The 'Patripassians', a branch of Sabellianism, held that when it came to suffering, God the Son was just another name for God the Father. We have seen in Justin's *Dialogue* that in their debate Trypho embraced a Sabellian stance; it was the one and only God of Israel who revealed himself to the Patriarchs and to Moses under different guises or modalities of an Angel or a flame of fire, but not in diverse realities. For Justin, on the other hand, the veritable subject of divine revelation described in Scripture as the Angel of the Lord or the fire in the burning bush was none other than the pre-incarnate Christ/Son or Word/*Logos* of God (see Chapter 8, pp. 184–6).

The only escape route away from the trap of suspected formal polytheism was by denying equal status to the various persons within the single Deity. Only the Father was fully *the* God; the Son was only the *second* or lower God, and the Holy Spirit, something vague and unspecific, floating somewhere below the Son. Such a standpoint entailing gradation – the term *hupodeesteros* ('inferior') is applied to the Son by Origen (*Against Celsus* 8.15) – was the conviction prevailing in the entire pre-Nicene church. It was already foreshadowed by the most advanced theological thinkers of the New Testament, Paul and John (1 Cor. 15:24–8; Jn 14:28).

This general view or *opinio communis*, held by all the leading lights in the church for two and a half centuries and reinforced and expressed with unquestionable clarity by Arius and his allies, was challenged, attacked and finally overturned by a minority of bishops with the backing of the emperor at the Council of Nicaea. Under the influential leadership of the two Alexandrians, Alexander and Athanasius, and with the even more weighty support of Constantine, the first ecumenical assembly of the church inaugurated an entirely new era in Christian thinking.

ARIANISM

To come down to tangible realities, as has already been stated, in 318 a big clerical row broke out in Alexandria, the capital of speculative thinking in the Christian church in the late third/early fourth century. Arius, a priest of Libyan origin, who was in pastoral charge of the Baucalis quarter of the city, advanced sharply formulated teachings regarding Christ and his relation to God the Father which infuriated his bishop Alexander.

Nothing much has survived of the writings of Arius apart from excerpts from his letters and quotations from of a poetic work entitled *Thaleia*. In fact, all our information comes from citations of Arius by his arch-enemy Athanasius and other unsympathetic historians of a later vintage. He appears to have been a clear-minded man, who set out to bring to a head and sort out once and for all the current confusions and uncertainties of the theological terminology concerning Christ. Wittingly or unwittingly Arius stirred up a hornets' nest.

He was determined to put the *Logos*/Son firmly in his place. He ranked him unquestionably after and below the limitlessly powerful and pre-existent Father. The Son was not ungenerated, nor was he a part of the unbegotten Father. Unlike the Father who was unoriginated, the Son had an origin. The Son was nothing prior to his birth. He was definitely not a portion of the unbegotten Father; the Father produced him from non-existence (*Letter to Eusebius of Nicomedia*, cited in Epiphanius, *Panarion* 69.6). The coming into existence, the begetting and the birth of the Son did not arise from necessity, but were due to a decision of the Father, who was responsible for his generation. The Son did not exist in any shape or form before that moment: in short, he came after the Father and, consequently, he was not eternal. To claim that the Son was of the same substance as the Father would make of him a detached part of God, but God, being indivisible, cannot be partitioned, reduced in size or diminished

(*Letter to Alexander*, cited by Athanasius, *De Synodis* 16; *Letter to the Emperor*, cited in Epiphanius, *Panarion* 69.6).

Nothing is unclear in Arius' thinking, which is perhaps not a true desideratum in theology, nor is anything left unsaid. The Son is a creature, a *ktisma*; he is 'not true God ... he is God only in name' (quoted in Athanasius, *Orationes contra Arianos* 1.6). In his poetic work, *Thaleia*, Arius declared, 'The number One (the Monad, the Father) always existed, but the number Two (the Dyad, the Son) did not exist before it was brought into existence.' Father, Son and Holy Spirit formed 'a Trinity of unequal glories' (quoted in Athanasius, *De Synodis* 15).

Arius' bishop, Alexander of Alexandria, held exactly the opposite views. God was always Father; the Son was not a creature or a product derived from non-existence, but as the true *Logos* of God he was begotten from all eternity, *homoios kat' ousian*, that is to say, of a substance like that of the Father (*Letter to all the Bishops*, cited in Socrates Scholasticus, *Ecclesiastical History* 1.6). To force Arius to recant, Alexander presented him with a confession formula of orthodoxy, but the recalcitrant priest refused to sign it. The obvious consequence of the head-on clash was excommunication. In 319 Arius and all like-minded people were declared anathema, excluded from the communion of believers.

The crafty Arius promptly sought the assistance and protection of two highly influential bishops, both bearing the name of Eusebius: Eusebius of Nicomedia in Bithynia and Eusebius of Caesarea in Palestine. Both were sympathetic to his ideas. What is more, both were court prelates who had the emperor's ear, and shared a common dislike for Alexander of Alexandria. Predictably episcopal councils were summoned – one in Nicomedia and another in Caesarea – which declared Arius and his associates blameless. Naturally, complete confusion ensued.

THE COUNCIL OF NICAEA

It was then Constantine's turn to intervene. Having defeated the rival emperor Licinius, he conquered and set out to pacify the eastern half of his territories in 324. So he wrote letters to the quarrelling Alexander and Arius, and entrusted their delivery to Ossius, bishop of

Cordova, Constantine's chief adviser in ecclesiastical matters, who was to play a lead part in the drama in Nicaea. For the emperor, who not only was not a theologian but at that time not even a baptized Christian, the conflict appeared as the outcome of a frivolous argument between disputatious clerics. He decided therefore to put an end to the squabble at once, and in no uncertain terms ordered Alexander and Arius to effect instant reconciliation.

> For as long as you continue to contend about *these small and very insignificant questions*, it is not fitting that so large a portion of God's people should be under the direction of your judgment, since you are thus divided between yourselves. (Quoted in Eusebius, *Life of Constantine* 2.71)

Alexander and his sympathizers were unwilling to accept that the eternal generation of the Son of God was a triviality and consequently refused to revoke the excommunication of Arius. They went even further and in a council promptly assembled in Antioch early in 325, which was attended by Ossius but to which the supporters of Arius were not invited, they reaffirmed their position, and in addition they rather unwisely excommunicated Eusebius of Caesarea, the patron of Arius and a confidant of the emperor. Naturally Constantine was not pleased and was determined to sort out the chaos without further delay. He convoked and financed an assembly of the universal church, the first ever ecumenical council of Christianity. It was planned to take place in Ancyra (present day Ankara), but was later relocated to Nicaea in Bithynia (today's Iznik in Turkey on the eastern shore of Lake Iznik) as it was more convenient for the emperor and for the bishops arriving from the west. The excommunications of Eusebius of Caesarea and of Arius were cancelled and both attended the council.

Of the 1,800 invited bishops some 200 to 300 attended. Eusebius puts the number at 220. They were almost exclusively from the Greek East. The western church sent only six representatives: in addition to the Spanish Ossius of Cordova, the episcopal president of the council and Constantine's chief adviser on Christian affairs, the bishops of Gaul, Calabria, Pannonia and Carthage. There were two further priestly envoys representing Pope Sylvester of Rome, who did not turn up in person. The westerners were not greatly interested in this Oriental row, which they probably did not fully understand.

CHRISTIAN BEGINNINGS

The emperor solemnly opened the council on 20 May 325 with a Latin speech, which was immediately translated into Greek, and the proceedings went on till July. No direct records of the debates have been preserved, but it is clear that they were principally focused on the main topic of discord among the Greek churches: the nature and status of God the Son in relation to God the Father. It seems that the arguments were so ambiguous and ill-defined that with their own special slants applied here and there both parties could give their consent to the proposals with or without further glosses or mental reservations.

Eusebius of Caesarea endeavoured to pre-empt the argument and win over the whole assembly for his pro-Arian tendency by putting forward his own credal formula. Its text is contained in his *Letter to the Church of Caesarea*, written immediately after the council. Its section relating to Jesus, with no i's dotted or t's crossed, reads as follows:

> We believe ... in one Lord Jesus Christ the Word of God, God from God, Light from Light, Life from Life, only-begotten Son, first born of all creation, begotten from the Father before all ages, through whom all things have come into being, who was incarnate for our salvation; and took up citizenship among men, and suffered and rose the third day and went up to the Father and will come again in glory to judge the living and the dead. (Quoted in Athanasius, *De Decretis*)

At the end the anti-Arians, led by the Alexandrian duo, Alexander and Athanasius, came up with the magic formula applied to Christ/Son of God/*Logos*. They asserted that the Son was of the same substance or essence (*ousia*) as the Father, in one word he was *homoousios* or consubstantial with God.

The expression was not in common theological use before the council. It was not the brainchild of Alexander or Athanasius either, although they undoubtedly thought of the Father and the Son in terms of eternal correlation. Alexander spoke of the Father as the Father of the always-present Son on account of whom he is called Father. The Father engendered the only-begotten Son not in an interval, nor from nothing, but eternally and from his own substance (*Letter to all the Bishops* 3). Athanasius, in turn, defined the Son as the supremely perfect issue of the Father, the only Son who is the perfect image of the Father (*Contra Gentes* 46.59–61). Neither of them thought of using *homoousios* as a trump card. Arius sarcastically summarized his opponents' creed as nothing more than a statement that God was eternal, the Son was eternal and the Son was from God himself (quoted in Epiphanius, *Panarion* 69.6).

Where did the word *homoousios* come from? Since Adolf von Harnack (*The History of Dogma*, 1898) it is customary to argue that it was the president of the council, the Spanish bishop Ossius, who ushered in the omnipotent term. But the hypothesis is not without difficulties. The corresponding Latin *consubstantialis* does not seem to be attested in any of the surviving pre-Nicene sources. It is pointed out that in Tertullian's teaching, Father, Son and Spirit are said to be 'of one substance, status and power because they are one God' (*'unius substantiae et unius status et unius potestatis quia unus Deus'*, *Against Praxeas* 2.4). From this it is deduced that *homoousios* might be the Greek translation of *'unius substantiae'*, 'of one substance'. But this theory is shaky for two reasons. Latin sources of the period usually do not translate the Greek word, but transliterate it in Latin characters. In short, they give a transcribed *homoousios* rather than translate it as *'consubstantialis'*. For instance, Hilary of Poitiers' Latin version of the Nicene Creed has 'of one substance with the Father, in Greek *homoousios*' (*'unius substantiae cum Patre quod Graece dicunt homoousion'*). It is also questionable whether the 'heretic' Tertullian would have been chosen as their model by the orthodox bishops of Nicaea.

The most satisfactory, if somewhat surprising, solution seems to be that in a way it was Arius himself who brought the concept to the notice of the fathers of Nicaea. In a letter written in 320, and aimed at persuading Alexander of Alexandria to cancel his excommunication, Arius introduced the adjective *homoousios* into the Christological debate only to discard it straightaway as unsuitable for expressing the orthodox doctrine. It had already been rejected as inapplicable to God the Son by a third-century bishop of Alexandria, Dionysius (see Athanasius, *De Sententia Dionysii*, 18.2). In turn, Arius objected to the use of *homoousios* on account of its apparently Manichaean origin. Here is the relevant extract:

> [The Father] has begotten the only-begotten Son . . . [he] produced him not in appearance, but in truth, giving him existence by his own will . . . a perfect creature (*ktisma*) of God . . . a product (*poiêma*) of the

Father . . . no[t], as Mani taught, a *consubstantial* part (*meros homoou-sion*) of the Father. (Quoted in Athanasius, *De Synodis* 16)

All the same, with the novel notion of consubstantiality, Arius unwittingly presented his opponents with a standard around which they could rally and utter the battle cry embroidered on it: the Son is '*homoousios*'. So, together with the phrase 'only-begotten of the Father, that is of the substance of the Father', the untraditional term was inserted into the Creed on the insistence of the anti-Arian bishops, and all the members of the Council were ordered to sign the full text together with the four appended anathemas condemning the specific theses of Arius.

The English translation of the Creed of the Council of Nicaea, with the specifically anti-Arian sections printed in italics, runs as follows:

We believe in one God Father Almighty Maker of all things, visible and invisible.

And in one Lord Jesus Christ the Son of God, begotten as only-begotten of the Father, *that is of the substance of the Father*, God of God, Light of Light, true God of true God, begotten not made, *consubstantial with the Father*, through whom all things came into existence, both things in heaven and things on earth; who for us men and for our salvation came down and was incarnate and became man, suffered and rose again the third day, ascended into heaven, is coming to judge the living and the dead.

And in the Holy Spirit.

But those who say,
(1) 'There was a time when he did not exist',
and (2) 'Before being begotten he did not exist',
and that (3) 'He came into being from non-existence',
or who allege that (4) 'The Son of God is another hypostasis *or* ousia, *or alterable or changeable',*
these the Catholic and Apostolic church declares anathema.

Thus with this revolutionary new formula Jesus was recognized as fully divine and the truth about the essence of Christianity was finally defined . . . or was it? The words were slippery enough for the astute Greek pro-Arian clerics to find a way around their understanding, yet piously mark their consent with an Amen. In any case, because of the endorsement of the Creed by the emperor, refusal to sign the decree became a highly risky business as criminal penalties threatened dissenters (see Fergus Millar, *The Emperor in the Roman* World, 1977, p. 598). So the prelates, who had no intention of getting on the wrong side of Constantine, found a way to fall into line. Both Eusebius of Nicomedia and Eusebius of Caesarea added their signatures to the document – the latter decided to do so, as he put it, 'for the sake of peace' – though they were definitely unhappy with the anathemas. Even Arius, who attended the council by order of Constantine, equivocated: he signed the Creed, but appended glosses to it. According to Eusebius of Caesarea, out of 220 fathers of the Council only two Libyan bishops remained obstinate. They were deposed and exiled. Arius, too, was dispatched to Illyria, no doubt on account of his critical glosses (see Sozomenus, *Ecclesiastical History* 1.21, 4–5). However, a couple of years later they all were allowed by the emperor to return and were reinstated in their offices. Constantine's letter to Arius is quoted by the church historian Socrates Scholasticus (*Ecclesiastical History* 1.25; see Millar, *Emperor in the Roman World*, p. 599):

> Constantinus Magnus Victor Augustus to Arius. Your Integrity was long since informed that you should come to my camp so that you may have the pleasure of the sight of us. I am surprised that this has not been done immediately. Therefore take the public transport and make haste to come to our camp, so that by gaining our goodwill and consideration you may be able to return to your native city. May God preserve you, beloved one. Given on 27 November [327].

Arius presented a written acceptance of the Nicene Creed, but on his return to Alexandria he was not welcomed by Athanasius, who in the meantime had inherited Alexander's episcopal office (Socrates Scholasticus, *Ecclesiastical History* 1.26–7).

Despite the decision obtained by the victorious pro-*homoousios* party, the Christological struggle continued for over half a century. At times the Arian opposition triumphed, as may be deduced from Jerome's ironical remark after the Council of Ariminum (Rimini) in 359, 'The whole world groaned and was surprised to find itself Arian' ('*Ingemuit totus orbis et Arianum se esse miratus est.*' *Altercatio Luciferiani et orthodoxi* 19 in Migne, *Patrologia Latina* 23, 181B).

The end came in 381 when Emperor Theodosius I made the profession of Arianism illegal. Thereafter consubstantiality carried the day and went on to feed the kind of philosophically based dogmatic evolution that was launched at Nicaea. The theologians carried on to underplay the image of Jesus of Nazareth, the itinerant preacher who in days long gone by was crisscrossing the rocky paths of Galilee, preaching the imminent arrival of the day of the Lord, and to overstress instead his shiny new identity as the consubstantial, co-eternal and co-equal only-begotten Son of God the Father. The Council of Ephesus in 431 specified that Christ's divinity and humanity were rooted in one single divine person, and the Council of Chalcedon in 451 condemned the monophysite heresy, and proclaimed that the single divine person of the *Logos* made flesh harboured two separate natures, one divine, the other human. For the monophysites, the divine nature of the incarnate Christ completely absorbed the human nature. But as the great twentieth-century theologian Karl Rahner noted, crypto-monophysitism has always dominated Christian religious thought (K. Rahner, 'Current Problems in Christology', 1961). In plain words, the nebulous speculative circle closed itself around a figure perceived, despite the vocal admission of his humanity, more and more as a transcendent God rather than a real human being of flesh and blood. From Nicaea until the age of the Reformation and beyond, the Christian religion was primarily governed by intellectual and indeed philosophical assent, by adherence to the orthodox dogma of the church.

By contrast, the piety preached and practised by Jesus, consisting of a total surrender of the self to God and a constant search for his Kingdom through limitless devotion and trust, was relegated to a supporting role. Charismatic Christianity was mostly kept away from the limelight, although occasionally it surfaced in a restricted form and not only in fringe movements like Montanism or millenarism or Quakerism, but also with ecclesiastical approval in the popular cults of miracle-working saints and Madonnas, and in more recent times and on a larger scale in the various branches of Christian Pentecostalism.

Christianity, as generally understood in the light of its Gentile development, is focused not on the genuine existential spiritual legacy of the Jewish Jesus, but on the intellectual acceptance of the divine Christ and his superhuman existence within the mystery of the church's triune Godhead.

I I

From Charisma to Dogma –
A Bird's Eye View

The aim of this study has been to follow step by step an amazing journey depicting the antecedents and the beginnings of Christianity. The investigation started with a sketch of charismatic Judaism from Moses to Jesus, necessary for the understanding of the religious message of the first-century Galilean rural holy man, and ended with his solemn proclamation by the universal church under the watchful eyes of the Roman emperor Constantine the Great as the eternal Son of God, consubstantial with the Father. All that remains now is briefly to recapitulate the evolutionary process and assess its significance.

The unfolding of the great adventure of the proper Christian beginnings in the spiritual history of mankind naturally falls into two unequal phases: the short Jewish opening period from AD 30 to *circa* 100 is followed by the Gentile development through the second, third and early fourth centuries up to the Council of Nicaea in 325 and beyond. The Synoptic Gospels and the first twelve chapters of the Acts of the Apostles, supplemented by the Judaeo-Christian tractate the Didache, correspond to the essentially Jewish stage, in which the message preached by Jesus and his original disciples was addressed to Jewish circles in Galilee, Judaea and Samaria. However, in many of the New Testament writings one can already detect efforts by Jewish authors to readjust the message to the requirements of a new Graeco-Roman pagan audience, the ultimate recipients of the apostolic teaching. Thus a gloss inserted in the Gospel of Mark (7:19) cancels for all church members the Mosaic dietary rules. Also the person ultimately responsible for the crucifixion, Pontius Pilate, is whitewashed in the story of the trial of Jesus in order to render the gospel account less unpalatable to listeners or readers in the Roman Empire, many of whom were filled with hostility towards the rebellious Jews in the final quarter of the first century AD.

THE JEWISH PHASE

The religion reconstructed from the Synoptic Gospels, a renewed version of prophetic-charismatic Judaism of the Old Testament age, is wholly devoted to preparing Jesus' Jewish followers for entry into the imminently expected Kingdom of God. In this eschatologically inspired religion attention is focused not on Jesus, but on God. For example, in the Synoptic Gospels Jesus never calls himself 'the Son of God'; he does not even appear to be keen on being designated as 'the Messiah'. His followers see in him a man of God, the miracle-working prophet and sage of the end time. The religion of Jesus demands no intellectual acrobatics, but a total self-surrender to God, the caring and loving Father in heaven.

Jesus' march at the head of his flock towards the promised Kingdom was brutally halted by the cross, but his death on Golgotha was not the end of the story. According to the Acts of the Apostles, having recovered from their shock a few weeks later at the first Pentecost, his disciples proclaimed Jesus as 'a man attested by God with deeds of power, wonders and signs' (Acts 2:22), that is to say, a charismatic prophet, who was recognized also as the crucified, risen and glorified Messiah.

The Didache or The Teaching of the Twelve Apostles is the only early literary witness of this exclusively, or almost exclusively, Jewish-Christian outlook outside the books of the New Testament. It is a unique landmark of post-apostolic non-Gentile Christianity, with a doctrine uninfluenced by Paul or John. It provides also a precious keyhole through which we can perceive a primitive portrait of Jesus. He is never described as the 'Son' or the 'Son of God'. In the Didache, as in the Acts of the Apostles, Jesus simply remains 'the Servant', who ministers to God and men as instructed by heaven. The Didache supplies the only comparative control mechanism outside the New Testament for assessing the advances of Christological speculation in the early Gentile church.

Still within the context of the Jewish religion, the casting of Jesus in a new mould began with Paul. Addressing a pagan audience ignorant of Judaism, he had first to explain to his public who Jesus was before transmitting his teaching to mostly low-class Greek men and women. As a result, it was the messenger rather than the message that became the subject of Pauline Christianity. Jesus' inspirational exhortation encouraging Jews to change their way of life was replaced by an expository exercise aimed not at God the Father, but at Christ, and at the significance of Jesus' death and resurrection, which Paul interpreted as atonement for sin and source of universal salvation. The Apostle of the Gentiles elevated the Prophet-Messiah of the Synoptic Gospels and Acts to the rank of a triumphant Son of God, a status granted to him by God after his resurrection. *Qua* Son of God, he was soon expected at his Second Coming to be revealed as the Lord of the living and the resurrected dead. Paul transformed the God-centred religion of Jesus into a Christ-centred Christianity.

A further major change occurs in the Fourth Gospel. While its historico-geographical setting remains Galilee and Judaea, its readership and atmosphere, like those of the authentic Pauline letters, are not Jewish, but Greek. The hero of the Fourth Gospel is no longer the Galilean holy man of the Synoptic Gospels and the Acts of the Apostles, but a celestial Saviour in temporary exile on earth. Jesus is the Son of God, not just metaphorically as Jews would understand the idiom, but the incarnate eternal Word or *Logos*, sent into the world to redeem not just the Jews, but the whole of mankind. By using the *Logos* terminology of Plato and Philo of Alexandria, the author of the Johannine Prologue opens a new mystical-philosophical perspective which is to leave a deep imprint on future Christian thinking in subsequent centuries. John has made the charismatic prophet Jesus wholly unrecognizable by lifting him from earth to heaven and from time to eternity. Nicaea would be unimaginable without the Graeco-Roman conceptual core of the Fourth Gospel.

THE GENTILE PHASE

The new theological thinking along exclusively Gentile-Christian lines was initiated by the Apostolic Fathers in the first half of the second century. The trend is characterized by the reshaping of the image of Jesus following non-Jewish patterns, by the allegorical interpretation of the Greek Old Testament, which Christianity took over from Hellenistic Judaism, and by a growing theological, as distinct from concrete historical, anti-Judaism. Such a transfer of a doctrinal message from one civilization into another, known as acculturation, may be successful if it avoids a fundamental distortion of the original ideas. But if it fails to do so, as seems to have been the case of Gentile Christianity, it is bound to produce a slant unpalatable to Judaeo-Christians and disturbing for historians.

The new perception within Christianity first manifests itself in the Epistle of Barnabas. Written for Gentile Christians, it shows the influence of Paul and John, but displays in addition a typically strong anti-Jewish animus. The Jesus of Barnabas, like the Jesus of John, has ceased to be Jewish; indeed, 'the Jews' are his enemies. He is simultaneously the earthly Son of Man and the eschatological as well as celestial Son of God, who participated in the work of creation long before his descent to earth. Although he is not expressly designated as 'God', his human body is seen as a deliberately assumed concealment of his underlying divine character, for without such a benevolent protective disguise he would have been unable to accomplish his task as no one could have contemplated his face and have survived.

The first major hurdle, before which Paul stopped short and John hesitated, was swiftly crossed by the Apostolic Fathers; they mustered enough courage to call Jesus God. Ignatius played the lead role in regularly employing the term, but the author of 2 Clement was no less brave and Pliny the Younger's Christians singing hymns to Christ as God testified to the usage of the title on the popular level. Some of the traditional terms, such as 'Son of God', 'High Priest' and 'Saviour' were further refined. The Son was seen in the company of God the Father since before the ages and in Jesus it was God who manifested himself in human form. Moreover, the incarnate Christ was real and not just apparent as the Docetist heretics maintained. The true humanity of the Redeemer is emphasized in Ignatius' rudimentary historical creeds, and under Pauline inspiration salvation is directly linked to the blood of Christ. A definitely non-Jewish theology, inspired by Hellenic ideas, is taking shape by the middle of the second century.

At approximately the same time, in the wake of Plato, Philo of Alexandria and their offspring, the Prologue of John, a philosophical concept finds its way into Christianity through the Epistle to Diognetus. There the revelation of truth is accredited to the Word/*Logos* portrayed as the divine 'Craftsman', the Demiurge, who was God's instrument in the creation of the world.

The first stage of Gentile-Christian development was distinguished by the launching of new Graeco-Roman ideas alien to Judaism but without any serious attempt at rationalization and systematization. The Apostolic Fathers affirmed that the incarnate Christ was God and man, but did not try to show how those two notions could hang together. The apologists, theologians and Bible interpreters from the mid-second to the mid-third century took charge of this task and sufficiently advanced its solution to allow the Council of Nicaea in 325 to come up with a revolutionary solution.

A Christian theology formally linked to Platonic philosophy, a system totally different from Jesus' non-speculative mode of thinking, was born with the apologist Justin Martyr. A professional philosopher and expert in the Greek Bible, he was well equipped to offer a rational defence of beleaguered Christianity against the persecuting Roman state and Trypho's self-confident Judaism. A philosophically grounded *Logos* doctrine borrowed from the Johannine Prologue was Justin's main contribution to the development of Christian thought. It led to the final elevation of Jesus to divine status with eternal pre-existence and participation in the work of creation. Furthermore, not only was Justin the first to elevate Christianity to the pedestal of the only true philosophy, he was also the pioneer of a systematic presentation of the fulfilment of biblical prophecy in Christ, in particular regarding the prediction by Isaiah of what Christians understood as a virginally conceived Emmanuel or 'God with us'. The importance of charisma manifest in the power revealed through the action of Christian exorcists was still stressed in the mid-second century.

Anti-Gnostic polemics furnished a further opportunity to formulate Christian thought in regard to the incarnate Christ's genuine humanity. Marcion and Valentinus were refuted along the philosophical-theological path by Justin, Irenaeus, Tertullian and Origen. In a different style, deploying the typological exegesis of the Old Testament, Melito of Sardis marshalled a moving poetic imagery for demonstrating the authentic corporeality of the redeeming Son of God. Thus were foreshadowed the major themes of the later Christological debate in the church: the simultaneous divinity and humanity of Christ, the problem of his divine and human natures, and his temporality and eternity.

The overall evaluation of Christology as affecting the various aspects of theological thinking in the church made further giant steps thanks to Irenaeus in the late second century. Christian belief was profoundly affected by his anti-Gnostic affirmation of the validity of the Old Testament in the redemptive 'economy' of biblical history, and in his idea of inverse 'recapitulation' of the roles of Adam and Eve in Jesus and Mary, perfecting Paul's vision in the Epistle to the Romans.

Further progress in proving the genuineness of the human nature assumed by the eternally begotten *Logos*/Word or *Sermo*/Discourse of the supreme Deity was achieved by Justin, Irenaeus and Tertullian within the framework of anti-Gnostic apologetics. At the same time all the main concepts of fourth- and fifth-century theology moved to the foreground of reflection: person, substance, union, distinction, and Trinity. The definition of Christianity as perfect *Gnosis*, the knowledge embodying every other true form of wisdom, supplied – thanks to a major insight of Clement of Alexandria – a fresh form of neutralization of Gnosticism.

By the mid-third century the summit of pre-Nicene Christian thought was reached with Origen, the sage whose work epitomized all existing philosophical, scriptural and theological knowledge. He produced the most advanced defence of the figure of Jesus against Jewish and pagan attacks, as well as a considerably polished *Logos* doctrine in regard to the creation. Creation was necessary from all eternity because of the infinite goodness of God, which could not express itself without spiritual or material objects to love. So the Son/*Logos* through whom God created and who as Word was God's instrument of revelation had also to be generated from eternity. Moreover, his assumption of a real human nature enabled him to become the revealer of the Father to humans, and through his suffering, death and resurrection to achieve their redemption.

Logical thinking on the part of Origen, starting from the idea of limitless divine goodness, which required creation, leads also to the universality of salvation. It was to encompass not only the righteous, but also (after due expiatory suffering) the wicked, the damned and Satan. Without the closing of hell, God, the loving Father of the universe, with his Son next to him, cannot truly be all in all. The logic of the teaching of Jesus supports Origen's conclusion, but another New Testament tradition visibly contradicts it, envisaging a last judgment with eternal damnation opposed to everlasting salvation. At the end, probably wrongly, the champions of a fiery perpetual Gehenna had the upper hand.

By the start of the fourth century the church, although not yet wholly ready, was pressed to make up her mind. The divine quality of Christ, the Son of God, his closeness to God the Father, his pre-existence and role in the creation of the universe were generally agreed by all the leading thinkers. They also agreed on a lack of equality between the Father and the Son. Even Origen was adamant: the Father was '*the* God', the Son was only 'God'; he was 'second God', placing himself below the Master of the universe. Every single mouthpiece of Christian tradition from Paul and John to Origen firmly held that the Father was in some way above the Son. The ante-Nicene church was 'subordinationist' and did not believe in the full co-equality and co-eternity of Father, Son and Holy Spirit.

The issue came to a head with Arius and his crystal-clear formulation of early Christian 'orthodoxy' in regard to Christ's relation to God, a theological orthodoxy which echoed the New Testament. In Arius' creed, the eternal and unbegotten Father stands above all and exists without origin. The first-begotten Son has an origin. He was generated by a decision of the Father, not out of necessity, and before that decision he did not exist. He is not truly eternal. He is God in name only and not in full reality.

Theologians have often vilified Arius. His doctrine has been characterized as 'a mess of presumptuous theorizing ... a lifeless system of unspiritual pride and hard unlovingness' (H. M. Gwatkin, *Studies in Arianism*, 1900, p. 274). It is therefore refreshing to discover that the late Canon Maurice Wiles, former Oxford Regius Professor of Divinity, had the courage to publish an article, 'In Defence of Arius' (1962), in which he endeavoured to rehabilitate to a certain extent the despised heresiarch. He called Arius' teaching 'an inadequate account of the fullness of Christian truth', but, he added, the same conclusion 'is true to some degree of every Christian theologian, ancient or modern'.

All the evidence we possess of nearly three centuries of theological thinking on the subject would suggest that, after some give and take, a creed quietly voicing Arius' ideas would have commanded a substantial majority among the bishops assembled at Nicaea. Yet the dogma of consubstantiality (*homoousia*) triumphed, no doubt thanks to the clever politicking of the party led by Bishop Alexander and Athanasius, which succeeded in winning over to their side the all-powerful emperor. After some ebbing and flowing, belief in the consubstantiality of the Son with the Father ultimately prevailed in the fourth-century church, and the profession of this belief became the authenticating stamp of post-Nicene Christianity.

Yet it is impossible to ignore the colossal difference between the Christ concept of Nicaea and the Christology that preceded the council. The idea of consubstantiality never occurred to any of the leading representatives of Christianity prior to 325; it would have indeed sounded anathema. By contrast, after 325 the claim of inequality between Father and Son amounted to heresy. After that surprising doctrinal volte-face, membership of the church primarily depended on adherence to the Nicene Creed. Intellectual assent to dogma gained precedence over the heart's openness to charisma urged by the historical Jesus.

At the end of this journey, those readers who wonder where they now stand should remember that in the sixteenth century the rediscovery by Renaissance scholars of the ancient sources of classical civilization forced Christians to return to the Bible for a revitalization and purification of their faith. This revolution first created Protestantism, but subsequently spread over the whole spectrum of the churches. It would seem that by now it has reached, or will soon reach, a stage when a fresh revival will be called for, a new 'reformation', zealous to reach back to the pure religious vision and enthusiasm of Jesus, the Jewish charismatic messenger of God, and not to the deifying message Paul, John and the church attributed to him.

Postscript

I would like to end with two afterthoughts. The first is a teaser: what would the historical Jesus of Nazareth have made of the Council of Nicaea? A legend preserved in the Babylonian Talmud (Menahot 29b) may suggest an answer.

According to this legend, Moses, on his arrival in heaven, heard God praising the wisdom of the future Rabbi Akiba and obtained permission from the Almighty to attend a lecture given by him. Sitting in the back row of the classroom, he listened attentively to the eloquent exposition of the teacher and the lively questions of the audience, but had no idea what the argument was about until Akiba, hard pressed by a clever pupil, declared that his words were patently true as they repeated a *halakhah le-Mosheh mi-Sinai*, doctrine given by God to Moses on Sinai.

Would Jesus, hearing about his consubstantiality with the Father, be as perplexed as Moses of the legend was when confronted with the rabbinic interpretation of his Law?

However, to finish on a serious note, let me quote Goethe's moving lines, echoing Judaism, Jesus and pre-Nicene Christianity as well as the theology of Islam:

> *Jesus fühlte rein und dachte*
> *Nur den Einen Gott im Stillen;*
> *Wer ihn selbst zum Gotte machte*
> *Kränkte seinen heil'gen Willen.*

> Jesus felt purely and thought
> only of the One God in silence;

Whoever makes him into God
does outrage to his holy will.

('Poems of West and East' – *West-östlicher Divan*, 1819)

Select Bibliography

CLASSICAL SOURCES

Josephus, Flavius, *The Jewish War* – *The Jewish Antiquities* – *The Life* – *Against Apion*, in *Josephus with an English Translation* I–IX, by H. St J. Thackerary and L. H. Feldman, Loeb Classical Library, London/New York, 1926–65.

Philo of Alexandria, in *Philo with an English Translation* I–X, by F. H. Colson and G. H. Whitaker, Loeb Classical Library, London/New York, 1962.

Pliny the Younger, *Letters* I–II, by B. Radice, Loeb Classical Library, London/New York, 1969.

Tacitus, Cornelius, *Annals with an English Translation*, by J. Jackson, Loeb Classical Library, London/New York, 1937.

CHARISMATIC JUDAISM

Blenkinsopp, J., *A History of Prophecy in Israel*. SPCK, London, 1984.

Bokser, B. M., 'Wonder-Working in the Rabbinic Tradition: The Case of Hanina ben Dosa', *Journal for the Study of Judaism* 16 (1985), pp. 42–92.

Büchler, A., *Types of Jewish-Palestinian Piety from 70 B.C.E. to 70 C.E.: The Ancient Pious Men*. Jews' College Publications, London, 1922.

Gerth, H. H. and Wright Mills, C. (eds.), *From Max Weber: Essays in Sociology*. Routledge, London, 1991.

Green, W. S., 'Palestinian Holy Men: Charismatic Leadership and Rabbinic Tradition', *Aufstieg und Niederand der römischen Welt*, ed. W. Haase, II. 19, 2 (1979), pp. 619–47.

Grey, R., *Prophetic Figures in Late Second Temple Jewish Palestine: The Evidence from Josephus*. Oxford University Press, New York, 1993.

Jaffé, D., 'L'Identification de Jésus au modèle du Hasid charismatique galiléen', *New Testament Studies* 55 (2009), pp. 218–46.

Safrai, S., 'Jesus and the Hasidim', *Jerusalem Perspective* 42–4 (1994), pp. 3–22.

Sanders, E. P., *Judaism: Practice and Belief, 63 BCE–66 CE*. SCM, London, 1992.

Schürer, E., Vermes G. et al. (eds.), *The History of the Jewish People in the Age of Jesus Christ* I–III. T. & T. Clark, Edinburgh, 1973–87.

Segal, J. B., 'Popular Religion in Ancient Israel', *Journal of Jewish Studies* 26 (1976), pp. 1–22.

Taylor, J., ' "Roots, Remedies and Properties of Stones": The Essenes, Qumran and Dead Sea Pharmacology', *Journal of Jewish Studies* 60 (2009), pp. 226–44.

Vermes, G., 'Hanina ben Dosa', *Journal of Jewish Studies* 23 (1972), pp. 28–50; 24 (1973), pp. 51–64.

—, *Jesus the Jew*. Collins, London, 1973/ SCM Classics, 2001.

—, *Jesus in the Jewish World*. SCM, London, 2010.

—, *The Complete Dead Sea Scrolls in English*. Penguin, London, 2011.

—, 'Jewish Miracle-workers in the Late Second Temple Period', in M. Brettler and A. J. Levine (eds.), *Jewish Annotated New Testament*. Oxford University Press, New York (2012).

Weber, M., *Ancient Judaism*. Free Press, Glencoe Ill., 1952.

JESUS

Alexander, P. S., 'Jesus and the Golden Rule', in J. H. Charlesworth et al. (eds.), *Hillel and Jesus*. Fortress, Minneapolis, 1997, pp. 363–88.

Allison, D. C., *Jesus of Nazareth: Millenarian Prophet*. Fortress, Minneapolis, 1998.

Barr, J., 'Abba isn't Daddy', *Journal of Theological Studies* 39 (1988), pp. 28–47.

Bauckham, R. J., *Jesus and Eyewitnesses: The Gospels as Eyewitness Testimony*. Eerdmans, Grand Rapids, 2008.

Benedict XVI/J. Ratzinger, *Jesus of Nazareth, Part 2, Holy Week*. Catholic Truth Society, London, 2011.

Borg, M. J., *Jesus, A New Vision: Spirit, Culture and Discipleship*. HarperSanFrancisco, San Francisco, 1987.

—, *Jesus in Contemporary Scholarship*. Trinity Press International, Valley Forge, 1994.

Bousset, W., *Kyrios Christos: A History of the Belief in Christ from the Beginning of Christianity to Irenaeus*. Abingdon, Nashville, 1970.

Brown, R. E., *The Birth of the Messiah*. Doubleday, New York, 1999.

Bultmann, R., *Primitive Christianity in its Contemporary Setting*. Thames & Hudson, London, 1956.

Casey, M., *From Jewish Prophet to Pagan God: The Origins and Development of New Testament Christology*. James Clarke, Cambridge, 1991.

—, *From Jesus of Nazareth: An Independent Historian's Account of his Life and Teaching*. T. & T. Clark, London, 2010.

Charlesworth, J. H., *Jesus within Judaism*. SPCK, London, 1989.

Charlesworth, J. H. (ed.), *Jesus' Jewishness: Exploring the Place of Jesus in Early Judaism*. Crossroad, New York, 1991.

—, *Jesus and the Dead Sea Scrolls*. Doubleday, New York, 1993.

—, *Jesus and Archaeology*. Eerdmans, Grand Rapids, 2006.

—, *The Historical Jesus: An Essential Guide*. Abingdon, Nashville, 2008.

Charlesworth, J. H. and Johns, L. L. (eds.), *Hillel and Jesus*. Fortress, Minneapolis, 1997.

Collins, A. Y. and Collins, J. J., *King and Messiah as Son of God*. Eerdmans, Grand Rapids, 2008.

Collins, J. J., *The Scepter and the Star: The Messiah of the Dead Sea Scrolls and other Ancient Literature*. Doubleday, New York, 1995.

Crossan, J. D., *The Historical Jesus: The Life of a Mediterranean Jewish Peasant*. HarperSan Francisco, San Francisco, 1991.

Davies, S. L., *Jesus the Healer: Possession, Trance, and the Origins of Christianity*. SCM, London, 1995.

Dunn, J. D. G., *Jesus and the Spirit*. SCM, London, 1975.

—, *Jesus Remembered*. Eerdmans, Grand Rapids, 2003.

Ehrman, B. D., *Jesus: Apocalyptic Prophet of the New Millennium*. Oxford University Press, New York, 1999.

Evans, C. A., *The Routledge Encyclopedia of the Historical Jesus*. Routledge, New York/London, 2010.

Flusser, D. and Notley, R. S., *The Sage from Galilee: Rediscovering Jesus' Genius*. Eerdmans, Grand Rapids, 2007.

Frederiksen, P., *From Jesus to Christ: The Origins of the New Testament Image of Jesus*. Yale University Press, New Haven/London, 1988.

Hahn, F., *The Titles of Jesus in Christology*. Lutterworth Press, Cambridge, 1969.

Harvey, A. E., *Jesus and the Constraints of History*. Duckworth, London, 1982.

—, *Strenuous Commands: The Ethic of Jesus*. SCM, London, 1990.

Hengel, M., *The Son of God: The Origin of Christology and the History of Jewish-Hellenistic Religion*. SCM, London, 1976.

—, *The Charismatic Leader and his Followers*. T. & T. Clark, Edinburgh, 1981.

Jeremias, J., *The Prayers of Jesus*. SCM, London, 1977.

Käsemann, E., *Essays on New Testament Themes*. SCM, London, 1964.

Klausner, J., *Jesus of Nazareth: His Times, his Life and his Teaching*. Allen & Unwin, London, 1925.

Lee, B. J., *The Galilean Jewishness of Jesus: Retrieving the Jewish Origins of Christianity*. Paulist Press, New York, 1988.

Mason, S., *Josephus and the New Testament*. 2nd edn, Hendrickson, Peabody, 2003.

Meier, J. P., *A Marginal Jew* I–IV. Doubleday, New York/Yale University Press, New Haven, 1991–2009.

Moore, D. F., *Jesus, An Emerging Jewish Mosaic: Jewish Perspectives, Post-Holocaust*. T. & T. Clark, New York/London, 2008.

Neusner, J., *A Rabbi Talks with Jesus*. McGill-Queens University Press, Montreal, 2000.

Otto, R., *The Kingdom of God and the Son of Man*. James Clarke, Cambridge, 2010.

Perrin, N., *Rediscovering the Teaching of Jesus*. SCM, London, 1967.

Sanders, E. P., *Jesus and Judaism*. SCM, London, 1985.

—, *The Historical Figure of Jesus*. Penguin, London, 1993.

Schäfer, P., *Jesus in the Talmud*. Princeton University Press, Princeton, 2007.

Schweitzer, A., *The Quest of the Historical Jesus*. SCM, London, 2000.

Smith, M., *Jesus the Magician*. Gollancz, London, 1978.

Taylor, J. E., *The Immerser: John the Baptist within Second Temple Judaism*. Eerdmans, Grand Rapids, 1997.

Theissen, G., *Sociology of Early Palestinian Christianity*. Fortress, Minneapolis, 1978.

Theissen G. and Merz, A., *The Historical Jesus: A Comprehensive Guide*. SCM, London, 1998.

Twelftree, G. H., *Jesus the Exorcist*. Mohr Siebeck, Tübingen, 1993.

—, *Jesus the Miracle Worker*. InterVarsity, Downers Grove, 1999.

Vermes, G., *Jesus the Jew*. Collins, London, 1973/ SCM Classics, 2001.

—, *Jesus and the World of Judaism*. SCM, London, 1983.

—, *The Religion of Jesus the Jew*. SCM, London, 1993.

—, *The Changing Faces of Jesus*. Penguin, London, 2001.

—, *Jesus in his Jewish Context*. SCM, London, 2003.

—, *The Authentic Gospel of Jesus*. Penguin, London, 2004.

—, *Who's Who in the Age of Jesus*. Penguin, London, 2005.

—, *Jesus: Nativity – Passion – Resurrection*. Penguin, London, 2010.

—, *Searching for the Real Jesus*. SCM, London, 2010.

—, *Jesus in the Jewish World*. SCM, London, 2010.

Wright, N. T., *The Resurrection of the Son of God*. Fortress, Minneapolis, 2003.

Zeitlin, I. M., *Jesus and the Judaism of his Time*. Polity Press, Oxford, 1988.

NASCENT CHRISTIANITY

Aune, D. E., *Prophecy and Early Christianity in the Mediterranean World*. Eerdmans, Grand Rapids, 1983.

Barrett, C. K., 'The Interpretation of the Old Testament in the New', in P. R. Ackroyd and C. F. Evans (eds.), *The Cambridge History of the Bible*. Cambridge University Press, Cambridge, 1970, pp. 412–53.

Broadhead, E. K., *Jewish Ways of Following Jesus: Redrawing the Religious Map of Antiquity*. Mohr Siebeck, Tübingen, 2010.

Charlesworth, J. H., *The Bible and the Dead Sea Scrolls. Vol. III: The Scrolls and Christian Origins*. Baylor University Press, Waco, 2008.

Crossan, J. D., *The Birth of Christianity*. HarperCollins, New York, 1998.

Haenchen, E., *The Acts of the Apostles: A Commentary*. Westminster, Louisville, 1971.

Horbury, W., *Jewish Messianism and the Cult of Christ*. SCM, London, 1998.

Hurtado, L.W., *Lord Jesus Christ: Devotion to Jesus in Early Christianity*. Eerdmans, Grand Rapids, 2003.

Juel, D., *Messianic Exegesis: Christological Interpretation of the Old Testament in Early Christianity*. Fortress, Philadelphia, 1988.

Knight, J., *Christian Origins*. T. & T. Clark, London, 2008.

Lüdemann, G., *Early Christianity in Traditions in Acts*. SCM, London, 1989.

—, *The Acts of the Apostles: What Really Happened in the Earliest Days of the Church*. Prometheus, Amherst, 2005.

Sanders, E. P. (ed.), *Jewish and Christian Self-Definition. Vol. I: The Shaping of Christianity in the Second and Third Centuries*. SCM, London, 1980.

Vermes, G., *Scrolls, Scriptures and Early Christianity*. T. & T. Clark, London, 2005.

PAUL

Bauckham, R. J., *God Crucified: Monotheism and Christology in the New Testament*. Pater Noster, Carlisle, 1998.

—, *Jude and the Relatives of Jesus in the Early Church*. T. & T. Clark, London, 2004.

Boyarin, D., *A Radical Jew: Paul and the Politics of Identity*. University of California Press, Berkeley, 1997.

Davies, W. D., *Paul and Rabbinic Judaism*. Fortress, Philadelphia, 1980.

Dunn, J. D. G., *The Theology of Paul the Apostle*. Eerdmans, Grand Rapids, 1998.

Goodman, M., *Mission and Conversion: Proselytizing in the Religious History of the Roman Empire*. Clarendon, Oxford, 1994.

Hengel, M., *The Pre-Christian Paul*. SCM Press, London, 1991.

Hengel, M. and Schwemer, A. M., *Paul between Damascus and Antioch*. SCM Press, London, 1997.

Loisy, A., *Paul, Founder of Christianity*. Prometheus Press, Tonbridge, 2002.

Lüdemann, G., *Paul, The Founder of Christianity*. Prometheus Books, Amherst, N.Y., 2002.

Meeks, W., *The First Urban Christians: The Social World of the Apostle Paul*. Yale University Press, New Haven, 1983.

Sanders, E. P., *Paul, the Law and the Jewish People*. SCM Press, London, 1977.

—, *Paul and Palestinian Judaism*. SCM Press, London, 1977.

Segal, A. F., *Rebecca's Children: Judaism and Christianity in the Roman World*. Harvard University Press, Cambridge, Mass., 1986.

Sherwin-White, A. N., *Roman Society and Roman Law in the New Testament*. Clarendon, Oxford, 1963.

Stendahl, K., *Paul Among Jews and Gentiles and Other Essays*. Fortress, Philadelphia, 1976.

Theissen, G., *The Social Setting of Pauline Christianity: Essays on Corinth*. Fortress, Minneapolis. 1982.

Tomson, P. J., *Paul and the Jewish Law*. Fortress, Philadelphia, 1990.

Vermes, G., *Scripture and Tradition in Judaism*. Brill, Leiden, 1961.

Wiles, M., *The Divine Apostle: The Interpretation of St. Paul's Epistles in the Early Church*. Cambridge University Press, Cambridge, 1967.

JOHN

Ashton, J., *Understanding the Fourth Gospel*. Oxford University Press, Oxford, 1991.

—, *Studying John: Approaches to the Fourth Gospel*. Clarendon, Oxford, 1998.

Ashton, J. (ed.), *The Interpretation of John*. 2nd edn, Continuum, London, 1998.

Barrett, C. K., *The Prologue of St. John's Gospel*. Athlone Press, London, 1971.

—, *The Gospel According to John: An Introduction with Commentary and Notes on the Greek Text*. 2nd edn, SPCK, London, 1978.

Boismard, M. E., *Le Prologue de Saint Jean*. Cerf, Paris, 1953.

Brown, R. E., *The Gospel According to John I–XII*. Doubleday, New York, 1966, 1970.

Bultmann, R., *The Gospel of St. John: A Commentary*. Blackwell, Oxford, 1971.

Culpepper, R. A., *Anatomy of the Fourth Gospel*. Fortress, Minneapolis, 1983.

—, *The Gospel and Letters of John*. Abingdon, Nashville, 1998.

Dodd, C. H., *The Interpretation of the Fourth Gospel*. Cambridge University Press, Cambridge, 1965.

Feuillet, A., *Le Prologue du quatrième évangile*. Desclée de Brouwer, Paris, 1968.

Hengel, M., *The Johannine Question*. SCM, London, 1989.

Kittel, G., 'Lego/Logos': 'Word and Speech in the New Testament', *Theological Dictionary of the New Testament* IV. Eerdmans, Grand Rapids, 1967, pp. 100–136.

Loisy, A., *Le Quatrième Évangile*. Emile Nourry, Paris, 1921.

Schnackenburg, R., *The Gospel According to St John* I–III. Seabury Press, New York, 1980–82.

POST-APOSTOLIC CHRISTIANITY: GENERAL LITERATURE

Altaner, B., *Patrology*. Herder/Nelson, Freiburg/Edinburgh-London, 1960.

Barnard, L. W., *Studies in the Apostolic Fathers and in their Background*. Blackwell, Oxford, 1966.

Bousset, W., *Kyrios Christos: A History of the Belief in Christ from the Beginning of Christianity to Irenaeus*. Abingdon, Nashville, 1970.

Carleton Paget, J., *Jews, Christians and Jewish Christians in Antiquity*. Mohr Siebeck, Tübingen, 2010.

Chadwick, H., *The Early Church*. Penguin, London, 1967, rev. edn 1993.

—, *The Church in Ancient Society: From Galilee to Gregory the Great*. Oxford University Press, New York, 2002.

Cross, F. L. and Livingstone, E. A. (eds.), *The Oxford Dictionary of the Christian Church*. 3rd edn, Oxford University Press, Oxford, 1997.

Crossan, J. D., *The Birth of Christianity*. HarperCollins, New York, 1998.

Daniélou, J., *The Theology of Jewish Christianity*. Darton, Longman & Todd, London, 1964.

Dunn, J. D. G., *The Partings of the Ways between Christianity and Judaism and their Significance for the Character of Christianity*. SCM, London, 1991.

Dunn, J. D. G. (ed.), *Jews and Christians: The Parting of Ways, AD 70–135*. Mohr Siebeck, Tübingen, 1989.

Edwards, M., *Tertullian, Adversus Marcionem*. Clarendon, Oxford, 1972.

Edwards, M. and Goodman, M. (eds.), *Apologetics in the Roman Empire: Pagans, Jews and Christians*. Oxford University Press, Oxford, 1999.

Frend, W. H. C., *The Rise of Christianity*. Fortress, Philadelphia, 1984.

Goethe, J. W. von, *West-Eastern Divan* (transl. Edward Dowden). Dent, London, 1914.

—, *Poems of West and East: West-östlicher Divan*. Peter Lang, Bern, 1998.

Goodman, M., *Rome and Jerusalem*. Penguin, London, 2007.

Grant, R. M., *Gnosticism and Early Christianity*. Harper & Row, New York, 1966.

Grillmeier, A., *Christ in Christian Tradition. Vol. 1, From the Apostolic Age to Chalcedon (451)*. 2nd rev. edn, Mowbrays, London/Oxford, 1975.

Grypeou, E. and Spurling, H., *The Exegetical Encounter between Jews and Christians in Late Antiquity*. Brill, Leiden, 2009.

Hanson, R. C. P., 'Biblical Exegesis in the Early Church', in P. R. Ackroyd and C. F. Evans (eds.), *The Cambridge History of the Bible*. Cambridge University Press, Cambridge, 1970, pp. 412–53.

Harnack, A. von, *The History of Dogma* IV. Williams & Norgate, London, 1898.

—, *Marcion: The Gospel of the Alien God*. Labyrinth Press, Durham, N.C., 1990.

Kleinknecht, H., '*Lego/Logos*': 'The Logos in the Greek and Hellenistic World', *Theological Dictionary of the New Testament* IV. Eerdmans, Grand Rapids, 1967, pp. 77–91.

Lake, K. (transl.), *Eusebius, Ecclesiastical History* I–II. Loeb Classical Library, Harvard University Press, Cambridge, Mass., 1926.

MacCulloch, D., *A History of Christianity: The First Three Thousand Years*. Penguin, London, 2010.

Millar, F., *The Emperor in the Roman World (31 BC–AD 337)*. Duckworth, London, 1977.

Rendel Harris, J., *Testimonies* I–II. Cambridge University Press, Cambridge, 1916–20.

Segal, A. F., *Two Powers in Heaven. Early Rabbinic Reports about Christianity and Gnosticism*. Brill, Leiden, 1977.

Simon, M., *Verus Israel: A Study of the Relations between Christians and Jews in the Roman Empire (AD 135–425)*. Oxford University Press, Oxford, 1986.

Stevenson, J. and Frend, W. H. C. (eds.), *A New Eusebius: Documents Illustrating the History of the Church to AD 337*. Baker Academic, Grand Rapids, 2012.

Suggs, M. J., 'The Christian Two Ways Tradition', in D. E. Aune (ed.), *Studies in New Testament and Early Christian Literature*. Brill, Leiden, 1972, pp. 60–74.

Taylor, M., *Anti-Judaism and Early Christian Identity: A Critique of the Scholarly Consensus*. Brill, Leiden, 1995.

Young, F. and Mitchell, M., *The Cambridge History of Christianity I: Origins to Constantine*. Cambridge University Press, Cambridge, 2005.

DIDACHE AND BARNABAS

Audet, J.-P., *La Didachè: L'Instruction des apôtres*. Études Bibliques, Gabalda, Paris, 1958.

Carleton Paget, J., *The Epistle of Barnabas: Outlook and Background*. Mohr Siebeck, Tübingen, 1994.

del Verme, M., *Didache and Judaism: Jewish Roots of an Ancient Christian-Jewish Work*. T. & T. Clark, Edinburgh, 2005.

Draper, J. A. (ed.), *The Didache in Modern Research*. Brill, Leiden, 1996.

Ehrman, B. D., *The Apostolic Fathers I–II*. Loeb Classical Library, Harvard University Press, Cambridge, Mass., 2003.

Kraft, R., *Barnabas and the Didache. The Apostolic Fathers III*. Nelson, New York, 1965.

Lake, K., *The Apostolic Fathers I–II*. Loeb Classical Library, Heinemann, London, 1912–13.

Louth, A. and Staniforth, M., *Early Christian Writings: The Apostolic Fathers*. Rev. edn, Penguin, London, 2004.

Niederwimmer, K., *The Didache*. Hermeneia, Minneapolis, 1998.

O'Loughlin, T., *The Didache: A Window on the Earliest Christians*. Baker Academic, Grand Rapids, 2010.

Prigent, P., *Les Testimonia dans le christianisme primitif: L'Epître de Barnabé I–XVI et ses sources*. Gabalda, Paris, 1961.

Van der Sandt, H. and Flusser, D., *The Didache: Its Jewish Sources and its Place in Early Judaism and Christianity*. Compendia Rerum Iudaicarum ad Novum Testamentum 5, Van Gorcum, Assen, 2002.

CLEMENT, IGNATIUS, POLYCARP, HERMAS AND DIOGNETUS

Brent, A., *Ignatius of Antioch: A Martyr-Bishop and the Origin of Episcopacy*. Continuum/T. & T. Clark, New York, 2007.

Camelot, P. T., *Ignace d'Antioche: Lettres*. Sources chrétiennes 10, Cerf, Paris, 1969.

Ehrman, B. D., *The Apostolic Fathers I–II*. Loeb Classical Library, Harvard University Press, Cambridge, Mass., 2003.

Grant, R. M., *Ignatius of Antioch*. Nelson, Camden, N.J., 1967.

Grant, R. M. and Graham, H. H., *First and Second Clement*. Nelson, Camden, N. J., 1965.

Joly, R., *Hermas: Le Pasteur*. Sources chrétiennes 53, Cerf, Paris, 1958.

Lake, K., *The Apostolic Fathers I–II*. Loeb Classical Library, Heinemann, London, 1912–13.

Louth, A. and Staniforth, M., *Early Christian Writings: The Apostolic Fathers*. Rev. edn, Penguin, London, 2004.

Marrou, H. I., *A Diognète*. Sources chrétiennes 29, Cerf, Paris, 1951.

Osiek, C., *The Shepherd of Hermas*. Fortress, Minneapolis, 1999.

Richardson, C., *The Christianity of Ignatius of Antioch*. Columbia University Press, New York, 1935.

Schoedel, W. R., *Polycarp, Martyrdom of Polycarp*. Nelson, Camden, N.J., 1967.

—, *Ignatius of Antioch: A Commentary on the Letters*. Hermeneia. Fortress Press, Philadelphia, 1985.

JUSTIN, MELITO AND IRENAEUS

Barnard, L. W., *Justin Martyr: His Life and Thought*. Cambridge University Press, Cambridge, 1967.

Bonner, C. (ed.), *The Homily on the Passion*, Studies and Documents 12. University of Pennsylvania, Philadelphia, 1940.

Chadwick, H., 'Justin Martyr's Defence of Christianity', *Bulletin of the John Rylands Library* 47 (1965), pp. 275–97.

—, *Early Christian Thought and the Classical Tradition: Studies in Justin, Clement, and Origen*. Clarendon, Oxford, 1966.

Edwards, M. J., 'On the Platonic Schooling of Justin', *Journal of Theological Studies* 42 (1991), pp. 17–34.

Hall, S. G. (ed.), *Melito of Sardis, On Pascha and fragments*. Clarendon, Oxford, 1979.

Houssiau, A., *La christologie de Saint Irénée*. Duculot, Gembloux, 1955.

Lukyn Williams, A. (ed.), *Justin Martyr: The Dialogue with Trypho*. SPCK, London, 1930.

Minns, D. and Parvis, P. (eds.), *Justin, Philosopher and Martyr, Apologies*. Oxford University Press, Oxford, 2009.

Rajak, T., 'Talking at Trypho', *The Jewish Dialogue with Greece and Rome: Studies in Cultural and Social Interaction*. Brill, Leiden, 2001, pp. 511–33.

Rousseau, A. et al. (eds.), *Irénée de Lyon, contre les hérésies*. Sources chrétiennes, 152–3, 210–11, 263–4, 293–4. Cerf, Paris, 1965–82.

Skarsaune, O., *The Proof from Prophecy: Study in Justin Martyr's Proof-Text Tradition*. Brill, Leiden, 1987.

Testuz, M., *Méliton de Sardes, Homélie sur la Pâque: Manuscript du IIIe siècle*. Papyrus Bodmer 13. Bibliotheca Bodmeriana, Cology-Genève, 1960.

TERTULLIAN, CLEMENT OF ALEXANDRIA AND ORIGEN

Barnes, T. D., *Tertullian: A Literary and Historical Study*. Oxford University Press, Oxford, 1985.

Chadwick, H., *Early Christian Thought and the Classical Tradition: Studies in Justin, Clement, and Origen*. Clarendon, Oxford, 1966.

Chadwick, H. (ed.), *Origen: Contra Celsum*. Cambridge University Press, Cambridge, 1980.

Clark, E. A., *The Origenist Controversy*. Princeton University Press, Princeton, 1992.

Crouzel, H., *Origen*. T. & T. Clark, Edinburgh, 1998.

de Lange, N., *Origen and the Jews*. Cambridge University Press, Cambridge, 1976.

Evans, E. (ed.), *Q. Septimii Florentis Tertulliani: De carne Christi liber*. SPCK, London, 1956.

Glover, T. R. (ed.), *Tertullian, Apology*. Loeb Classical Library, Heinemann, London, 1931.

Hanson, R. C. P., 'Origen as Biblical Scholar', in P. R. Ackroyd and C. F. Evans (eds.), *The Cambridge History of the Bible*. Cambridge University Press, Cambridge, 1970, pp. 454–89.

Harl, M. et al. (eds.), *Origène, Traité des principes (Peri Archôn)*. Études Augustiniennes, Paris, 1976.

Kannengiesser, C. and Petersen, W. L., *Origen of Alexandria: His World and Legacy*. Notre Dame University Press, Notre Dame, Minn., 1988.

Mondésert, C. and Caster, M. (eds.), *Clément d'Alexandrie, Les Stromates*. Sources chrétiennes 463. Cerf, Paris, 2001.

Osborn, E., *Clement of Alexandria*. Cambridge University Press, Cambridge, 2005.

Souter, A. (ed.), *Tertullian, Against Praxeas*. SPCK, London, 1919.

Waszink, J. H. (ed.), *Tertullian: The Treatise against Hermogenes*. Longmans, London, 1956.

NICAEA

Ayres, L., *Nicaea and its Legacy: An Approach to Fourth-Century Trinitarian Theology*. Oxford University Press, Oxford, 2004.

Bardy, G. (ed.), *Eusèbe de Césarée, Histoire ecclésiastique*. Sources chrétiennes 31, 41, 55, 73. Cerf, Paris, 1952–60.

Barnes, M. R. and Williams, D. H. (eds.), *Arianism after Arius*. Continuum/T. & T. Clark, Edinburgh, 1993.

Barnes, T. D., *Constantine and Eusebius*. Harvard University Press, Cambridge, Mass., 1981.

Brakke, D., 'Athanasius', in P. F. Esler (ed.), *The Early Christian World* II. Routledge, New York, 2000, pp. 1102–27.

Cameron, A. and Hall, S. (transls.), *Eusebius: The Life of Constantine*. Oxford University Press, Oxford, 1999.

Gwatkin, H. M., *Studies in Arianism*. 2nd edn, Bell, London, 1900.

Hanson, R. C. P., *The Search for the Christian Doctrine of God: The Arian Controversy, 318–381*. T. & T. Clark, Edinburgh, 1988.

Kannengiesser, C., *Arius and Athanasius: Two Alexandrian Theologians*. Variorum Reprints, London, 1991.

Kannengiesser, C. (ed.), *Athanase d'Alexandrie, sur l'incarnation du Verbe*. Sources chrétiennes 199, Cerf, Paris, 2000.

Rahner, K., 'Current Problems in Christology', *Theological Investigations* I. Darton, Longman and Todd, London, 1961, pp. 149–200.

Thompson, R. W. (ed.), *Athanasius: Contra Gentes and De Incarnatione*. Clarendon, Oxford, 1971.

Wiles, M. F., 'In Defence of Arius', *Jounal of Theological Studies* 13 (1962), pp. 339–47.

—, *Archetypal Heresy: Arianism through the Centuries*. Oxford University Press, Oxford, 1996.

Williams, R., *Arius: Heresy and Tradition*. SCM, London, 2001.

Williamson, G. A. (ed.), *Eusebius, The History of the Church from Christ to Constantine*. Penguin, London, 1965, rev. edn 1989.

Index